Foundations of Western Civilization II: A History of the Modern Western World
Part I

Professor Robert Bucholz

THE TEACHING COMPANY ®

PUBLISHED BY:

THE TEACHING COMPANY
4151 Lafayette Center Drive, Suite 100
Chantilly, Virginia 20151-1232
1-800-TEACH-12
Fax—703-378-3819
www.teach12.com

ISBN 1-59803-177-5

Robert Bucholz, D.Phil.

Professor of History, Loyola University of Chicago

Robert Bucholz was born March 17, 1958, in Los Angeles, California. He received his undergraduate education in history at Cornell University, where he also earned his letter in cross-country and track. He graduated in 1980, magna cum laude and Phi Beta Kappa, whereupon he received a Keasbey Memorial Scholarship for study at Oxford University. At Oxford, Bucholz studied under G. V. Bennett and P. G. M. Dickson. He took his doctorate in modern history from Oxford in March 1988. He taught at Cornell, UCLA Extension, Cal State Long Beach, and Loyola-Marymount Universities before joining the faculty in history at Loyola University of Chicago in 1988. He currently holds the rank of professor.

At Loyola, Dr. Bucholz teaches both halves of the Western Civilization survey, as well as upper-division courses in Early Modern (Tudor-Stuart) England, English Social History, and Early Modern London. He has received several awards for his teaching, most notably, in 1994, in the first year of its presentation, the Sujack Award for Teaching Excellence, the College of Arts and Sciences' highest such award. He was also the Honors Program Faculty Member of the Year in 1998 and 1999.

Dr. Bucholz's primary research interest is the English court and royal household for the period from 1660 into the 19th century. He is the author of *The Augustan Court: Queen Anne and the Decline of Court Culture* (Stanford, 1993); with Sir John Sainty, KCB, *Officials of the Royal Household, 1660–1837*, 2 vols. (Institute of Historical Research, London, 1997–1998); and, with Professor Newton Key of Eastern Illinois University, *Early Modern England, 1485–1714: A Narrative History* (Blackwell, 2003). He is the project director of the Database of Court Officers, which contains the career facts of every person who served in the British royal household from the restoration of the monarchy in 1660 to the death of Queen Victoria in 1901. The database was launched online by Loyola University in 2005.

In 1997, Dr. Bucholz was named Prince of Wales Foundation Scholar for Architecture in America, which led, in turn, to his being invited to speak on the etiquette of the public rooms and the experience of going to court in the 17th and 18th centuries to Royal Collection Studies at Windsor Castle in September of that year. (Dr. Bucholz's week-long stay at Windsor coincided with the death and funeral of Diana, Princess of Wales.) This talk was repeated in 2000 and published in 2001 in *The Court Historian*. Dr. Bucholz's work has been solicited and commented upon by HRH, the Prince of Wales.

Dr. Bucholz is past president of the Midwest Conference on British Studies and the organizer of the Center for Renaissance Studies/Society for Court Studies Seminar on Courts, Households, and Lineages at the Newberry Library, Chicago. Dr. Bucholz is occasionally asked to comment on British history and the activities of the British royal family to the Chicago media, most notably "Chicago Tonight" with John Calloway and "Extension 720" with Milt Rosenberg.

Table of Contents
Foundations of Western Civilization II:
A History of the Modern Western World
Part I

Foundations of Western Civilization II:
A History of the Modern Western World

Scope:

Wherever we come from, whatever we believe, however we make a living, Americans are all, to a greater or lesser extent, inhabitants of a land shaped by the last five centuries of Western history and culture. Over those five centuries, the Western world has seen a profound transformation. How did the decentralized agrarian princedoms of medieval Europe become great industrial nation-states? How was the power of disease and superstition dealt a blow by Western science and technology? How and why did absolutism yield to democratic liberalism? Why did Europe produce two great antagonistic economic systems, capitalism and communism? How did Westerners conquer half the world, then lose it? Why did the Western world erupt into two world wars, then a cold war in which Europe found itself the prize between two superpowers? To what extent have Europeans learned to work together for their common good; to what extent do they remain divided by history and culture? Overall, has their legacy to the wider world been positive or negative?

This course will explore the ideas, events, and characters that molded Western political, social, religious, intellectual, cultural, scientific, technological, and economic history during the tumultuous period between the 16th and 20th centuries. The course begins by explaining the geographical, philosophical, political, religious, and economic background to the modern Western world. It then examines, in turn, the crisis of the 17th century, absolutism and constitutionalism, the wars of the 18th century, the Enlightenment, the French and American Revolutions and the spread of liberal ideals, nationalism, the Industrial Revolution, socialism, imperialism, the Russian Revolution, two world wars, communism, fascism, de-colonization, the collapse of the Soviet bloc, democratization, and globalization and other issues confronting contemporary Western society. Frequent reference to contemporary philosophy, literature, the arts, and biography will help us define these explosive centuries and understand how we are their heirs.

Lecture One
The Importance of the West

Scope:

Why study the West? What is distinctive about Western Europe and its culture? What did the West contribute to modern society and culture? This lecture posits that, for all its diversity, modern American society, in particular its assumptions and forms of expression, is very much a product of the last 500 years of European history and culture. Our system of government, our economic structures, our science and technology, and much of our literature, art, and music are based on or react to European models forged in the crucible of modern Western history. Far from being a history of "dead white men," the story of the West is the road map that tells us where we came from and what obstacles we have erected for ourselves in the journey ahead.

Outline

I. This course will explore the history of Western Europe from the 16th century to the present day. This period, arguably, has done more to shape our world than any other period.

    A. Americans are all, to a greater or lesser extent, inhabitants of a world shaped by the last five centuries of Western history and culture.

    B. Auditors and viewers might object to a course on the modern West on the following grounds:

        1. Some might say that the events of five centuries ago (and in between) are not really relevant to our ever-changing world.

        2. Others might object that dead Europeans have little to tell the inhabitants of such a diverse a country as ours.

II. What reasons could we list for not studying the West?

    A. There are many other histories and cultures worth studying, and many of us in North America can trace our backgrounds and ancestors to these non-European cultures.

    B. Western or European civilization cannot be viewed as inherently superior to these other civilizations and cultures.

1. If measured by technological advance, Western civilization clearly wins (at the moment).
2. If the measurement is society's ability to coexist with the natural world, then other societies do better.

III. Why, then, should we study the West?

    A. One answer is that European thinkers, traditions, conflicts, and experiments produced our system of government, our economic structure, and much of our art.

    B. Above all, European culture produced certain ideas that have become pillars of our culture:

        1. "All men are created equal."
        2. "No taxation without representation."
        3. "The people united can never be defeated."
        4. A free press.
        5. Limited government.
        6. Innocence until proof of guilt.
        7. Judgment by a jury of peers.

    C. Far from celebrating dead white men, these ideas have given the world its most powerful tools to achieve justice and freedom.

    D. It is important not to overdo this notion of Europe's gifts to the world.

        1. Europeans have spent an awful lot of time fighting and killing each other and other non-Europeans in wars, revolutions, and general inhumanity to other humans—sometimes over these ideas.
        2. The continuing tensions in Northern Ireland, the Balkans, Chechnya, and elsewhere are noteworthy.

    E. Still, European ideals of and debates about equality, justice, class, reason, science, and technology remain at the center of our struggle for a more just world.

IV. Who am I to tell you this story?

    A. I am a professor of British history at Loyola University of Chicago, where I have taught this course every year for the past 15 years.

B. More information is located in the professor biography of this booklet, or look me up on The Teaching Company Web site, www.teach12.com.

C. In the meantime, the basic point to make is that this is very much a course presented by an American to Americans, both north and south.

V. What is the underlying philosophy of the course?

A. For most of the past 500 years, the history of the West has been told as if it was the story of its kings and queens, premiers and dictators.

B. Within the past half-century, though, historians have come to realize that there were between 100 million and 1 billion *other* people in Europe whose stories need to be told.

   1. Great movements and great events meant nothing unless great numbers of ordinary people were caught up in them.

   2. Most people in European history never saw a king, voted in an election, or even fought a war.

   3. Instead, they spent most of their time worrying about the same things that we worry about: growing up, falling in love, getting a job, rearing children, putting food on the table, staying healthy, and coming to terms with death.

   4. This, too, is a story worth telling.

C. European historians have also come to realize that their history cannot be understood outside the context of the histories of Asia, Africa, or what historians have increasingly come to call the Atlantic world.

D. Finally, this is a story that must be told with a view to what came before, if only because Europe did not begin in 1500.

   1. In fact, what this course is really about is how we stopped being medieval and became modern.

   2. Therefore, to help auditors and viewers place this period in a larger *chronological* context, this course will provide background lectures for the period before 1500, covering:

      a. The geography of Europe.

b. The intellectual inheritance of the Middle Ages, in particular, a hierarchical worldview called the *Great Chain of Being*.

c. A series of developments that began to undo the Great Chain of Being at the dawn of modern Western history.

VI. The course consists of 48 lectures, divided as follows:

A. The course begins with eight lectures that provide crucial background information.

1. The first lecture will address the geography of Europe from 1500–2000.

2. The second lecture will address what Europeans thought about their world in around 1500.

3. The next six lectures address developments between 1500 and 1650 that were destroying the medieval worldview and laying the groundwork for the modern world. These developments include:

a. Renaissance Humanism.

b. The rise of centrally governed nation-states.

c. The discovery of the New World.

d. The invention of the printing press.

e. The Protestant Reformation and the Wars of Religion.

f. The Rational and Scientific Revolutions.

B. Lectures Ten through Fifteen examine a crisis in European leadership in the 17th century.

1. Lecture Ten explains that the French responded to the crisis by embracing absolutism.

2. Lecture Eleven and Twelve explain how the English responded by embracing constitutional monarchy.

3. Lectures Thirteen through Fifteen chronicle how, after 1688, Britain, France, and their allies went to war with each other periodically for more than a century to determine the mastery of Europe, imperial control of the Americas, and commercial control of the Far East.

C. Lectures Sixteen through Eighteen focus on the *Ancien Régime* on the verge of the French Revolution (1600–1789).

1. Lecture Sixteen explains how Europeans of different classes lived their lives in the century before the French Revolution.

2. Lectures Seventeen and Eighteen explain the Enlightenment and two very different responses to its ideas: enlightened European despots and the American Revolution.

D. Lectures Nineteen through Twenty-One address the French Revolution and its aftermath (1789–1815).

1. Lectures Nineteen and Twenty explain the causes and course of the French Revolution to the rise of Napoleon.

2. Lecture Twenty-One addresses the Napoleonic Empire, its collapse, and the Congress of Vienna of 1815.

E. Lectures Twenty-Two through Twenty-Six address possibly the most significant watershed separating us from our ancestors, the Industrial Revolution (1760–1850), and three great intellectual reactions to it: Liberalism, Romanticism, and Socialism.

F. Lecture Twenty-Seven presents scientific advances of the 19th century and its effect on the perceptions of men and women.

G. Lectures Twenty-Eight through Thirty-Two address the long-term causes of World War I.

1. Lectures Twenty-Eight and Twenty-Nine deal with nationalism in Europe, resulting in the unifications of Italy and Germany.

2. Lecture Thirty addresses the scramble for worldwide empire among the European powers.

3. Lecture Thirty-One discusses the second Industrial Revolution, the growing rivalry between Britain and Germany, and their eventual arms race.

4. Lecture Thirty-Two explains the Alliance system, designed by Bismarck to prevent war, but which actually helped cause war following the events at Sarajevo in 1914.

H. Lecture Thirty-Three examines European society and culture on the eve of World War I.

I. Lectures Thirty-Four through Thirty-Seven address World War I, the Russian Revolution, and the war's aftermath (1914–1919).

J. Lectures Thirty-Eight through Forty-Two offer the history of Europe between the wars (1919–1939).

  1. Lecture Thirty-Eight deals with the 1920s and the Great Depression.

  2. Lecture Thirty-Nine addresses the Soviet Union under Lenin and Stalin.

  3. Lecture Forty presents the rise of Fascist Italy and Nazi Germany.

  4. Lecture Forty-One examines the Holocaust.

  5. Lecture Forty-Two traces the approach of World War II.

K. Lectures Forty-Three and Forty-Four present World War II (1939–1945).

L. Lectures Forty-Five through Forty-Seven address postwar Europe (1945–2005), including:

  1. The reconstruction of Europe and the Cold War.

  2. The European embrace of Democratic Socialism.

  3. The fall of the Soviet Union and rise of the European Union.

M. The final lecture addresses the meaning of European history.

Supplementary Reading:

M. B. Chambers, et al., *Western Experience*, Introduction.

Questions to Consider:

1. What is civilization?

2. What is the West? Is it confined to Europe or does it include the Americas? Oceania? The world?

Map of Europe (2005)

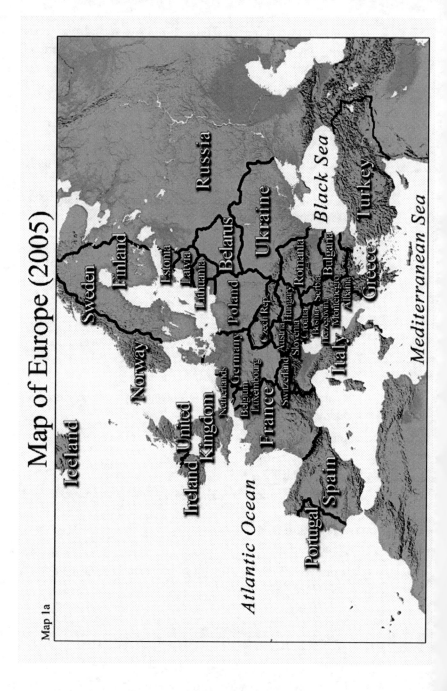

Lecture One—Transcript
The Importance of the West

Welcome to one of the great intellectual experiences of your life. That rather bold statement has nothing to do with me and my limited talents. It has everything to do with the subject that you have so wisely chosen to study. Together, we will explore the history that has arguably done more to shape your world than any other: that of Western Europe from the 16th century to the present day.

Wherever we come from, whatever we believe, and however we make a living, Americans are all to a greater or lesser extent inhabitants of a world shaped by the last five centuries of Western history and culture. Over those five centuries, the Western world has seen a profound transformation, which raises some questions: How was it that the decentralized agrarian principalities of Medieval Europe became great industrial nation-states? How and why did Absolutism rise and then yield to democratic Liberalism? How did Western science and technology create the first industrialized economies and reduce the power of superstition and disease? Why did Europe produce two great antagonistic economic systems, Capitalism and Communism? Why did westerners conquer half the world and then lose it? And above all, has this legacy been, on the whole, positive or negative?

This course will explore the ideas, events, and characters that molded the political, social, religious, intellectual, cultural, scientific, and economic history during the most tumultuous period between the 16th and 21st centuries. We will examine Absolutism and the challenges it provoked; the Enlightenment; the French and American Revolutions; the spread of Constitutionalism, Liberalism, and Nationalism; the Industrial Revolution; Socialism; Imperialism; the Russian Revolution; two World Wars; Fascism; Communism; decolonization; the collapse of the Soviet bloc; democratization; and the issues confronting contemporary Western society. Along the way, we will encounter some of the most brilliant thoughts, fascinating stories, and intriguing people that the whole soap opera of human history has to offer.

"But Professor Bucholz," you might well ask, "How relevant is that soap opera, really, to the very real dramas that we face today at the dawn of the 21st century? What do dead Europeans have to tell us about our problems? In any case, isn't it our particular genius as Americans that we have escaped from the past and that, as the most powerful society in the history of the planet, we can make our own reality?"

I have a rather long answer for that. In fact, the whole course is sort of an answer to that. But let's start with a basic fact. This is a course in European history. I say that without apology. I know, and I hope that you know, that there are many histories, and many "herstories," if you will, that are deep, rich, and well worth studying. I mean, of course, those of the native cultures of East Asia, the subcontinent of India, Africa, the Middle East, and North and South America. Many of us in North America can trace our backgrounds and ancestors to these non-European cultures.

So aren't they more relevant to our lives than the culture sometimes dismissed as that of "dead white men?" What do we have in common with French peasants of the 18th century? Or English workers of the 19th century? Or Russian soldiers of the 20th century? We have quite a bit in common, as it turns out, as I hope to demonstrate.

But in the meantime, let me state unequivocally that I don't teach this course either here, before the cameras and microphones, or at my university because I think Western civilization or European culture is inherently superior to, more advanced than, or better than these other civilizations. Quite frankly, I don't think that you can rate civilizations like college football teams. (If you read the sports section in January, you know you can't even do that with any degree of reliability.)

If measured by technological advance, sure, Western civilization clearly wins, at least right now. But if we were to measure a society by, say, its ability to coexist with the natural world, those of Native Americans and Mongolian tribesmen would actually look a lot better than ours. So we fall back on the old question: Why should we study the West? Why should Americans concern themselves with the history of Europe? Because, like it or not, it was from Europe— European thinkers, European traditions, European conflicts, European experiments—that we in the West derived our system of government—democracy, for most western countries. The organization of our society into classes, our economic structure (Capitalism), our literature, much of our art and music, and the media of our public discourse (television, radio, newspapers, and novels) are all by and large, for the most part, European inventions.

Above all, certain core ideas were developed during the course of European history and reached fruition during the period of our course: the notion that all men—and now all women—are created equal; no taxation without representation; the people united can never be defeated; a free press; a limited government; and the idea that those accused of crimes are innocent until proven guilty, and they are entitled to be judged by a jury of their peers.

Far from celebrating dead white men, it is these ideas that have given the world the most powerful tools to fight the hegemony of European empires, and for all people of all colors to achieve justice and freedom. When oppressed or disenfranchised groups such as the poor, women, racial or ethnic groups, the disabled, and gay men and women in any of the five continents argue for justice and equality, they argue over and with these very concepts.

In the United States, they have been enshrined in the Declaration of Independence and the U.S. Constitution, which were written by men like Madison and Jefferson, who were themselves, in a figurative sense, students of John Locke, Montesquieu, and the histories of 17th and 18th century Europe. Indeed, ultimately they were students of the Magna Charta, Roman law, Socrates, Plato, Aristotle, and the Bible.

If I may, I would like to take just one American example: Martin Luther King. Most years, I teach this course in the spring. We usually begin around mid-January, which means that the first lecture—this lecture—generally falls around the time of the Martin Luther King holiday. Now it may seem off-topic, but I'd like you to consider for a moment the life of this one rather extraordinary American. He was named for his father, a Baptist preacher, who was, of course, named for the great 16th century Protestant reformer, Martin Luther.

He is Dr. Martin Luther King because he earned a doctorate at Boston University. The university, in the sense of an institution that awards degrees or credentials for academic knowledge, is, of course, a European invention dating back to the Middle Ages. He received his doctorate for a dissertation on the German-American theologian Paul Tillich.

Now Tillich was a graduate of the University of Breslau in Germany. In World War I, he fought on the German side. He was dismissed from his post at the University of Frankfurt and eventually forced to flee Nazi Germany to America. Eventually he taught at Harvard and the University of Chicago. Can we agree that his life spans many of the great controversies and issues of the first half of the 20th century?

King was also profoundly influenced by Mahatma Gandhi, the great Indian political leader; but—and this is often forgotten—a he was a graduate of an English law school in 1888. I could argue that Gandhi's entire life boiled down to forcing the British to live up to the enlightened democratic ideals that he had learned from them. So here's another life with a profound impact on Western civilization.

King's writings and speeches, like Tillich's, demonstrate deep knowledge of Christian scripture, but also the profound influence of much intervening culture. They are positively drenched with the language and cadences of the King James Bible, Shakespeare, the Founding Fathers, English Common Law, Jesus, and Gandhi. His appeals to justice, equality, and non-violence are rooted in similar fights in European history.

So here is this great American—perhaps, if one measures by what he accomplished, the greatest American of the 20th century—of African descent and yet himself a product through and through of Western culture and its turbulent history.

Now, I don't want to oversell this idea of Europe's gifts to the world. If you pay attention to this course, or just watch the news, you will know that Europeans have spent an awful lot of time fighting over and against these very ideas, and often killing each other and other non-Europeans in wars, revolutions, and general inhumanity to their fellow humans. One notes continuing tensions often leading to ruthless violence in Northern Ireland, the Balkans, and Chechnya. There are continuing European debates about anti-Semitism, immigration, public welfare, and Europe's role in the world; the latter, in part, a bitter legacy of European Imperialism.

In the last lecture, I want to suggest that the Europeans may actually have found their way past some of these issues in a way that Americans might want to study. But in the meantime, and in any case, despite these disputes and madnesses, I remain convinced that European ideals of and debates about equality and inequality, justice and injustice, class and power, reason and revelation, and science and technology remain our world's "last best hope"—to quote an American president, himself named after an English county (that's Lincoln) and steeped in the King James Bible and the traditions of English Common Law—to achieve a society with "liberty and justice for all." That alone seems to me a pretty good reason for spending time on this story, these ideals, and the place and peoples that forged them.

Okay, fine, I think I've sold you on this; but what gives me the right and the background to tell you this story? Well, I am a professor of British history at Loyola University of Chicago, where I have taught this course every year for the past 15 years. If you want to know more details about me, you can read them in the booklet or look me up on The Teaching Company website.

In the meantime, I want to make two basic points about myself. It should be obvious by now from my accent that I am an American. This is very much a course presented by an American for his fellow Americans. I like to think that my own long apprenticeship in studying this people and culture have given me a pretty good insight into what Americans are likely to know and not know, and what they are likely to be interested in and not interested in, about the history of Western civilization. If I'm wrong, you'll undoubtedly find ways of letting me know.

The second thing I'd like to do here is issue a little bit of a disclaimer. This course covers a lot of ground: the whole of human life across an entire continent and its extensions across the globe for five centuries. Anyone who teaches this course has to know about 16th century theology, the 19th century factory system, U-boats, British parliamentary politics, the experience of French peasants and Russian serfs, and the internal problems of Ulster, Kosovo, and countless lands beyond Europe. So if I sometimes seem less than omniscient, I hope that you will forgive me, as I, too, remain a student of Western civilization.

On the other hand, if I often seem biased toward Western Europe, Great Britain in particular, that is more conscious and a result of both circumstance and conviction. The circumstance is that my specific area of research is Great Britain during the Tudor and Stuart period. That is what Loyola originally hired me to teach. This is the part of the world whose history I know best. I can't help that. The conviction, though, is that of all the countries of the West, it is Britain—British political and social institutions—from which we in America have derived most of our heritage. The proof is to follow.

So what's the underlying philosophy of the course? I've been sneaking it in on you. That may seem an odd question: Does history really need an underlying philosophy? History is pretty straightforward, isn't it? You begin at the beginning and march on to the end, one darn thing after another, in chronological order, don't you?

Fifty years ago, I might very well have launched in with Ferdinand and Isabella bankrolling Columbus, or Henry VIII beheading his wives, or Louis XIV building Versailles. (All these people had issues, by the way.) I would then have carried on through the dynastic and political changes in Europe with special attention to Napoleon, Bismarck, Hitler, Stalin, and Churchill, and left off with the fall of the Soviet Union and the foundation of the European Union.

That is, for most of the past 500 years, the history of the West has been told as if it were the history of about 12 people; that is, the history of kings and queens and premiers and dictators. Now, let me reassure you, you will be getting plenty of kings and queens and premiers and dictators. They are undoubtedly one of the reasons you signed up for the course and you can't beat them for ringing declarations and shocking pronouncements. Elizabeth I proclaimed, "I have the heart and stomach of a king, and of a king of England, too!" Louis XIV bypassed anatomy altogether to declare, "I am the State!" Frederick the Great one-downed him after reading his Voltaire and asserting, "I am the servant of the State." Otto von Bismarck spurned even assertions themselves with, "The great questions of time are not decided by speeches and majority decisions, but by iron and blood."

The example of Louis XIV reminds us that kings and queens are great for scandal. Henry VIII had his six wives and Louis XV had his mistresses (Madame du Pompadour's power will feature in this course). They are also great for fascinating anecdotes. One of my favorites is Maria Theresa. In 1740, with Austria and Hungary surrounded and beset by enemies, she goes to the Hungarian Diet with her children and she holds them up to the Diet and says, "You must defend these children. You must defend this dynasty." One of those children grew up to become Emperor Joseph II, who was famous for telling Mozart, who had just written *The Marriage of Figaro*, that it had, "Too many notes." Another great anecdote is that of Napoleon crowning himself. There's also Wilhelm I and the Ems Dispatch and, of course, Churchill, Churchill, Churchill. These are all great stories and sources of great stories.

Within the past half-century, however, historians have come to realize that they are not the whole story, because at any given time there were between 80-800 million other people in Europe whose stories need to be told. The problem with making this course a story of kings and queens (and in my view, the problem with biography as history generally) is that it creates the impression that the histories of great nations were simply manifestations of the plans, passions, and whims of about 12 or 20 people.

Sometimes that may seem to be true. Take one of the most important events described in this course, the Reformation. It was obviously catalyzed by Martin Luther's doubts about the Catholic doctrine on indulgences. But do we really believe that if Luther hadn't had those doubts or kept his mouth shut that there wouldn't have been a Reformation? Or that once he decided to nail the 95 theses on the Wurtemburg church door, the whole thing happened like clockwork? The first ignores a growing movement, often among ordinary people, that seems to have wanted Reformation in Europe. The second ignores the immense loyalty or inertia that many Europeans had for Catholicism.

Put another way, historians have come to realize that European history is not simply the working of the rulers on the ruled, but a sort of dance between them, in which each partner is sometimes led and sometimes followed. They have also come to realize that great events like the Reformation, wars, and revolutions often took generations to affect the great mass of the people, if at all.

One of the reasons Luther and the German princes could get away with starting the Reformation was that most people didn't seem to notice that it was happening. Nothing changed in their churches for quite some time, or in their daily lives for even longer. This reminds us that the great mass of people in early modern Europe never saw the king or Cardinal Richelieu. They cared not a fig for political or theological controversies. They never read or even heard of Shakespeare, Goethe, or Marx.

They occupied themselves the way most of us do most of the time—in the mundane business of living. That is, they spent most of their time worrying about the same things that you and I worry about: growing up; making friends; getting a job; finding the next meal; falling in love; getting married; having children and then worrying for the rest of your life about what's going to happen to them; the aches, pains, and illnesses that come with life; and finally, dying—and what that might actually mean.

The traditional history of wars, treaties, laws, and scandals—the one we all learned or were bored by in high school—ignored these stories. We will remember them. By remembering them, we call the people of the past to live again. We give them a kind of immortality. We also remind ourselves that their problems were real and their solutions to those problems were not necessarily as crazy as they can sometimes appear to be to us smug moderns. Finally, we remind ourselves that we, too, will someday be the stuff of history.

Therefore, I will be at frequent pains to remind you that the history of Europe is not simply the story of kings and queens, or their ministers, or their relations with diets, parliaments, or estates. It is also the story of every man, woman, and child who lived, loved, fought, and died in Europe during the period covered by our course. This story must be told from the bottom up as well as from the top down.

This story must also be told side-to-side, for European historians have also come to realize that their history cannot be understood outside of the context of the histories of other places such as Asia, Africa, or what historians have increasingly come to call the Atlantic world. I want to be clear about this. I repeat: this is a course about Europe. Though America is the intellectual heir of the West, it too big a topic for this course to address American, Canadian, Mexican, Latin American, or Caribbean history in any detail. Though Africa, Asia, and the Middle East have been profoundly influenced by the West, they deserve histories of their own. These places will enter our story as Europe enters theirs, for good or ill.

Finally, this is a story that must be told with a view to what came before, if only because Europe didn't begin in 1500 or 1600. In fact,

©2006 The Teaching Company Limited Partnership

what this course is really about is how Europeans stopped being medieval and became modern.

To understand that, we have to address the medieval inheritance. That brings me to the question of how exactly the course will be structured. The course consists of 48 lectures, divided, after the one I'm giving now, as follows. First, there will be eight lectures of background. I believe in a lot of pedestal before I erect my statue. We will begin with the geography of Europe and a sort of Cook's Tour of Europe as this course opens. This lecture will explain how geography is, in my view at least, destiny; that is, how and why climate and topography made the development of Western Europe different from that of eastern Europe, and the development of northern Europe different from that of the South.

We'll then look at how European history has been affected by mountain ranges, rivers, and bodies of water and islands. We'll look at Europe's relative distribution of natural resources, such as water, timber, coal, and other minerals. Finally, to give you a better understanding of the physical environment inhabited by early modern Europeans, we are going to pay a visit to a typical (but non-existently typical) village.

We will then continue with a lecture on the mental world of Europeans around 1500. We'll examine their universe, their society, and how their economy and politics were supposed to work. This is a lecture on a construct known as the Great Chain of Being. That will be followed by six lectures on those developments between 1500–1600 or so that were actually destroying the Great Chain of Being—destroying the old medieval worldview. Those six developments are Renaissance Humanism; the rise of centrally governed nation-states; the discovery of the New World; the invention of the printing press; the Protestant Reformation and the wars of religion that followed from it; and the rational and scientific revolutions.

It is at that point that we are ready to begin the course proper in terms of the development of modernity. We will follow the pedestal lectures with lectures on the crisis of the 17th century and a series of wars sometimes called the Second Hundred Years' War, that were fought between Britain and France following that crisis. We will talk about why there was such a crisis. We will talk about the French response to it, which was to embrace Absolutism. We'll talk about the English response, which was to embrace Constitutionalism, and why those two great political systems had to clash. Those clashes would last right into the 19th century and wouldn't end until Wellington met Napoleon on the field at Waterloo. At stake was the mastery of Europe, imperial control of the Americas, and commercial control of the Far East.

Those lectures will be followed by three on the *Ancien Régime* on the verge of the French Revolution. We'll talk about the European class system in the 18th century and how Europeans of all classes lived their lives in the century before that revolution. We'll talk about really basic mundane things like birth, upbringing, education, courtship, marriage, disease, and how people faced death.

We will then talk about how the philosophers of the Enlightenment sought to reform the *ancien régime*. Then we'll talk about two very different responses to their writings: those of the enlightened despots of Europe, but also the American Revolution, which provided a blueprint for other revolutions.

That reminds me that the next set of lectures (three of them) will cover the French Revolution and its aftermath, the Napoleonic Empire. This will be followed by five lectures on the Industrial Revolution: its causes, consequences, and the three great intellectual responses to it—Liberalism, Romanticism, and Socialism. This will be followed by a lecture on the culture of the 19th century, emphasizing the impact of science on how people thought of man and how people thought of women.

This will be followed by two lectures on Nationalism and its consequences. These will follow revolutions in Greece, France, Italy, Germany, and the Austro-Hungarian Empire, and culminate in the unification of Italy in 1861 and that of Germany in 1871. They will also take note of the fact that nationalistic tensions continued in the Balkans. That will help to explain why within half a century Europe will be plunged into World War I.

The next four lectures will cover the long-term causes of what Europeans still call the Great War. We'll talk about European Imperialism, industrial rivalry during the second Industrial Revolution, the Anglo-German arms race, and Bismarck's European alliance system, which was designed to prevent war. In addition, there will be a lecture on the cultural life of Europe at the turn of the 20th century.

This will be followed by four lectures on the Great War and the Russian Revolution (1914–1918), in which I will make the argument that World War I did to Europe what perhaps Vietnam did to our politics and our culture. This will be followed by four lectures on the period between the wars (1919–1939) covering the Treaty of Versailles and the League of Nations, the Great Depression, the rise of the Soviet Union, the rise of Fascist Italy and Nazi Germany, the Holocaust, and the approach of World War II.

We will then give World War II itself two lectures, followed by two lectures on post-war Europe, including its reconstruction, the cold war, the end of European empires and Colonialism, the European embrace of Democratic Socialism, the fall of the Soviet Union, and the rise of the European Union. The final lecture will be on the meaning of European history and civilization in which I will muster all my wisdom and eloquence.

This course intends to provide an understanding of the political, social, and cultural history of Europe over these five centuries. It will also explore the ramifications of that history for the rest of the world, including the United States. This is obviously a terrific story. In the course of these 48 lectures, we will encounter numerous kings, presidents, premiers, and dictators; countless wars; a religious reformation; a scientific, a commercial, a financial, and four major political revolutions (the English, the American, the French, and the Russian, and we might throw in as well the Velvet Revolution, which brought down the Soviet Union and its satellites).

We will also encounter numerous small riots and rebellions and amazing works of art and culture: *Utopia, The Prince, The Sistine Chapel, Don Quixote, King Lear*, the King James Bible, *Leviathan, Principia, The St. Matthew Passion, The Night Watch, Candide*, Diderot's *Encyclopedia, Faust, Don Giovanni*, Beethoven's symphonies, *Frankenstein, Madame Bovary*, Impressionism, Realism, *The Ring of the Nibelung*, Verdi's *Falstaff*, Mahler's symphonies, *The Rite of Spring, The Brothers Karamazov, War and Peace, Ulysses, The Wasteland, The Trial, Guernica, 1984, Night*, and *The Gulag Archipelago*.

We will encounter the lives of popes and kings, but also subjects and citizens, including Ferdinand and Isabella, Henry VIII, Francis I, Charles V, Philip II, Columbus, Luther, Galileo, Pascal, Descartes, Michelangelo, James I, Cardinal Richelieu, Gustavus Adolphus, Cromwell, Marlborough, a host of Louises (XIII, XIV, XV, and XVI), Newton, Locke, Voltaire, Rousseau, Frederick the Great, Catherine the Great, Robespierre, Napoleon, Nelson, Wellington, Watt, Brunel, Bessemer, Adam Smith, Malthus, Ricardo, Bentham, Mill, Wollstonecraft, Wordsworth, Blake, Shelley, Goethe, Beethoven, Metternich, Garibaldi, Bismarck, the Kaisers, Nicholas and Alexandra, Gladstone, Disraeli, Florence Nightingale, Darwin, Mendel, Lister, Koch, Hegel, Marx, Einstein, Freud, Kierkegaard, Wittgenstein, Keynes, Lenin, Stalin, Mussolini, Hitler, Churchill, de Gaulle, Adenauer, Brezhnev, The Beatles, Sartre, Fellini, Thatcher, Gorbachev, Milosevic, and John Paul II—as well as a few Americans who left their mark on the Western world.

If those names mean anything to you, you must be nearly as excited as I am to be beginning this course. If they don't, I think maybe you need it. Either way, I welcome you to the History of Modern Western Civilization.

Lecture Two
Geography Is Destiny

Scope:

Where, exactly, is Europe? That is, what areas are considered part of the continent and what parts are not included? How have the physical realities of Europe and the Atlantic world shaped its peoples? Why are geography and climate destiny? Which parts of Europe were fertile or prosperous, which parts were barren? How did this affect patterns of population, immigration, diplomacy, and war? How did Europe tend to divide, politically and culturally? Why do mountains, rivers, and forests matter? As this course opens, Europe is still recovering from the demographic disaster of the Black Death. The lecture concludes with descriptions of city and village life and the role of the landlord.

Outline

I. If this is a course about Europe, what, exactly, does that mean?

    A. For the purposes of this course, *Europe* means the continent west of Asia, an area of about 4 million square miles that comprises about 35 countries.

    B. We will tend to concentrate on those parts of Europe that have had the greatest influence over our own American civilization.

        1. Toward the beginning of the course, we will spend a disproportionate amount of time on Italy, Spain, France, and the British Isles.

        2. Only in the 19th century will we shift our focus to Germany, Italy again, Eastern Europe, and Russia.

II. Geography is destiny.

    A. One way to approach the geography and even the politics of Europe is to think in terms of great axial divides (East/West, North/South) that operate as states of mind as much as they are geographic regions.

        1. The East/West border will shift:

    a. For the first half of the course, Western Europe will include everything west of the Rhine: the British Isles, Spain and Portugal, France, and the Scandinavian countries.

    b. Eastern Europe will include countless German and Italian states, Poland, the Baltic States, the Balkans, and Russia.

2. As the course progresses, sometime in the 19th century, the East/West dividing line will shift east to the Elbe or the Oder River.

    a. That is, as the region known as Germany unified and industrialized, it became more Westernized.

    b. It is possible that we are witnessing a similar shift "West" today among the former communist nations and Turkey.

3. If the dividing line East/West is as much political, economic, and cultural as it is topographic, this is equally true for Europe's North/South divide: the Alps.

B. Other natural features have had a profound effect on European history.

1. Mountains have been important as barriers to invasion and trade.

2. Forests can be barriers to invasion and produced their own unique economies and societies.

3. People who made their livings at sea were similarly outside the mainstream.

4. Water defines much of Europe via the coastline.

    a. Europe—which can be seen as a peninsula filled with peninsulas—is blessed with innumerable natural harbors.

    b. There is one great group of islands (the British Isles) and numerous smaller islands.

        i. The failure of invasions of Britain in 1588, 1805, and 1940 enabled a crucial subset of Western values to survive even when the rest of the continent seemed to go the other way.

        ii. But more often, the English Channel has been a highway for invaders and traders.

         iii. Iceland has been an important stopping point to America.
         iv. The Mediterranean Islands were strategic for trade and naval operations, especially Gibraltar.

    c. Rivers have also played a crucial role in European history.
         i. European diplomats and historians have tended to see them as barriers, e.g., the Rhine, Elbe, Rubicon, or Danube.
         ii. People on the move, though, have tended to see rivers as a means to penetrate the countryside and engage in trade.

  5. Plains are crucial for agriculture—and invading armies.

III. As for its climate, speaking latitudinally, Europe should be colder than it is.

  A. Northern Europe is famously cold.

  B. Western Europe is warmed by the Gulf Stream, leading to relatively mild climates.

  C. Southern Europe is warmed by the Mediterranean.

IV. Turning to demography, in 1500, the population of Europe was perhaps 80 million. (Today, it's more like 726 million.)

  A. The population of Europe was slowly recovering from the Black Death of the mid-14th century.

    1. Average life expectancy in Europe in 1500 was approximately 30 years.

    2. Old people were far rarer in this society than is the case today.

    3. Infant mortality was approximately 20 percent in the first year.

    4. Another 10 percent of children would die by age 10.

  B. The population only began to grow again around 1500, just as this course gets under way.

  C. The demographic disaster of the 14th and 15th centuries ironically led to a "golden age" for labor.

1. Few workers meant that the survivors could demand an end to serfdom, wages in exchange for labor, lower food prices, and lower rents.

2. Many landowners abandoned demesne farming (i.e., relying on profits from crops grown on their land) in favor of renting their land to peasants.

V. Less than 5 percent of the European population was urban.

    A. The largest city in Europe in 1500 was Constantinople, with nearly 400,000 people.

        1. The next largest city was Paris with a population of 200,000, followed by Naples and Venice at 100,000.

        2. The populations of London, Amsterdam, Moscow, Lisbon, Madrid, Rome, and Florence were approximately 50,000.

    B. Next in rank came provincial cities, such as York, England; Milan, Italy; and Berlin, Prussia, all of which had populations of several thousand inhabitants.

    C. Cathedral cities (e.g., Salisbury, Rheims) and market towns (e.g., Antwerp, Bruges, King's Lynn, Dortmund, Lyon) had populations of several hundred.

VI. The vast majority of European people lived in the countryside on manors and villages of fewer than 500 inhabitants, sometimes as few as 50.

    A. The manor contained two impressive buildings:

        1. The lord's manor house or castle.

        2. A church made of stone.

            a. The church was the religious center of the village. In most European states, there was no diversity of religion.

                i. The West was dominated by what we today call Roman Catholicism.

                ii. In the East, all people were required to worship in one of the Christian Orthodox faiths.

            b. The church was also the social center of the village.

3. A cluster of small, two-room huts likely to be made [often using a technique called "wattle and daub"] of anything that would stick together, including mud, straw, and animal manure.
   a. Houses of more prosperous peasants might be of stone or wood.
   b. Most people had few possessions.
   c. Personal privacy was an unknown concept.
   d. Animals provided milk, cheese, and wool.

B. Finally, surrounding the village, were the fields, arranged in long strips, where the villagers worked.

VII. The work engaged in by European people in 1500 varied by location.

A. In town, most people sold goods or services.

B. In upland areas or swamps, people made their livings by sheep farming or dairy farming; spinning wool, flax, or hemp; or quarrying.

C. Port towns contained fishermen, shipwrights, carpenters, sailmakers, dock workers, and customs officials.

D. Most villages depended on arable farming.
   1. The big tasks of late-medieval farming (ploughing, soughing, and harvesting) were organized communally.
   2. Men were joined by women and children at peak times (planting, harvest).
   3. At other times, the women cooked, sewed, fetched water, spun, or wove wool.
   4. Children tended animals and, when older, looked after younger children.

VIII. The landlord owned nearly all the land in the neighborhood.

A. He commanded a vast income from the sale of produce, mineral wealth, and, above all, rents from his tenants.

B. Control of the land implied control of the church, thanks to the fact that the landlord owned the land on which the church was built.

C. The landlord could demand from his tenants not only rents but also taxes, exclusive hunting and fishing rights, labor services (*corvée*), military service during war, and certain seignorial rights (*droits du seigneur*).

D. Often, the king would ask the landlord to use this power to maintain order in the countryside.

E. Paradoxically, the landlord's local importance might draw him to London or Paris to attend the King's Council and court, or to sit in Parliament, the Estates General, or the Cortes.

F. Fortunately, late medieval theology argued that those entrusted with such power had a paternal responsibility to provide their tenants with legal, military, and economic protection, paternal care, and hospitality.

G. Clearly, land was the key to power.
   1. By virtue of owning land, aristocrats owned all those little villages that housed most of the people of Europe.
   2. By virtue of owning all those little villages, it could be said that, despite the end of serfdom, they owned the lives and futures of all the people living within their domain.

H. The class of men who owned all this land and wielded all this power over all these people was tiny.

IX. To understand why the rest of the population put up with these inequalities, we will have to turn from the physical world of Europeans in 1500 to their mental universe.

Supplementary Reading:

D. Herlihy, *Women, Family and Society in Medieval Europe: Historical Essays, 1978–1991*.

Carlo Ginzburg, *The Cheese and the Worms: The Cosmos of a Sixteenth-Century Miller*.

Questions to Consider:

1. What are the cultural limits of Europe?

2. Why was land the hallmark of wealth, social status, and power for most of European history?

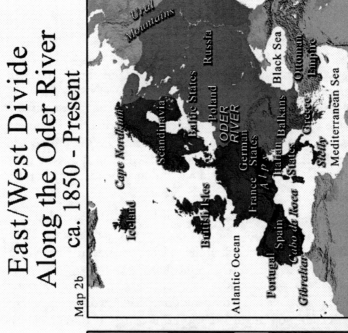

East/West Divide
Along the Rhine River
ca. 1500

Map 2a

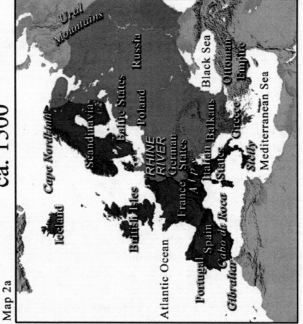

East/West Divide
Along the Oder River
ca. 1850 – Present

Map 2b

Lecture Two—Transcript
Geography Is Destiny

Like I was said in Lecture One, this is a course about modern Europe. We could spend a lot of time debating about what the word "modern" means and, in fact, the first half of my course will be offering my argument. As it turns out, Europeans spend a lot more time debating what "Europe" means. For example, in the summer of 2004, the website of the European Union asserted that, "Turkey lies on the very edge of the European continent, and the prospect of its joining the E.U. raises questions about where to draw the ultimate boundaries of the European Union." In other words, they don't even know.

For the purposes of our course, Europe means the continent west of Asia from the Ural Mountains in the east to Cabo da Roca, Portugal in the west, but also including the Atlantic islands to Iceland. It runs from Cape Nordkyn, Norway in the north to Gibraltar, Sicily, Greece and, maybe as we need it, Turkey in the south. That's about four million square miles. By the way, unless you won your geography bee in school, you might want to have a map of Europe handy for this particular lecture.

Depending on the period covered, that comprises about 35 countries. If this is a problem for the E.U., it is one for the history professor as well, especially the teacher of Western civilization. This course will tell a story about Europe, in particular its rise to modernity. It will not tell every story about Europe, however, nor the story of every part of Europe. Rather, we are going to be concentrating on those parts of Europe that tended to change most rapidly and dramatically from their medieval origins—politically, economically, and intellectually—and which thus had the greatest influence over our own American civilization. In other words, we are going to be concentrating mainly on Western Europe.

Towards the beginning of the course, we will spend a disproportionate amount of time on Italy, Spain, France, and the British Isles, in part because these countries are most associated with those developments that launched the modern world: the Renaissance, the Reformation, and the scientific and rational revolutions. This is also in part, however, because these were the countries facing west, and so had the most to do with what became us.

By the way, the Americas, Africa, Asia, and Oceania will enter into our story often, for they have affected and been affected by Europe profoundly. Later, we will add Germany, Italy again, and finally Russia. So even as a matter of how this course is organized, geography is destiny. What that means is that this course may be disappointing to those of you wishing detailed information about any one particular country, particularly if that country does not have a history of pushing its neighbors around or being pushed, or of aggressively pursuing intellectual or economic dominance. So, my apologies to partisans of the Baltic States, Scandinavia, Luxembourg, Andorra, Monaco, and even the Balkans, for much of the first half of this course. These places will enter into the course as they affect the larger story. Ironically, they are least likely to do so when they were behave or are left in peace.

Let's begin with some basic geography. One easy way to approach the geography and even the politics of Europe is to think in terms of great axial divides: east versus west and north versus south. I want to stress that these are states of mind and cultural categories as much as they are geographic regions. For example, the east/west border in our course is going to shift. For the first half, Western Europe will comprise everything west of the Rhine: the British Isles, Spain, Portugal, France, the Scandinavian countries, and (I know that this is geographically incorrect) Italy. Eastern Europe will include countless German states, Poland, the Baltic States, the Balkans, and Russia.

As the course progresses, however, sometime in the 19th century, that east/west dividing line is going to shift east to the Elbe or Oder River. In other words, as the region known as Germany (it didn't unify as a country until 1871) industrializes and becomes a cultural leader, looking to the industrializing West instead of the still feudal East, it will shift and become a Western country. This is a sign that geographical designations are constructs; they are based as much on culture as they are on physical topography. It is possible that we are witnessing a similar shift "west" today among former Communist nations and Turkey, who is in that process of joining the E.U.

If the east/west dividing line is as much political, economic, and cultural as it is topographic, this is equally true for Europe's north/south divide: the Alps. North of the Alps, it's colder and agriculture involves heavy grains. People excel at indoor activities. South of the Alps, it tends to be warmer, they grow citrus, olive oil, and wine, and people can spend more time outdoors. Southern Europe is also culturally different, because its location provided a lot more contact with Africa and Islamic civilizations of the Middle East.

Other natural features have had a profound effect on European history. Mountains have been important as barriers to invasion and trade. The Pyrenees separate France and Spain, crucially in the 17th century and will do so again during the 1930s and 1940s. In Britain, the Pennines and mountainous regions of Wales and Scotland help to explain why those two countries were actually culturally and ethnically different from England. When the Anglo-Saxons came over, they didn't get there (or at least they didn't get there for several centuries).

Forests also act as barriers. The Ardennes and Argonne on the French and German border will figure especially in the Franco-Prussian War and World Wars I and II. Less dramatically, because forests are isolated and not conducive to arable farming, they will develop their own unique economies. People will live in small settlements. Sometimes those settlements will be mobile. They'll engage in pastoral sheep farming, not arable farming. They'll do a lot of hunting.

That's a problem, because forests in many European countries were owned by the king and set aside for his own hunting. Therefore, to hunt was to poach, and to be a hunter was to be an outlaw. So, forest people, like gypsies, will be considered outsiders and almost a counterculture for most of our course.

People who got their livings at sea—fishermen, merchants, and pirates—were also outside the mainstream. That reminds us that water defines much of Europe. To get back to geography or the physical aspect of geography, first Europe is a peninsula. In fact, it is a peninsula filled with other peninsulas. This implies that it is surrounded on three parts by water and that it has lots of natural harbors, which of course are conducive to seafaring and trade.

In terms of islands, there is one great group and numerous smaller islands. The great group of islands is, of course, the British Isles.

Legend has it that the fact that Great Britain and Ireland are a series of islands has prevented invasion and preserved the unique cultures of these places. It's certainly true that in 1588 the Spanish Armada, in 1805 Napoleon, and in 1940 Hitler were all thwarted in their plans to invade Great Britain because of the English Channel. The failure of those invasions was crucial, for it enabled an important subset of Western values to survive, even when the rest of the continent seemed to go the other way.

But I always like to remind my students that more often, the English Channel has been a highway for both invaders and traders. There have been lots of successful invasions of Great Britain. The one everybody knows about is 1066. The one we are going to talk about took place as recently as 1688, when the Dutch under William III invaded. This has led to a never-ending debate in Britain about the degree to which Britain is part of Europe. The British can very easily now cross under the Channel to join their continental brethren.

Iceland will be an important stopping point on the way to America. Mediterranean islands will be strategic for trade and for naval operations. Malta and Crete will be important naval bases, especially during the World Wars. Then of course, there's Gibraltar, the famous "Gateway to the Mediterranean." It was won by Great Britain from Spain during the War of the Spanish Succession at the beginning of the 18th century. The fact that the Union flag still flies over Gibraltar is a real sore point to Spain and subject to periodic negotiations today.

Perhaps the liquid feature of geography that matters most in European history would be rivers. European diplomats and historians have tended to see rivers as barriers: the Rhine, the Elbe, the Rubicon ("crossing the Rubicon" is, of course, an important phrase in our culture), and the Danube. Peoples on the move, however, have tended to see them as highways and a means for early settlers to penetrate the countryside. The Germanic tribes penetrated into the Roman Empire along the Danube. The Celts and Anglo-Saxons penetrated into England on the Thames. And, of course, the Vikings used the Rhine to get into the heart of Europe. Later, during our period certainly, rivers have been very important for trade. The Tiber, Rhine, Thames, and Seine have all been crucial to the economies of their respective country.

Plains are crucial for agriculture. There are three great plains in Europe to know about: the eastern plain that stretches from East Germany through Poland to Russia; eastern France; and the midland plain in England. Altogether, they form Europe's breadbasket. Plains, by the way, are also very useful highways for invaders, as for example Napoleon's and the Germany armies would prove during the Napoleonic Wars and World War II.

Let us now turn to climate. Speaking latitudinally, Europe should be a lot colder than it is. London sits at the same latitude as Hudson's Bay. Northern Spain sits at the same latitude as Chicago. Now, northern Europe (Scandinavia, North Germany, Russia) is famously cold, but Western Europe is warmed by the Gulf Stream; so Western Europe experiences a relatively mild climate. The weather in England is famously never very good, but it's also never very bad— never very cold, never very warm—and so very good for growing heavy grains. Southern Europe, warmed by the Mediterranean, is of course good for citrus, olive oil, and winemaking.

I'd now like to talk about the demography of Europe—the population, or people, who make up this place and culture. If we were to take a field trip to early modern Europe—Europe in 1500— the first thing we would notice is the relative lack of people, especially as compared to today. I should perhaps explain that because this course is about the rise of modern Western civilization, and because I believe that modernity was beginning well before 1600 or 1700, I am going to choose as my baseline year here 1500.

In 1500, the population of Europe was maybe 80 million. Today, it's more like 726 million. That implies tremendous growth, but, of course, that growth was slower than any other continent in the history of the planet during that time. In fact, the population of Europe is now in decline.

Even during the Middle Ages, the population of Europe had once been much larger, but in 1347–1350, the Black Death (named for the black patches it left on the skin, and which was probably bubonic plague, although historians still argue about this) had swept into Europe, killing anywhere from two-fifths to one-half of the population. What has that got to do with 1500? That population continued to dwindle for a century and then only slowly began to grow back, beginning around 1450–1500.

There are many things to hold back the population of Europe at this course of the game. Periodic recurrences of the plague happened between 1361–1722. The last outbreak was at Marseille, France. There was a host of additional bacterial and viral infections and exotic epidemic diseases to which Europeans were prone. Remember that late medieval people and early modern people had no understanding of the connections among hygiene, germs and disease. In fact, we oftentimes don't actually know what diseases attacked them. They had weird names like the "sweating sickness" or the "bloody flux." They had no recourse to modern antibiotics. As a result, this period has been called the "golden age of bacteria."

Famine was also something that Europeans had to deal with, usually as a result of bad harvests. About one out of four harvests was bad, and one out of six so bad as to induce famine. While few people actually starved, the scarcity of food lowered resistance to disease, and that sent death rates up.

Clothing and housing were barely adequate to keep one warm and dry. Most people had one, flea-infested suit of woolen clothes and linen underwear, which was the only part of their clothing that they washed regularly. They lived in flimsy huts made of mud and straw, as we'll see towards the end of this lecture. They were subject to accidents, fire, and drowning. Nobody knew how to swim. Violence was also common in the early modern period in the form of war and assault, as we will see.

As a result, the average life expectancy in Europe in 1500 was about 30 years. The young were not spared. Infant mortality ran about 20% in the first year. This included 5% of babies that were stillborn and another 10% of children who would die by the age of ten. This has led some historians to postulate that parents avoided emotional investment in their children, but that is a very controversial concept among historians. What is certain is that this population only began to recover again after 1500.

The demographic disaster of the 14th and 15th centuries had tremendous economic consequences. Ironically, the "golden age of bacteria" was also a "golden age for labor." You see, if you managed to survive the Black Death, you were part of a very small labor force that was very much in demand. These people who were left could demand an end to serfdom. They could demand to be paid in wages.

They could demand lower food prices and lower rents. That was good news for agricultural workers and terrible news for landowners, who had to find other ways of raising money. What they did was they sometimes abandoned farming themselves and instead, they rented to peasants and let them farm the land. Sometimes they would throw the peasants off their land in a process called "enclosure," and revert to sheep farming. This was a process that was much criticized at the time. If you've ever read More's *Utopia*, you know this.

Finally, some aristocrats sought economic gain through war and plunder. The period before 1500 sees a rash of wars fought among kings and aristocrats, such as the Hundred Years' War between France and England (1337–1456); the Wars of the Roses in England (1455–1485); numerous smaller campaigns in Poland and Prussia; infighting among Italian cities; and dynastic and religious wars in Spain.

Where did people live? Less than 5% lived in towns. The largest city in Europe in 1500 was Constantinople, but that had only 400,000 people. Only a few other cities approach the size of, say, Birmingham, Alabama, or Stockton, California today: Paris had 200,000, Naples had 150,000, and Venice had 100,000. Then there was a clutch of smaller cities at about 50,000: London, Amsterdam, Moscow, Lisbon, Madrid, Rome, and Florence. Note the high number of these that are Italian; we'll come back to that.

Below that level of town, cathedral, county, and market towns might house several hundred. I'm referring to places like Salisbury in England, Rheims in France, Bruges, Dortmund, or Lyon. Some of these towns were not very urban. They were just a couple of cross streets surrounded by fields with a market square. They would often swell during holiday periods or during markets to twice their normal size. They were all dependent on trade and that meant they were vulnerable to war and epidemic.

In any case, most people didn't live in towns. The vast majority of Europeans lived in villages of less than 500 inhabitants, and sometimes as few as 50. Let us imagine that in our quest to find the people of Europe at the beginning of our course, we have trekked across forest and field looking for human habitation. We would find the continent mostly empty and green, but perhaps in the distance we would spy the towers of a castle, a windmill, or most likely the steeple of a village church. Any of these would tell us that we had stumbled upon the estate of a great landlord known as a "manor."

There are probably two impressive buildings on this manor. The first would be the lord's manor house. It might be near the center of the village or up on a hill. Actually, if this lord has lots of manors, his manor house might be on another manor. It might be an impressive castle or a big timber frame house.

But the building that would draw our attention rather more magnetically, I think, is the church. The church was virtually the only stone building in town apart from that manor house. It was the religious center of the village, where Sunday services were held and holy days—about 40 of them—were celebrated. Similarly, all the important rites of passage of one's life took place there—one's birth at baptism, one's marriage at matrimony, and one's death at one's funeral.

This church has no competition. There's one church per village. In most of Europe, there is only one legal religion. In the West, before about 1550, it was what we today call Roman Catholicism. In the East, it was one of the Christian Orthodox faiths. So, on Sundays, Holy Days, and funerals, the entire village turns up to hear the Latin or Greek mass, performed behind an altar screen, and to hear a homily in the vernacular.

That homily is probably the only religious instruction and the only news that these people get. I want to make three points about it. First, most people were probably illiterate—about 95% of the population. There were no newspapers, television, radio, or Internet. The local priest was almost certainly selected and remains employed by the landlord. In other words, he's giving you the news, but he's giving you the news the landlord wants you to have. He's giving you the company line.

After mass, there's likely to be some sort of party or socializing. Sundays and holy days are the only days these people have off from working in the fields. There might be a church ale or the feast associated with a particular saint. On Sundays and holidays, people would engage in football and stickball. They would drink ale while sitting on the tombstones surrounding the village church.

There are a couple points to make here. One is that the entire village is present, even past generations, because given the Catholic doctrine of Purgatory, there is a sense in which the living villagers are still praying for the people over whose graves they are drinking the ale and playing the football. The second point to make is that obviously the church is the social as well as the religious center of the village. Contemporaries would actually have been shocked at the way we draw a line between those two things.

After the excitement of the day, we might accompany the villagers down their one dirt track to their homes. These were likely to be small two-room huts or shacks. They're made of basically anything that will stick together: mud, straw, animal manure, etc. As a result, they are pretty flimsy and easily destroyed and washed away any time it rains. More prosperous peasants might at this stage be able to afford a small house of stone or wood. All of these houses had thatched roofs and dirt floors. There might be one wooden door but few or no windows, because windows let in the cold. On entering one of these hovels, our eyes take some time to adjust to the darkness because of the lack of light and the smoke. When our eyes do adjust, they would see a hearth in the center. Please don't think of a cheery brick fireplace; rather, I want you to imagine an indoor campfire. This was the family's main source of light and heat and its main implement for cooking.

When the harvests were good, the average peasant's diet was pretty well balanced, if not particularly mouth-watering: rough brown bread, pea soup, cheese, meat on very rare occasions, and ale or wine.

Looking around the room, we might spy some possessions: a few pots and pans, a table and some stools, a chest, a candleholder, some candles, and a few articles of clothing. People slept on rushes, or mattresses that were stuffed with straw. Admittedly, they spent most of their time working outdoors, but at night and in the winter they lived their entire lives in these cramped conditions and very much in each other's company. In other words, modern notions of privacy did not pertain. Everything that takes place within a family would have taken place in front of the entire family.

If the family was lucky, it might have a second room to shelter the animals. Otherwise, during winter, you bring the animals in with you. Animals are so valuable and so necessary for survival that you can't risk their death in a frost. They provide milk, cheese, and wool that might keep this family solvent or even alive during the hard times of winter.

Finally, surrounding the village, were the fields where the villagers worked. Let's talk a little bit about work. The work of early modern European people was, of course, dependent upon where they lived. In town, most people sold goods or services. Merchants acted as middlemen for grain, cattle, or wool. Craftsmen made and sold cloth, shoes, barrels, and candles. They shoed horses if they were blacksmiths, or ground grain if they were millers.

To do so, they had to belong to the local guild, which made sure that any merchant or craftsman was a member. You couldn't trade outside the guild. They made goods by hand and on spec rather than keeping a ready stock. You would go in and order a pair of shoes. They lived above their shops with their families and apprentices who helped with the work.

Port cities contained all the crafts and trades that we associate with seafaring: fishermen, shipwrights, carpenters, sailmakers, dockworkers, and customs officials. In upland areas, or swamps, people made their livings with sheep or dairy farming; they spun wool, flax or hemp; they engaged in quarrying.

Most villagers, however, depended upon arable farming. Surrounding the village would be a plot of common land. On this, you could graze animals and you could also play sports and games. Each villager's rented land would be arranged in long strips in a haphazard manner. You might have several strips that didn't connect with each other. You may be wondering, "Why strips? Why not the neat squares that we today see from airplanes when we look down on farms?"

The idea behind the long strip was that it was easier to plow. At the end of the Middle Ages, the standard beast of burden was an ox. I have to admit that I don't have a lot of experience with oxen, but I am told that oxen are not easily turned around. You don't want to be negotiating those four corners. You want to get behind that thing and plow all day in one direction.

Men went out to the fields where they hoed, plowed, sowed, pruned, harvested, and winnowed. There, they were joined by women and children at peak times—planting in the spring and harvest in the fall. They worked sun-up to sundown, which implied longer hours in summer and shorter but colder hours in winter. At other times, the women cooked, sewed clothes, fetched water, and spun or wove wool. Again, these supplemental sources of income might be the difference between economic or even physical survival and poverty or death. Children looked after the animals and, when older, looked after the younger children. This was a very common way for children to die; animals can gore children. Accidents were very frequent.

Before we leave these people, it is worth remarking that this manor and village would be their entire world. Most villagers will never saw a city. They never touched the ocean. They never passed the borders of their county. Being such a small community, everyone will know everyone else, and everyone else's business. Peer pressure must have been immense. Our modern notions of privacy would have been entirely foreign to these people. All would have been conscious of the fact that they were not masters of their own destinies.

Who was? The landlord on the hill overlooking the village. He might actually live many miles away or he might be in a manor house from which he could view his peasants. In any case, he was the person who determined their fate. The landlord might have been a great nobleman, a prosperous squire, or a minor gentleman. He might have owned many manors across the county or just this one. He might have lived on the estate or at a great distance, but what is certain is that he had tremendous power over his tenants.

First, he commanded a vast income. He owned nearly all the land in the neighborhood, and that land yielded an income from harvesting its crops, exploiting its mineral wealth, and above all collecting the rents of the tenants who lived and worked on it. In addition, the landlord probably owned the best mill for the grinding of grain and the best oven for the baking of bread. He's got you coming and going. You pay rent to grow grain on his land that you then have to pay him to grind and bake.

Control of the land also implied control of the church, since it's probable that the landlord names the priest—and can also fire the priest—from that local chapel. He could demand from his tenants not only rents, but taxes that could be paid in produce like wheat, butter, or a certain number of chickens a year. He had exclusive hunting and fishing rights. He could demand *corvée:* annual service of a few days a year for building roads and the upkeep of his estate. He could demand military service in time of war and even, by custom, the sexual favors of any young woman on his land. If you know the plot of *The Marriage of Figaro*, you know that this is an important plot point. These rights were called the *droits du seignior*, or seignorial rights.

Often, the king would ask him to use his power to maintain order in the countryside as a local official. Paradoxically, that local importance might draw him to the capital to attend the king's council and court, or to sit in Parliament, the Estates General, or the Cortes.

Given his immense power, it is probably fortunate that medieval theology argued that great landowners had a paternal responsibility to take care of their tenants. We'll talk more about that in the next lecture. In the meantime, it should be obvious that being a landlord gave tremendous power.

If you remember one thing about Europe in 1500, it should be that the people who mattered in 1500, 1700, and beyond owned land. By virtue of owning land, they owned all those little villages and all those little lives of the people who lived in them.

The second thing that you should remember is that the proportion of people who owned land was very small, less than 10% of the population. The highest nobility, with sometimes 30% of the land, amounted to less than 0.5% of that population. All of which should raise a question: Why did the other 99.5% of the population put up with it? As my students like to ask me, "Why didn't they just rebel?" As we shall see, sometimes they did; but by and large, they did not. If they did not, it has something to do with the way they constructed their universe in their heads. To explain why they didn't rebel, I now have to talk about the Great Chain of Being.

Lecture Three
Culture Is Destiny

Scope:

The Great Chain of Being posited an ordered, hierarchical universe in which every creature—especially humans—was placed in a particular rank by God. To rebel against that order, even to try to rise higher than one's place at birth, was, thus, to challenge God's own mandate. But as Europe emerged from the Middle Ages, the Great Chain of Being was being challenged and strained by forces in politics, society, religion, and culture. Those forces will be the subject of the next six lectures.

Outline

I.   Geography is destiny, but culture is, too. How people perceive their reality is at least as important as the physical and social topography discussed in the last lecture.

II. In 1500, most European men and women were what we would call Catholics today.

 A. All European men, women, and children were taught that God created the universe, ordered it, and was active in its everyday working.

 B. When asked to describe their universe or its parts, late medieval commentators fell back on metaphors.

  1. One of their favorite metaphors for society was that of the body politic.

  2. A more comprehensive metaphor (because it took into account God and all the creatures in his universe) was the one that historians later dubbed the *Great Chain of Being*. (Note: I also discuss the Great Chain in my Teaching Company course entitled *History of England from the Tudors to the Stuarts*.)

 C. Europeans generally believed in the Ptolemaic universe; a series of concentric spheres with the Earth in the center.

1. Copernicus published *De Revolutionibus Orbium Coelestium* (*On the Revolutions of the Celestial Spheres*) in 1543, but his ideas would only begin to gain ground around 1600.

2. In 1500, most people still believed that, moving from the outer sphere inward, the universe consisted of the stars, the planets, the Sun, the Moon, and, at the center, the Earth; at the center of Earth were the flames of hell.

D. As this implies, when they thought about the inhabitants of that universe, they thought of a hierarchy, arranged as follows:

1. The celestial hierarchy consisted of God, angels, man, animals, plants, and stones.

2. There are five things to remember about this system.

    a. Those at the top of this hierarchy were closer to God than those at the bottom.

    b. Humankind is halfway down the chain, suspended between the angels and the animals.

    c. Apart from God, each of the ranks in the chain could be further divided.

        i. Angels were divided into nine ranks.

        ii. The animal, plant, and stone hierarchies could be similarly divided.

        iii. And so with man: king, aristocrats, peasants, laborers, and the poor.

        iv. These ranks can be further subdivided.

        v. Every rank might be further divided into families, with the genders ranked.

        vi. In theory, every single creature and object in God's universe could be placed, precisely, in this hierarchy.

    d. The top of each part of the chain is analogous to the head of the whole chain, God himself.

        i. Clearly, the people of Europe in 1500 were obsessed with order.

        ii. By the same token, their greatest fear was disorder.

     e. The chain is a chain, not a ladder. Because the chain was considered to be God's plan, it was a grave sin to attack the chain, disobey one's superiors, rebel against the king, or even try to rise to another rank!

E. Clearly, European society in 1500 valued order, not opportunity; conformity, not originality; community, not individuality.

    1. The top three ranks of the human chain represented less than 10 percent of the population.

    2. That 10 percent owned perhaps 50 percent of the land in Europe and possessed nearly 100 percent of the power.

    3. We might well ask why the other 90 percent of people put up with this system.

F. This system was drilled into the people of Europe from the pulpit every Sunday.

    1. After all, it explained their universe and probably did prevent disorder that they would otherwise have been unable to stop.

    2. Imagine what a European from 1500 would think of the violence, noise, and chaos of our world.

G. Another explanation for widespread acceptance of the chain can be found in two related beliefs designed to mitigate the worst effects of inequality: paternalism and deference.

    1. Paternalism was the belief, also taught from every pulpit in Europe and often embodied in proclamation and law, that those at the upper end of the chain had a responsibility to look after those below them.

    2. Deference, that is, allegiance, obedience, and respect, was the attitude that the lower orders were supposed to display toward those at the top of the chain.

H. Thus, in the European universe of 1500, every man, woman, and child knew where he or she stood. Or did they?

III. The chain was an ideal of order and stability, but life is ever messy and mutable. As our course opens, the ideal of the chain fit less and less well with the realities of European life.

A. The composition of the various ranks changed.

1. The nobility were supposedly the oldest, most distinguished families in Europe.
   a. But some noble families were upstarts, receiving their titles through royal favor or court service, rather than military service, as in the past.
   b. Other families died out or were deprived of their titles on conviction of treason.
   c. As a result, the oldest families were, in fact, constantly renewed with new blood.
2. Peasants rose and fell with fluctuations in the economy and fluctuations in the weather.
3. Some people fell out of the chain entirely by forming chains of their own that did not seem to fit into the main social hierarchy.

B. Cities had their own chains, consisting of the mayor; aldermen, burghers, or members of the town council; citizens or freemen (that is, members of the guild); journeymen, apprentices, and so on; and everybody else.
   1. It was difficult to figure how to fit this chain into the main one.
   2. Cities were places where capitalism flourished.
      a. People could grow rich very fast and, thus, rise in status.
      b. People could grow poor very fast and, thus, fall in status.
   3. Cities were places of relative anonymity.
      a. It was harder to tell who was who, and who belonged to whom in a city.
      b. Unlike the parish and village, everybody did not know everybody else.
      c. It was possible to escape one's rank in the main chain by going to the city.
   4. Thus, the economic and social fluidity of cities made nonsense of the chain.

C. In the East (Russia and portions of Southern Europe ruled by the Ottoman Empire), the Orthodox Churches were subordinate to the civil authority, but in the West, the Roman Catholic Church had its own chain: the pope, archbishops, bishops, priests, sisters, and the laity. This Church hierarchy, too, raised problems for the chain.

    1. If the pope was the Vicar of Christ, and the emperor or king was God's lieutenant, who was superior? That is, while these two leaders usually agreed, what if they did not?

        a. During 1309-1374, the King of France more or less abducted the papacy to Avignon ("Babylonian Captivity of the Church"), which led many people to view the papacy as a tool of the French monarchy.

        b. During the Great Schism of 1374-1417, there was more than one pope. Two separate sets of cardinals elected popes, and each one excommunicated the other. During this time, some rulers encouraged their subjects to question papal authority.

    2. During the Middle Ages, a growing chorus had criticized both the doctrine and practice of the Church.

        a. The Church regarded such critics as heretical, enforcing discipline, with the cooperation of kings, by burning heretics at the stake.

        b. There remained a small minority of Christians, though, who wanted a more democratic, less hierarchical Church.

        c. What would happen if the king ever agreed with them?

D. These problems were inevitable given the tensions between the chain and the reality of European medieval life.

E. But as Europe entered the 16th century, it was beginning to experience six new challenges that would eventually smash the chain and lay the groundwork for the modern world.

    1. Renaissance Humanism.

    2. The rise of centrally governed nation-states.

    3. The discovery of the New World.

    4. The invention of the printing press.

5. The Protestant Reformation and its consequence, the Wars of Religion.
6. The Rational and Scientific Revolutions.

Supplementary Reading:

M. B. Chambers, et al., *Western Experience*, chapter 11, sections III–IV.

A. O. Lovejoy, *The Great Chain of Being: A Study of the History of an Idea*.

Questions to Consider:

1. Why did Europeans continue to cling to the Great Chain of Being even as it failed to reflect reality?

2. To what extent do attitudes associated with the chain survive today?

Diagram 3a

Great Chain of Being

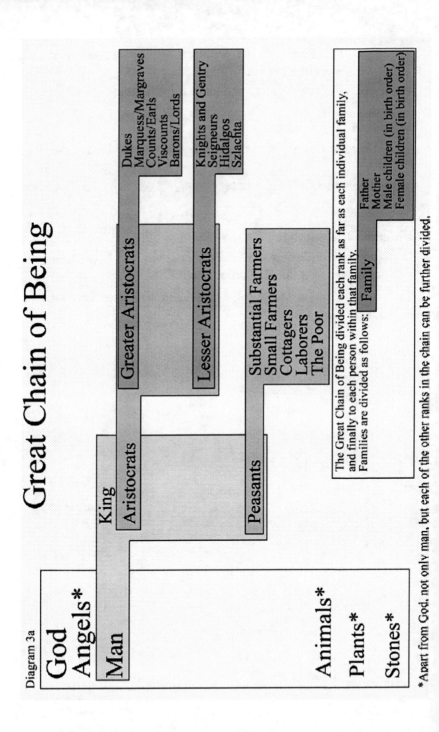

God

Angels*

Man
- King
- Aristocrats
  - Greater Aristocrats
    - Dukes
    - Marquess/Margraves
    - Counts/Earls
    - Viscounts
    - Barons/Lords
  - Lesser Aristocrats
    - Knights and Gentry
    - Seigneurs
    - Hidalgos
    - Szlachta
- Peasants
  - Substantial Farmers
  - Small Farmers
  - Cottagers
  - Laborers
  - The Poor

The Great Chain of Being divided each rank as far as each individual family, and finally to each person within that family. Families are divided as follows: Family
- Father
- Mother
- Male children (in birth order)
- Female children (in birth order)

Animals*

Plants*

Stones*

* Apart from God, not only man, but each of the other ranks in the chain can be further divided.

Lecture Three—Transcript
Culture Is Destiny

In the last lecture, we examined the physical and social topography of Europe in about the year 1500. The physical world, geographical realities, spatial relationships, and material culture are all very important parts of history. After all, didn't we say that geography was destiny? These things are less than half of the story, however. Sometimes they can be downright misleading if you fail to understand how the people of a specific time and place constructed their world mentally and made sense of it in their heads.

If I may be allowed a personal reflection to start this lecture: one of my frustrations with the way history is done in the movies is that very often you find that producers or directors brag about getting the costumes and uniforms exactly right and the last rivet down on the battleship that they are portraying in this film. Then he or she will fill characters' heads with thoughts they never would have thought and their mouths with words they never would have spoken, because he or she did not take the time to understand their worldview and the mental universe that existed at the time. We will not make that mistake.

If geography is destiny, then culture is reality—or how people perceive their reality. This is a fact that we as Americans need to know as we interact with other cultures and the values of other peoples. In short, you don't understand them if you don't understand their worldview.

This lecture will address the worldview of Europe circa 1500, which means that it will deal with the medieval inheritance in philosophy and theology. Specifically, it will lay out a late medieval ideal called the Great Chain of Being and the social hierarchy that it implied. Here I should probably issue a warning. If you have ever taken a course from me—this goes for virtually every student I have ever taught—you have probably heard a lecture on the Great Chain of Being. If you want to skip to the next tape, you are free to do so.

This lecture will then explain why that ideal of society was under strain as our course opens. This will require discussion of Europe's economic base, its religious structure, and its political arrangements at the end of the Middle Ages. Put another way, I'm going to explain the universe to you as it was envisioned—at least at the dawn of our course—from the celestial bodies down to earth and from God himself down to the lowliest peasant, the tiniest creature, and the most infinitesimal pebble.

In 1500, most European men and women were what we would today call Roman Catholic, at least in Western Europe. That was about to change during the 16th century, thanks to the Protestant Reformation. Even in 1600, however, Protestants and Catholics shared or reacted against a common set of assumptions dating back to the Middle Ages. All European men, women, and children were taught about and, so far as we know, all believed in God. Atheists as we know them were virtually unknown; perhaps it was not thought of, or perhaps it was just a very dangerous opinion to express. By the way, after about 1550 or so, the term "atheist" will generally mean a Protestant if you're a Catholic, or a Catholic if you're a Protestant.

All Europeans believed, further, that God created the universe, ordered it, and was active in its everyday working. "There's a special providence in the fall of every sparrow," as Shakespeare would have it. When asked to describe their universe or its parts, late medieval commentators fell back on metaphors. One of their favorite metaphors was that of the "body politic." That is, they thought of the English or French state as a body, with the king as the head; the aristocracy, who bore arms as the arms and shoulders; and the tenant farmers and the poor, as the legs and smelly feet.

A more comprehensive metaphor, for it took into account God and all the creatures in his universe, was the one which later historians have dubbed "The Great Chain of Being." When late medieval and early modern men and women thought about the universe, they generally thought of it as the Ptolemaic universe; that is as a series of concentric spheres with Earth in the middle center. Copernicus would publish *On the Revolutions of the Heavenly Bodies* in 1543, but his ideas would only begin to gain ground around 1600.

In 1500, most people still believed that, moving from the outer sphere inwards, there were the stars, the planets, the sun, the moon, and at the center, Earth. At the center of Earth were the flames of hell. This implies that when they thought about the inhabitants of the universe, they thought hereto of a hierarchy arranged as follows: God, who dwelt everywhere but especially beyond the stars, as he is referred to in the Beethoven *Ninth*; angels, who traversed the heavens between God and man; man, who dwelt erect on the Earth;

animals, on the Earth but closer to it (remember, these are Europeans—they don't have elephants or giraffes—most animals really are closer to the Earth than most Europeans are); plants are closer still if we ignore trees; and finally stones, which are literally on the Earth.

There are five things that I want you to remember about the Great Chain of Being. Number one: as should be obvious, those at the top of this hierarchy were closer to God than those at the bottom. Thus, church steeples aspired to Heaven. The one at St. Paul's Cathedral in London rose over 500 feet before it burnt down in 1666. Thus, when one attends a royal palace, one ascends to meet the sovereign—one goes up to be closer to God. Thus, the souls of the damned dwelt at the center of the Earth, in the molten core of Hell, farthest removed from God's mercy, both spiritually and physically.

The second thing I want you to remember about the Chain is that humankind is halfway down the Chain, suspended between the angels and the animals. Contemporaries thought that each rank in the Chain partook a little bit of the rank above it and a little bit of the rank below it. Therefore, man was both half angel and half beast. By the way, I'm going to be using the term "man," politically incorrect as it is, because that is the term that contemporaries would have recognized. Theologians and moral commentators were deeply aware of the fact that man could go either way—animal or angel. In the words of Francis Bacon, "A man's nature runs either to herbs or to weeds; therefore let him seasonably water the one, and destroy the other."

The third thing I want you to remember about the Chain is that, apart from God, each of the ranks in the Chain can be further divided. Thus, medieval theologians didn't just think of angels. Anyone who has read their Dante or was raised in the old Roman Catholic Church will know that there aren't just angels. There are seraphim, cherubim, thrones, dominations, virtues, powers, principalities, archangels, and angels.

The animal hierarchy, too, could be similarly divided. Is not the lion the king of the beasts? Is not the eagle nobler than the sparrow? The whale greater than the codfish? Plants, too, could be ranked from the mighty oak to the lowly fern. As for stones, are not diamonds a girl's best friend? Far closer to divine beauty than, say, granite or a grain of sand? And so, with man.

Man, too, is arranged in a hierarchy as follows: at the top, the king, followed by aristocrats, great landowners, peasants, laborers, and the very poor, who might be said to have fallen out of the Chain. I'd like to examine each of these ranks in greater detail. They'll be the social ranks with which we start this course.

First, there's the king, or in Germany, the Holy Roman Emperor. He was the fount of justice and honor. He was "God's Lieutenant on Earth." We're going to be talking a lot about kings in this course. I'm going to move over them pretty quickly, but for now it's important to remember that he is not only the most socially prominent person, but probably the wealthiest person in this society.

Below the king are aristocrats. I'm going to divide these into greater aristocrats, usually the titled nobility (those who bear the ranks of duke, marquis, count, earl, viscount, or baron), and what I'll call "lesser aristocrats," namely, smaller landowners. The first thing to note about these people, apart from their titles, is that they command vast incomes. They are very wealthy and often have multiple estates. The way they started off was probably as the king's soldiers, and they earned those estates through warfare. They want to preserve their estates as much as possible, so they generally leave their holdings to the eldest male. This is the process known as *primogeniture*.

They also used to build castles and many still live in them in 1500, but they are becoming obsolete thanks to gunpowder and artillery. From this point, increasingly, they build great chateaux and country houses, which emphasize luxury rather than military preparedness.

Their great wealth and importance in the country imply office and also large regiments of servants. A great aristocrat is serviced by estate managers, chaplains, household servants of all kinds, tenants, political allies, clients, and hangers on. His web extends out into the countryside. In fact, it could be argued that his castle or country house is not just a fortress, but also a sort of mini-court.

The lesser aristocracy would include knights and gentry in England, *seigneurs* in France, *hidalgos* in Spain, *Junkers* in German, and the *szlachta* in Poland. These people usually have just one estate or maybe a couple. Their income provides a comfortable existence facilitated by maybe a dozen servants. As our period wears on, however, many of them, particularly in Eastern Europe, will grow poorer. This rank oversaw the day-to-day local government for the king. They serve as tax collectors and local judges, and raise the militia.

Below them come the peasants. Perhaps I ought to say a word about this word. This has come to mean in our language anyone in a subservient position. People who have bosses like to think of themselves as being peasants. In its original meaning, however, it meant someone who lived in the country. Think of the derivation from *pays*, *paesano* (a countryman), or *patria*. You can't be a peasant and live in the city.

Peasants can also be divided between substantial peasants and, for want of a better term, lesser or poorer peasants. In England, a substantial peasant would be called a "yeoman." This person would have pretty secure tenure of their land. Either they own it or they have a lease that can't be broken. They might have several farms. In other words, the richest yeoman is oftentimes as wealthy as the poorest nobleman. They might employ several servants to work them, but the difference is that a yeoman farmer will share in that work. He'll go out and help with the plowing and harvesting. These people made a small but comfortable living. In England, they could vote for members of Parliament, specifically for the House of Commons. They were the backbone of rural society. They served on juries and commanded the local militia.

Below them were small farmers, what an Englishman might call a "husbandman." These are probably renters. They don't own land and their tenure is not secure. They employ a few servants on a seasonal basis and make very small amounts of money. In England, they would make perhaps £10 a year. To give you a sense of scale, a great nobleman in 1500 in England might make several hundred pounds a year.

Cottagers were even smaller than husbandmen and rented a small cottage with no farm attached. They make just a few pounds a year. They scrape by on the edge of subsistence.

Below the ranks of the peasants, I would include laborers. Laborers had no homes of their own. As in *Green Acres,* for those of you who remember that show, these are people who probably live in the barn.

They may actually do seasonal work at various locations. They may not be permanently attached to a family.

In general, talking again about peasants, it was better to be a peasant or laborer in Western Europe than in Eastern Europe. In Eastern Europe, peasants and laborers were serfs. They were not free. They were tied to the land. That always conjures up images, particularly in undergraduate minds, of people with dog collars literally leashed to the land. What it means is that they couldn't leave without their landlord's permission. French peasants were free, but they had few rights and the law was harsher towards them than it was towards aristocrats. They were heavily taxed, unlike the clergy and nobility. English peasants were free and had a vote. They were less heavily taxed.

Finally, below this level came the poor, who had no permanent residence or visible means of support. The last four groups below the level of nobility formed the bulk of rural society.

Another point I want to make, which is tied up in the point about divisions, is that all of these ranks can be further subdivided. For example, the titled nobility are divided into dukes (usually related to the king), marquises or margraves, counts (or earls in England), viscounts (or *vicomte* in France), and barons. They were further divided by the order in which they received their title.

The Chain also implies a hierarchy of genders, as well as social rank. In other words, every single family that we have described could be divided into men and women, followed by male children in birth order, followed by female children in birth order. Biologically, women were considered to be inferior men. Medieval theology followed Aristotle in believing that the female is a misbegotten male. Theologically, a lot of scripture was deployed to justify that supposed inferiority. Legally, socially, and economically, the status of women in Europe was most often tied to whichever man they "belonged to"—their fathers until they married, and then their husbands. If a woman lost her male—her father or her husband—she was considered quite dangerous. European society didn't know how to handle unattached women, as it didn't know how to handle unattached men.

The fourth thing I want you to remember about the Great Chain of Being is that the top of Chain is analogous to the head of the whole

Chain: God himself. In other words, the king in the country, the father in the family, the lion among beasts, and, of course, the professor in the classroom all represent God and were placed at the top of their respective chains by God. They wield God's power in his stead and so were to be obeyed as God himself.

Clearly, the people of Europe in 1500, or at least their leaders, were obsessed with order. Their fondest desire was apparently to be able to place every single being and every single speck of matter in its proper place in the celestial hierarchy. By the same token, their greatest fear was disorder, and that brings me to the fifth thing I want you to remember about the Great Chain of Being: it was a Chain, not a ladder. To attack the Chain, disobey your superiors, rebel against your king, sass your professor, or even to rise from the place that God had appointed for you to live your life was to commit treason against God. It was to violate the fundamental laws of the universe. This is a very hard thing for us moderns to understand. We spend all of our lives trying to do better than our parents. We go to university for precisely that reason. For any creature to attack its superior in the Chain was to unhinge the universe.

In a famous speech from *Troilus and Cressida,* Shakespeare argues:

> The heavens themselves, the planets, and this center [Earth]
> Observe degree, priority, and place,
> Insisture, course, proportion, season, form,
> Office and custom, in all line of order; ...
> ...But when the planets,
> In evil mixture to disorder wander,
> What plagues, and what portents, what mutiny,
> What raging of the sea, shaking of the earth,
> Commotion in the winds! Frights, changes, horrors,
> Divert and crack, rend and deracinate,
> The unity and married calm of states
> Quite from their fixture!

In the next few lines, Shakespeare alludes to the contemporary belief in astrology by moving from the celestial to the earthly:

> O when degree is shak'd,
> Which is the ladder to all high designs,
> The enterprise is sick! How could communities,
> Degrees in schools, and brotherhoods in cities,

Peaceful commerce from dividable shores,
The primogenitive and due of birth,
Prerogative of age, crowns, sceptres, laurels,
But by degree, stand in authentic place?
Take but degree away, untune that string,
And, hark, what discord follows!

Clearly, European society in 1500 valued order, not opportunity; conformity, not originality; and community, not individuality. When we consider that the top two ranks of the human chain represent only about 1% of the population, yet own maybe 50% of the land in Europe and nearly 100% of its power, it kind of makes you wonder why didn't the other 99% just rebel?

There were a few reasons for that. One was education. This is what they heard from the pulpit every Sunday. Remember that every person is required to attend the parish church. There were few or no competing religions. In 1500, only Jews were tolerated in some parts of Europe, but this was rare. The local landlord appointed the pastor. Having had this system drummed into them from childhood on a weekly basis, having grown up being told it was God's plan, and knowing no alternative, it became as instinctual to them as our belief in competition, ambition, and advancement by merit is to us.

After all, it explained their universe and it probably did prevent disorder that they would otherwise have been impotent to stop. As Shakespeare argues, the alternative might have been disastrous. Imagine what Europeans from 1500 would think of our world. Would they embrace its disorder, constant change, and opportunity; or would they find it violent, noisy, cold, and chaotic? Would they not find plenty of confirmation of Shakespeare's prediction of anarchy and misery?

There's another reason, however, that people accepted the Great Chain of Being. There were two related beliefs designed to mitigate the worst effects of inequality: paternalism and deference.

Paternalism was the belief, also taught from every pulpit in Europe, that those at the upper end of the Chain had a responsibility to look after those below them. After all, if a father was like God, God was also a loving father. If those at the top of the Chain represented and, in some sense, embodied him, wielding his power, surely they also bore his responsibility to look after his creation. Like God, those at the top of the Chain were to watch paternally over their flocks, by offering military protection in time of war; justice in the royal and manorial courts; jobs and economic assistance in hard times (you're supposed to take care of your tenants); and hospitality at the holidays, when the manor house might be opened up to everyone.

In return, the common people below them in the Chain were supposed to provide deference. By deference, I mean allegiance, obedience, and respect. They did this by attending church on Sunday; paying their taxes and tithes to the church; obeying God's law, the king's law, and church (or canon) law; and obeying their landlords, employers, and fathers. They gave their landlords the seignorial rights we mentioned in the last lecture: a set amount of their produce, annual service to build roads and repair farm buildings, refraining from hunting and fishing, and even tolerating the sexual advances of the landlord on their wives and daughters.

They also expressed deference by gestures such as bowing, curtseying, tipping their cap, and "giving the wall." Let me explain "giving the wall:" say I happen to see a social superior walking down the street. Let's say I see the Duke of Richmond (I don't know why he's on foot since he can afford a carriage, but here he comes). I'm clearly a social inferior because I'm just a college professor. My job as he approaches is to give him the wall. That means that I must step into the street. If we remember that the street was also the common sewer and that I am stepping into the muck to show my respect for a social superior, could there be any more eloquent indication of just how hierarchical this society is?

In the European universe of 1500, God was in his Heaven, the king sat on his throne, the landlord held sway in his manor house, fathers of all ranks were universally respected and obeyed, and university professors were treated with the dignity and esteem sadly lacking in these our own times. Everyone else stepped into the muck at their behest. Every man, woman, and child in Europe knew where they stood and stand they would, hat in hand, in the presence of a social superior.

Or would they? It always strikes historians that when contemporaries write about the Great Chain of Being and the body politic, they always sound anxious. The Chain was an ideal. It represented order and stability; but life is never ideal, neat, or stable. It is messy and changes constantly. As our course opens, the ideal of the Chain fit less and less well with the realities of European life.

Take social mobility, the idea that everyone is not supposed to move—there's supposed to be no social mobility. Take the nobility. These are supposedly the oldest, most distinguished families in the realm, who received their lands ages ago from the king for military service. By 1500, however, an awful lot of those families had died out, and people tended to receive their land not necessarily for going to war for the king, but by being a good royal servant at court (a "courtier"). These courtiers are very often viewed with resentment as upstarts.

Other nobles are deprived of their titles not only because their lines die out, but because they have engaged in rebellion or perhaps performed an act of treason that might mean forfeiting their estates. In other words, what I am telling you is that noble families rose and fell all the time.

Peasants, too, rose and fell with fluctuations in the economy, fluctuations in the weather (i.e. bad harvests), and fluctuations in the season (laborers thrown out of agricultural work annually during winter). Of course, some people fell out of the Chain entirely; that is, they didn't live on the land under the paternal care of a landlord.

This brings me to cities. Cities had their own chains. They would have a mayor, followed by aldermen, burghers, and a town council. Underneath them, there are the citizens, or freemen (that is, full members of the guild), followed by journeymen and apprentices trying to break into the guild, followed by everybody else. You could live in a city and not be a citizen; citizens were tied to the guild.

Where did that fit into the Great Chain of Being? Where would you put the mayor of Bremen, who is probably a merchant? Is he above a gentleman? He works with his hands, which is something that gentlemen don't do. What of a prosperous attorney? Or a struggling tailor? Where do they fit? The Great Chain said nothing about them; so the basis of their status is wealth, not birth. That didn't fit the principles of the Great Chain of Being.

Cities are places where capitalism flourishes. That means people can grow rich very fast—they can rise in status—and they can grow poor very fast—fall in status. Both played havoc with the notion that God placed people in immutable ranks.

Cities are places of relative anonymity. How does anyone know what rank you are? You can move to a city and change your rank. You can pretend to be something you're not. Unlike a parish in a village, where everyone else knows everyone else's business, nobody knows you in a city. Thus, the economic and social fluidity of cities make nonsense of the Great Chain of Being.

Then there's the Church. In the East—Russia and portions of southern Europe ruled by the Ottoman Empire—the Orthodox churches were subordinate to the civil authority. In the West, however, the Roman Catholic Church had its own chain: the pope followed by archbishops, bishops, priests, sisters, and the laity. That meant that nearly every person in Christendom was actually part of at least two chains.

This Church hierarchy, too, raised problems for the Great Chain of Being. Take the papacy: if the pope was the Vicar of Christ and the emperor or king was God's Lieutenant on Earth, then which one outranked the other? If these two leaders usually agreed, what would happen if they didn't? In fact, during the Middle Ages, popes and kings had clashed frequently over matters like who appointed the bishops, and whether a civil court could try a churchman for murder or collect taxes from him.

Though the pope had won a number of concessions in the 12th and 13th centuries, his prestige took a big hit in the 14th. First, when the King of France more or less abducted the papacy to Avignon between 1309–1374. This is known as the Babylonian Captivity of the Church. During this period, many people viewed the papacy as a tool of the French monarchy, which reduced the sense of the pope being an impartial arbiter.

Then, during the Great Schism between 1374–1417, there was more than one pope. Two separate sets of cardinals elected popes. Each one excommunicated the other. During this period of time, some rulers actually encouraged the questioning of papal authority by their subjects. The upshot, of course, was a tremendous decline in the prestige of the papacy.

After the healing of the Great Schism, the Church remained powerful and wealthy, with thousands of parishes and clergy; but even that made the question more pressing. What would happen if kings and popes disagreed more profoundly?

Then there were the problems of corruption, discipline, and conscience in the Church. During the Middle Ages, there was a growing chorus that criticized both the doctrine and practice of the Church. Groups like the Albigensians, Lollards, and Hussites attacked the clergy for being too worldly, too concerned with power, and too remote from the faithful. The Church regarded such groups as heretical. Kings generally agreed and were often happy to burn them at the stake.

What would happen, however, if king and heretics ever agreed? Stay tuned. These problems were perhaps inevitable, given the tensions between the Chain and the reality of medieval European life.

As Europe entered the 16th century, however, it was beginning to experience six new challenges that would eventually smash the Chain and give rise to the modern world. These were Renaissance Humanism; the rise of centrally governed nation-states; the discovery of the New World, the invention of the printing press; the Protestant Reformation and its corollary, the Wars of Religion; and the rational and scientific revolutions. I would argue that these six changes created the modern world. Let us now turn to them.

Lecture Four
Renaissance Humanism—1350–1650

Scope:

The age of Michelangelo, Leonardo, More, Erasmus, Castiglione, and, especially, Machiavelli represented the first significant break from the medieval worldview. Beginning in late medieval Italy, artists and writers revived interest in the literary and historical (as opposed to the philosophical and religious) works of the Classical Age of Greece and Rome. The resulting emphasis on textual accuracy, literacy and education, and, above all, the human and the practical can be seen in new ideas about the qualifications of a gentleman, the role of women, and the expectations for a prince.

Outline

I. What were the ideas behind the Renaissance?

    A. Every freshman knows that *Renaissance* means "rebirth." But what was reborn?

    B. Beginning in the 14th century, mostly in Italy, intellectuals and artists began to be more interested in Classical (Greek and Roman) literature and art for its own sake.

        1. University scholars had long been influenced by Greece and Rome.

        2. The medieval interest in Classical writings had been limited to churchmen and university academics.

            a. Medieval scholars were not terribly interested in ancient authors per se.

            b. Rather, medieval schoolmen were largely interested in ancient authors for how their works could assist them in understanding Greek, Latin, and the rules of logic as laid down by Aristotle—all with a view to comprehending Scripture and, ultimately, God.

        3. But toward the end of the Middle Ages, scholars and artists began to grow interested in Greek and Roman authors for their own sakes and for what they might say about the human condition.

C. Although the Renaissance eventually spread north, east, and west, it is generally agreed to have started in Italy.

    1. Italy was perfectly placed to be the European entry point for goods (e.g., fabrics, spices), texts, and ideas from the fabled East.

    2. The resultant wealth, combined with the collapse of political control by the Holy Roman Empire, enabled the cities of Italy to gain independence and prosper.

    3. Later, after about 1500, the rest of Europe would bypass Italian trade routes and seek to abrogate Italian wealth. By 1559, Spanish victories largely put an end to the independence of most Italian city-states, though these wars would also allow Renaissance ideas to spread.

    4. Because Italian wealth centered on cities, Renaissance Humanism was, to start off with at least, an intensely urban phenomenon.

D. Far more important than the idea of rebirth of interest in Greece and Rome, the Renaissance saw a shift away from the study of abstract heavenly concerns (theology, philosophy) toward the real, the human, the concrete, and, above all, the individual.

II. Overall, Renaissance Humanism was a valuation of the human, perhaps not over the divine, but in tandem with it.

A. To see this valuation, all we need do is compare a medieval Madonna and child with a Renaissance example.

    1. Certainly, both artists would have seen their productions as glorifications of God.

        a. Humans were His creation.

        b. They were created in His image.

    2. But what strikes us about Renaissance images is how much they look like us.

B. These artistic changes began in the late Middle Ages.

    1. The painter Giotto gave greater weight and presence to the human figure in the 14th century.

    2. The sculptor Donatello studied Classical masters and attempted to put their principles into practice.

3. Italian architects (e.g., Michelozzi, Brunelleschi) rejected the Gothic and went back to simpler Classical forms in the 15th century.

4. Fifteenth-century artists such as Masaccio used mathematics and observation—as contemporary scientists do—to solve the problem of perspective.

5. At same time, the sculptor Ghiberti applied some of these principles to the magnificent east door for the baptistery at Florence.

6. Fra Angelico and Fra Filippo Lippi emphasized brilliant color and sensuality.

7. Castagno and Leonardo da Vinci studied anatomy.

8. This period saw the beginnings of portraiture. Rich Italian merchants and Renaissance princes wanted to be memorialized at the hands of such artists as Mantegna and Botticelli.

9. These trends culminated in the masterpieces of Leonardo, Michelangelo, and Rafael.

10. The ideals of the Renaissance spread north thanks in part to the printing press and the wars of the 15th and 16th centuries.

11. This culminated in the work of Holbein, the portraitist, in England and 17th-century Dutch painters such as Rubens, Van Dyck, and, later, Rembrandt.

12. Note that we know who these people are because artists now claimed and achieved far-ranging fame, e.g., sculptor Benvenuto Cellini's famous and self-glorifying autobiography (which in the 19th century became an opera by Berlioz).

C. But the real origin and greatest impact of Renaissance Humanism was in literature. Beginning in the 14th century, Europeans began to produce a new kind of literature, less about God and kings and more about human beings.

1. In Italy,

a. Dante Alighieri was a precursor with his *La divina commedia* (1307).

    b. Francesco Petrarca (1304–1374), known as Petrarch, was arguably the founder of Humanism, writing poetry and prose in both Latin and Italian.

    c. Giovanni Boccaccio (1313–1375) wrote the *Decameron*.

    d. Lorenzo de Medici patronized Italian poets, as well as painters and sculptors at his court.

2. In England,

    a. The *Canterbury Tales* by Chaucer (1342/43–1400) anticipated later developments, as Dante had done.

    b. Later Humanist works included the sonnets of Thomas Wyatt (1503–1542) and Henry Howard, Earl of Surrey (1517–1547), Spenser's *Faerie Queen* (1590–1609), Shakespeare's sonnets and plays, and Ben Jonson's poems and plays.

3. In Spain, *Don Quixote* (1605, 1615) by Cervantes (1547–1616) made fun of medieval notions of knightly conduct.

4. In France, the poetry of Ronsard (1524–1585), the political satire of Rabelais (c. 1494–1553), and the essays of Montaigne (1533–1592) all reflected Humanist values.

D. Music also experienced a Renaissance.

1. Church music remained important but grew increasingly polyphonic and complex.

2. Secular madrigals and motets, intended to be performed in people's homes, were a development of the songs of the medieval troubadours and do show a classical influence, e.g., Guillaume de Machaut, Orlando di Lasso, Don Carlo Gesualdo, Claudio Monteverdi.

III. Renaissance Humanism sought to change the world through education.

A. Humanist scholars were highly critical of medieval education, which was often deductive and unadventurous.

B. By extension, Humanist scholars were often highly critical of the medieval Church and its sometimes shabby logic and intolerance.

C. Humanist scholars advocated a reform and an extension of education beyond the clergy to gentlemen and, often, women.

D. They believed, like many Classical authors before them, that education was necessary to make good citizens.

    1. Some Humanist scholars advocated an education that went far beyond the clergy to encompass even women, e.g., Roger Ascham, who tutored Princess Elizabeth

    2. Aristocrats were no longer to be soldiers so much as ministers and officials, serving the prince in peacetime as well as in war.

    3. A good prince should, like the Medici or the Borgia, be well educated himself, employ those who were well-educated, and promote education and the arts. This would, in turn, promote civic virtue and glorify the rule of the prince.

    4. The latter impulse led to an explosion of Renaissance civic art, and pageantry, and buildings like St. Mark's in Venice, Brunelleschi's Duomo in Florence, St. Peter's in Rome, Fontainebleau and the Louvre in France, and Hampton Court in England.

E. The Renaissance de-emphasis of God for human concerns and human capacities, however, threatened to degenerate into a glorification of expediency over virtue.

IV. Castiglione and Machiavelli both wrote for their respective princes at the courts of Urbino and Florence.

A. Balthasar (Baldassare) Castiglione was a diplomat who published *Il libro del cortegiano* (*The Courtier*) in 1528.

    1. The successful courtier was to be impeccable in his manners, discreet in his behavior, and accomplished in the arts of peace and war.

    2. Above all, he was to insinuate himself into the confidence of his prince by telling him the truth—but in the most flattering way possible.

B. Niccolò Machiavelli (1469–1527) sought to advise the ruler himself in *Il principe* (*The Prince*), written in 1513 but published only posthumously in 1532.

1. *The Prince* was part of a long tradition called "Mirrors for Princes."
2. But Machiavelli gave this old genre a new Humanistic twist.
   a. In keeping with the Renaissance de-emphasis on the divine and emphasis on the human, Machiavelli's goal was not to make his prince a better person or get him into heaven.
   b. The goal was, rather, to keep the prince in power on Earth.
3. To stay in power, the prince would have to become adept at seeming to be and doing good, while actually doing whatever it takes to enhance his power.

V. A whole school of Christian writers, including Desiderius Erasmus and Thomas More, took a different tack from Machiavelli, prodding Renaissance princes to remember their responsibilities to their subjects and to the laws of God.

A. In 1509, Erasmus wrote a satire of the human condition and bad government in general called *In Praise of Folly*.

B. Thomas More wrote *Utopia* (1516), describing a mythical land that was far more just and rational than England.

VI. Shakespeare (1564–1616) and Montaigne (1533–1592) were the ultimate inheritors of this tradition.

A. William Shakespeare, in a series of plays written at the turn of the 17th century, explored the human condition from seemingly every angle.

B. Michel de Montaigne's *Essays*, written in the late 16th century, similarly examined the human condition from a wide variety of angles.

VII. Renaissance Humanism was dynamite for the old medieval worldview and the Great Chain of Being.

Supplementary Reading:

M. B. Chambers, et al., *Western Experience*, chapter 12, section III.

P. Burke, *The Italian Renaissance*.

J. Hale, *The Civilization of Europe in the Renaissance*.

Questions to Consider:

1. What did the wealth and political situation of Italy have to do with the Renaissance?

2. What is distinctly modern about Renaissance ideals? What is medieval about them?

Lecture Four—Transcript
Renaissance Humanism—1350–1650

In the last lecture, we learned that medieval theologians had forged an ingenious and comprehensive worldview called the Great Chain of Being. The Chain saw the Earth and its inhabitants as part of a much wider universe, arranged in a strict hierarchical order and presided over by God. The Chain purported to place every creature and every object in the universe in its proper place. Because that place had been assigned by God himself, to attempt to change one's place, let alone to attack the hierarchical concept overall, was to commit treason against God. The whole thing was, of course, a recipe for maintaining the status quo.

However, as Europe emerged from the Middle Ages in the 16th century, its inhabitants were neither sleeping nor standing still. The internal stresses and contradictions of the Chain were being exposed by all sorts of new developments that had the potential to change how Europeans thought. Slowly and subtly, Europeans were coming to question the received wisdom of the past and beginning to move about physically, socially, politically, and even in terms of religion. As a result, they would soon become less superstitious and more rational; less accepting of authority and more questioning; less apparently concerned with the next life and more with this one. All these habits of mind are characteristic of modernity. It could be argued that this tectonic shift began with the movement known as Renaissance Humanism.

There is a great line in the medieval portion of Woody Allen's *Everything You Always Wanted to Know About Sex But Were Afraid to Ask* that plays off our popular conception of the Renaissance. A court jester, played by Allen, is trying to bed the queen, played by Lynn Redgrave. One of his come-on lines is something like, "We'd better fool around now because before you know it, the Renaissance will be here, and we'll all be painting." When we think of the Renaissance, we do tend to think of painting. I'll get to painting and art in a minute, but far more important than lovely Madonnas and commanding Biblical statues was the set of ideas behind them.

What were the ideas behind the Renaissance? If you walk into class and say, "What does the word 'Renaissance' mean?" every freshman can all still tell you, "rebirth." Then you ask them what was reborn, and they're kind of lost. Beginning in the 14th century, mostly in Italy, intellectuals and artists began to be more interested in Classical (that is Greek and Roman) literature and art for their own sakes.

In fact, university scholars had long been influenced by Greece and Rome. Historians often refer to an earlier Renaissance of the 12th century, during which Islamic translations of Greek and Roman authors made their way into Europe as a result of the Crusades. University curricula came to be dominated by the study of Roman law; Greek and Roman grammarians and rhetoricians; and above all, Aristotle, who dominated the fields of philosophy, science, politics, and aesthetics. In fact, the Great Chain of Being is itself very much an Aristotelian conception.

Many historians today would de-emphasize the degree to which the Renaissance was a break from the past. They would argue that it was merely the logical outgrowth of these medieval trends. I would argue, however, that something new was going on in Europe around 1500. The medieval interest in Classical writings had pretty much been limited to churchmen and university academics. Those scholars were not terribly interested in what ancient authors could tell them about themselves or ancient times.

Rather, the medieval schoolmen were largely interested in pagan authors only for how they could assist them in understanding and communicating in Latin and mastering the rules of logic as laid down by Aristotle, all in order to assist in the great medieval project of comprehending scripture and therefore ultimately comprehending God.

Towards the end of the Middle Ages, however, scholars and artists began to grow interested in the great Classical writings, not only for how they could illuminate the Bible or even illuminate God, though both remained a preoccupation. They became more interested in these authors for their own sakes and for that of their own times. We see, along with the traditional emphasis on Greek and Roman philosophy, rhetoric and grammar; an increasing interest in Greek and Roman history; Plutarch's *Lives*; Livy's and Tacitus's histories; and later, Herodotus and Thucydides among the Greeks. There was also an increased interest in Greek and Roman poetry—Homer's *Iliad* and *Odyssey*, Virgil's *Aeneid*, the Odes of Horace, etcetera—for what they might say generally, not only about how to speak and write Latin, but about the human condition.

Something else is different in the century before 1500. Before, these works might have been studied in medieval universities to assist in Bible exegesis and rhetoric; after around 1400 and increasingly as the century wears on, they were being read and studied by kings, nobles, and merchants—not only as stories of value for their own sakes and in their own right, but for what they could tell Europeans of their Classical past and, more specifically, for advice on how to run states and live lives.

The movement is universally credited with starting in Italy. Why Italy? Italy was perfectly placed to be the European entry point for goods from the fabled East. That meant fabrics, spices, and medicines; but it also meant books. During the Middle Ages, it had been Italian traders who had followed the Crusaders into the Middle East and, when the fighting subsided, established contacts with Muslim governments and merchants in the Levant (that's what contemporaries call the eastern shore of the Mediterranean).

This wealth, combined with the collapse of political control by the Holy Roman Empire, especially in northern Italy, had enabled the cities of Italy to gain independence and then prosper toward the end of the Middle Ages. Do you remember how many of the most populous cities in Europe we've mentioned in previous lectures were Italian? Venice, Genoa, Milan, and Naples were all ports, while inland Florence became a manufacturing and banking center. The Medici were, in fact, the bankers to Europe.

Later, after about 1500, the rest of Europe would eventually either bypass the Italian trade routes when Portugal and Spain pioneered alternative routes to the East, or they would seek to take control of them. During the 15th and 16th centuries, both the Holy Roman Empire and the French fought over control of Italy. By 1559, the Spanish had largely won, putting an end to the independence of most Italian city-states. In the meantime, however, the contact borne of those wars would allow Renaissance ideas to spread.

In the meantime, you need to know that it was Italian wealth between 1250–1550 that made the Renaissance possible. Because that wealth was centered on cities, the Renaissance was, to start off with at least, an intensely urban phenomenon. It was also, I want to argue, an intensely human one. Implied in the rebirth of interest in Greece and Rome, the Italian Renaissance saw a shift away from the study of abstract heavenly concerns, such as theology and philosophy, towards the real, the human, and the concrete. History, after all, is full of the story of humans. Poetry is full of human emotions and, in the case of Roman poets like Ovid, lots of sex. I would also argue that this period and this movement sees a shift towards the individual. All of this explains why we speak not just of the Renaissance, but of Renaissance Humanism.

I want to be careful here. I don't want to overdo it. Theology and philosophy continue to be growth industries for European intellectuals, especially in northern Europe. Some of the greatest Humanist scholars applied their more critical scholarship (in other words, Humanist methods) to more accurate translations of the Bible and early Christian texts in a movement that came to be known as Christian Humanism. Christian Humanism is very important. It will be especially important for the Protestant Reformation.

One good example of a Christian Humanist is the great Dutch Humanist Desiderius Erasmus. He produced a new critical edition of the Greek New Testament, as well as a better Latin translation based on sounder classical scholarship than the old Latin Vulgate. He also sought reform of the Church through better education and scholarship. These are all Humanist values. He also sought reform through a critical examination of its core texts.

I would argue that even though he is a Christian Humanist, this reflects a change in attitude, from regarding the Bible and other texts received from the past as sacrosanct objects to understanding them as human documents with a history, which are subject to human error, and to which the individual could bring his or her critical faculties.

Overall, I see Renaissance Humanism, whatever else it might have been, as a valuation of the human and the individual, perhaps not over the divine, but in tandem with it.

Now let's get back to painting. To see that valuation, all you need to do is compare a medieval *Madonna and Child* with a Renaissance example, say one by Leonardo or Rafael. If you look at the Renaissance example, you should be struck by the greater facial and emotional expression; the amplitude and weight of the bodies (these people eat); and the attempt to get the features of childhood just right, even though that attempt is not always successful. When we see a Renaissance Madonna, we see a real individual with a history and feelings.

Another fine example is Michelangelo's *David*. Obviously, this work glorifies the human body and glorifies youth; but on some level it also glorifies this one particular person. Again, I don't want to overdo it. Contemporaries would certainly have seen these productions as glorifying God and the humans who were his creation, and created in his own image. By glorifying humans, we glorify God.

What strikes us today, however, is how much they look like real human beings—people you might actually see walking down the street. We see these qualities of individualism, humanity, and the portrayal of human emotion as early as the late Middle Ages, which explains why it is so hard to draw a line separating medieval from modern.

For example, the painter Giotto gave greater weight and presence to human figures as early as the 14th century. The sculptor Donatello studied classical masters and attempted to put their principles into practice. Italian architects rejected the Gothic and went back to simpler Classical forms in 15th century; for example, Michelozzi's Medici Palace in Florence, or Brunelleschi's churches at San Lorenzo and Santo Spirito.

In the 15th century, artists like Masaccio used mathematics and observation, like contemporary scientists, to solve the problems of perspective. At the same time, the sculptor Ghiberti applied some of these same principles to the magnificent east door for the Baptistery at Florence. Fra Angelico and Fra Filippo Lippi emphasized brilliant color and sensuality as Ovid might. Castagno and [Leonardo] da Vinci studied anatomy. In fact, this period sees the beginnings of portraiture. Rich Italian merchants and Renaissance princes wanted to be memorialized, and artists like Mantegna and Botticelli sought to do so with flattery, but also anatomical correctness; again, it was movement towards the human.

These trends culminated in masterpieces of Leonardo, Michelangelo, and Rafael. In particular, the work of Rafael—the School of Athens—is itself a tribute to Classical values because it enshrines all the great Greek and Roman philosophers and writers in one great picture.

These ideals eventually spread north, certainly by 1500, thanks in part to the printing press and also to war. They culminated in the work of the great portraitist based in England, Hans Holbein, and Dutch and Flemish painters before Rembrandt, such as Rubens and Van Dyck.

By the way, there is one additional human element here. Another hallmark of the Renaissance is that we know who these people are. During the Middle Ages, artists and architects did not claim or sign their works. It was all done for the greater glory of God. Now, artists claimed and achieved far-ranging fame. Vasari wrote *The Lives of the Most Eminent Italian Architects, Painters, and Sculptors*, published in 1568. Imagine a world in which people want to learn about the lives of these people. That says something about the elevation of the artists, but also an engagement with the human. The sculptor Benvenuto Cellini wrote a famous, self-glorifying autobiography, which in the 19th century became an opera by Berlioz.

This degree of self-consciousness and self-promotion would have been unthinkable outside of academia (academics always take credit) in the Middle Ages. I would argue, however, that the real origin and the greatest impact of Renaissance Humanism came not in the visual arts, but in literature. Beginning in the 14th century, Europeans began to produce a new kind of literature, which was less about God and kings and more about human beings.

In Italy, Dante Alighieri is a sort of precursor with *The Divine Comedy,* which first appeared around 1307. *The Divine Comedy* is clearly about celestial themes; but if you read the stories, especially of those condemned to hell, they are intensely human. They are written with an obvious veneration for Latin and for Virgil, but they are written in the vernacular so more people can read them.

Perhaps the real founder of Humanism was Francesco Petrarca, better known as Petrarch. He wrote in both Latin and Italian. His *Exemplary Lives* imitated Plutarch. His *Africa* celebrated the Punic Wars. He actually wrote letters to dead Classical authors like Cicero, which shows you how much he cared about them. At the same time, in his sonnets dedicated to his great unrequited love, Laura, he reveals a full range of human passion and emotion.

Giovanni Boccaccio wrote *The Decameron,* which was 100 very human and kind of racy stories told by citizens trying to take refuge from the plague. A century later, in 1487, Pico della Mirandola wrote an anthem for the Renaissance in his *Oration on the Dignity of Man.* In this short work, he imagines God placing man in the Great Chain of Being with these words:

> Adam, we give you no fixed place to live, no form that is peculiar to you, nor any function that is yours alone. According to your desires and judgment, you will have and possess whatever place to live, whatever form and whatever functions you yourself choose. All other things have a limited and fixed nature prescribed and are bounded by Our laws. You, with no limit or bound, may choose for yourself the limits and bounds of your nature. We have placed you at the world's center so that you may survey everything else in the world. …so that with free choice and dignity, you may fashion yourself into whatever you choose. To you is granted the power of degrading yourself into the lower forms of life, the beasts, and to you is granted the power, contained in your intellect and judgment, to be reborn into the higher forms, the divine.

In Florence, Lorenzo de Medici—*Il Magnifico*—patronized Italian poets as well as painters and sculptors at his court. These ideas spread beyond Italy, as I indicated before. In England, as early as the 14th century, Geoffrey Chaucer's *Canterbury Tales* anticipates later developments, as did Dante.

Later, in the 16th century, Humanist works included the sonnets of Wyatt and Surrey, Spenser's *Faerie Queen,* Shakespeare's sonnets and plays, and Ben Johnson's poems and plays. In Spain at the beginning of the 17th century, *Don Quixote* by Cervantes makes fun of medieval notions of knightly conduct. In France, the poetry of Ronsard, the political satire of Rabelais, and the essays of Montaigne wave the flag for Humanism.

In music, church music remained important. It's kind of hard to attribute any kind of Classical influence to the increasingly polyphonic and complex masses of Palestrina, Thomas Tallis, or

William Byrd. In secular music, however, we see a definite interest from the Classical side. Madrigals and motets were intended to be performed in people's homes. This is a development of the songs of the medieval troubadours, but all of them show a Classical influence—they are all based on Renaissance poetry. They emphasize human conflict, love, war, etc. and above all, the role of fortune (*Fortuna*) in people's lives. This is very Classical and not religious at all.

Examples are Orlando di Lasso, Carlo Gesualdo, and above all, Claudio Monteverdi. He was an Italian court composer who wrote the first, still-performed operas about 1600. They were all based on Classical stories such as *Orfeo*, *The Return of Ulysses*, and *The Coronation of Poppea*, yet filled with the human themes of love, loss, power, and ambition. In England, about the same time, we get the songs and motets of Byrd, John Dowland, and Orlando Gibbons. These songs are all dramatically expressed and full of unrequited love and powerful passion.

But Renaissance Humanism was about more than raw emotion. It sought to change the world. Humanist scholars were highly critical of medieval education, which emphasized that all knowledge was received from God through ancient authoritative texts like the Bible or Aristotle. Medieval scholars tended to believe that it was very hard, if not impossible, to add new knowledge and, therefore, scholarship should be based on deductive reasoning from the first principles contained in these prior authorities.

Humanist scholars often found the resultant scholastic logic to be shabby, intolerant, and incapable of fulfilling Pico della Mirandola's prediction. Humanist scholars advocated a reform of education. In effect, they wanted less theology, less abstract logic, less rote memorization of past knowledge, and less narrow professionalism. They were more open to new ideas, learning by observation and induction, and more willing to question first principles. They wanted more emphasis on history, poetry, and ethics, which is after all the human application of moral principles. Of course, they also wanted the examination and criticism of original texts.

They also wanted a practical education, not just so that people would express themselves better, but so that they would become good citizens. Indeed, some Humanist scholars advocated an education that went far beyond the clergy to encompass even women. The famous Humanist scholar Roger Ascham, for example, became a tutor to Princess Elizabeth. This is a period of time when women even down into the middle classes began to receive Classical educations. They believed, like many Classical authors before them, that education was necessary to make good citizens.

This is actually a problem for the Great Chain of Being, because the idea that you would educate people for good citizenship suggests the idea that people—citizens—can actually participate in government, and perhaps even make its decisions. Admittedly, most Humanist authors were more snobbish than this. They wanted to restrict participation only to the well educated; but even that is revolutionary. They see a world in which aristocrats were no longer supposed to be great warriors, but were increasingly government servants serving the prince in peacetime as well as war.

A good prince should, like the Medici or the Borgia, be well educated himself and employ those who are well educated. He should promote education and the arts, which would in turn promote civic virtue, and also glorify his rule. Practically speaking, that advice led to an explosion of Renaissance civic art and pageantry in the 15th and 16th centuries. We owe to this reforming impulse the great paintings and statuary of Venice, Florence, and Rome. Later, it would spread to the court of Burgundy, the Valois court of France, and the Tudor court. We owe to this impulse buildings like St. Mark's in Venice, Brunelleschi's Duomo in Florence, St. Peter's in Rome, Fontainebleau and the Louvre in France, and Hampton Court in England.

The de-emphasis of God for the human in these equations and the emphasis on human concerns and human capacities threatened to degenerate into a glorification of expediency over virtue, practicality over idealism, and success over morality. There is a dark side to Renaissance Humanism, and we see these themes come together in two of the greatest authors produced by the Renaissance courts of Italy: Castiglione and Machiavelli. One was light and one was dark.

Balthasar Castiglione was a diplomat who wrote [sic published] *Il libro del cortegiano (The Courtier)* in 1528. This book captured the imaginations of contemporaries. It was translated into many languages throughout the 16th century. What Castiglione's book, which is in the form of a dialogue, purported to do was explain how to rise into the innermost confidence of a great ruler—in other words, how to become Vernon Jordan, or Leon Panetta, or Karl Rove, or Karen Hughes—with all the power that that implies. In short, it was the world's first "dress for success" book.

The successful courtier was to be impeccable in his manners; discreet in his behavior; and accomplished in the arts of peace and war, including dancing, poetry, horsemanship, and swordsmanship. This fit him to be a companion to the ruler. Yet he was to wear these accomplishments lightly. Above all, he was to insinuate himself into the confidence of his prince by never being in the way or out of the way, and by telling him the truth, but in the most flattering way possible. Indeed, the whole point of these skills was to flatter the prince into listening to good advice—to flatter him into thinking that it was his idea all along.

It could be charged that Castiglione never really confronts the central tension here between truth and flattery, or between morality and success. Anyone in active life can tell you it is next to impossible to embrace both simultaneously. In fact, the Renaissance itself only barely began to confront the fact that it is next to impossible to be both godly and human at the same time.

Our next author would solve the problem by choosing one. His name is Niccolò Machiavelli and his great work is *The Prince* of 1532. Machiavelli doesn't bother with courtiers. He wants the prince to himself. In fact, he is part of a long tradition, going back to at least Seneca, of trying to teach princes how to rule. It's called the "Mirrors for Princes" tradition.

Machiavelli gives this old genre a new humanistic twist, however. In keeping with the Renaissance de-emphasis of the divine and emphasis on the human, Machiavelli's goal is not to make his prince a better person or get him into Heaven. It is rather to keep him in power on Earth and to strengthen that power.

Machiavelli's reasoning is intensely practical:

> My intention being to write something of use to those who will understand, I deem it best to stick to the practical truth of things, rather than to fancies. Many men have imagined republics and principalities that never really existed at all. [This is a hit at medieval schoolmen, by the way.] Yet the

way men live is so far removed from the way they ought to live, that anyone who abandons what is for what should be, pursues his own downfall rather than his preservation; for a man who strives after goodness in all his acts is sure to come to ruin, since there are so many men who are not good. Hence, it is necessary that a prince who is interested in his survival learn to be other than good, making use of this capacity or refraining from it according to need.

As this implies, a prince must become adept at seeming to be and do one thing, while actually doing what serves:

Therefore, it is not necessary for the prince to have all the good qualities I have enumerated, but it is very necessary to appear to have them.... And you have to understand this, that a prince, especially a new one, cannot observe all those things for which men are esteemed: being often forced, in order to maintain the state, to act contrary to fidelity, friendship, humanity, and religion. Therefore, it is necessary for him to have a mind ready to turn itself accordingly as the winds and variations of fortune force it; yet, as I have said above, not to diverge from the good if he can avoid doing so, but be able to do evil if constrained.

Is this the freedom of choice celebrated by Pico della Mirandola? Is this where we've ended up? A philosophy that began by elevating human beings has now, taken to this rational extreme, ended by reducing them and their lives to the level of beasts.

There were numerous reactions to Machiavelli's work. I could make an ahistorical argument here by saying that the two most profound ones were actually written before Machiavelli. They come from Erasmus and More. Erasmus had written a satire of the human condition and bad government generally, called *In Praise of Folly*, which was published [sic written] in 1509. Thomas More had written *Utopia* in 1516, describing a mythical land that was far more just and rational than England.

In each, Renaissance princes were prodded by satire to remember their responsibilities to their subjects and to the laws of God. Note that, while Erasmus's and More's aims are a lot closer to the tradition of the "Mirror for Princes" than Machiavelli, even here the appeal is to critical humor rather than abstract encomia. In other words, these works, too, were far more Humanistic than they were scholastic or medieval.

Perhaps the ultimate inheritors of the Humanist tradition were the Englishman William Shakespeare and the Frenchman Michel de Montaigne. Shakespeare, in a series of plays written at the turn of the 17th century, explores the human condition from seemingly every angle. His rulers try out Machiavelli; his courtiers try Castiglione; his comedies have the biting wit of Erasmus; and his tragedies, the sympathy for the human condition of Thomas More.

Like any good Humanist, Shakespeare knew his Classical authors and many of his plays center around issues of public morality that would have been familiar to Thucydides or Seneca. It is perhaps the ultimate Humanist compliment to say that scholars and playgoers have studied him in vain for hundreds of years trying to pin down exactly what it is Shakespeare believed. Like Machiavelli's ruler, his sympathies seem to shift with the winds.

Montaigne's *Essays,* written in the late 16th century, similarly examine the human condition from a wide variety of angles. Like all Humanists, he uses his critical faculties to advocate rational reforms. For example, "On the Education of Children" advocates reform of education along Classical lines. He also uses that questioning ability to be quite radical, however. In "Of Cannibals," he makes what must have been a shocking suggestion that Europeans were no better than the native peoples that they increasingly sought to conquer.

Note that in all these cases, the critical faculty of Humanism seems to point to a kind of moral relativism, or at least a refusal to flag wave for European culture as it then existed. Both would have been anathema to medieval thinkers.

To conclude, Renaissance Humanism was a movement that urged human beings to be more practical and less spiritual; more learned and less ignorant; more critical and less trusting; more involved and less subservient; more involved in the world and less concerned with what heaven thinks. Its emphasis on the critical and the practical were dynamite for the old medieval worldview and the Great Chain of Being.

In Machiavelli, it found a prophet who would not only create a new adjective, but would also continue to have a profound, if indirect, influence on how statecraft is pursued. We see that influence in the second great development that would attack the Great Chain of Being and give rise to the modern world: the rise of nation-states centrally governed by ambitious, powerful, charismatic, and Machiavellian Renaissance princes and kings.

Lecture Five
Renaissance Princes—1450–1600

Scope:

The Humanist emphasis on this world dovetailed nicely with the rise of a new kind of ruler who was ambitious, practical, and ruthless, typified by Henry VII, Henry VIII and Elizabeth I of England, Louis XI and Francis I of France, Charles V of the Holy Roman Empire, and Ferdinand, Isabella, and Phillip II of Spain. After establishing their dynasties, these men and women sought greater control of their governments, reduced the power of their barons and legislative assemblies, secured greater authority over the religious lives of their subjects, and sought to pay for it all by claiming trade routes to the Far East and the Americas.

Outline

I. Although we tend to think of medieval kings as powerful, in fact, their power was not absolute.

   A. A medieval king had to answer to or balance quite a few groups in the Great Chain of Being.

      1. First, he was subordinate to God and his angels.

         a. All medieval commentators agreed that the king's power came from God.

         b. This power was transmitted to the king through the Church at his coronation.

         c. Theoretically, this power could be revoked through excommunication.

         d. The most famous and enduring statement limiting the power of a lay ruler, the Magna Carta, was written by a bishop, Archbishop Stephen Langton.

         e. Popes might also claim to be at the top of the chain—the Vicar of Christ.

      2. Medieval kings created, enriched, and empowered nobles in order to have an army, but that meant that they created, enriched, and empowered a whole class of people who might rise up to challenge them.

    a. These so-created nobles often used their lands and the wealth they produced to build up independent power bases—hence, the modern usage of the terms *feudal* and *fiefdom*.

    b. They used their armies, not necessarily to defend kings or maintain peace, so much as to attack local towns or even the king himself, e.g., the Hundred Years War (1337–1456), in which a series of weak kings were taken advantage of by their vassals.

    c. To fight the barons, kings needed to hire mercenary armies, that is, armies paid occasionally rather than endowed with land permanently, as in feudalism.

        i. At first, kings allied with towns and their merchants. In return for loans and taxes, kings gave towns military protection and rights to hold markets or establish legal courts.

        ii. Eventually, it became too cumbersome to summon delegations of merchants to court to explain the king's difficulties on an ad hoc basis.

        iii. In the 13th–14th centuries, European kings began to institutionalize these meetings with both barons and townsmen. In England, these meetings came to be known as Parliament; in France, they were called the Estates General; in Castile, Spain, they were called the Cortes; and in the Holy Roman Empire, they were called the Diet.

        iv. But only in England and Spain did the tradition develop that laws and taxes had to be approved by these bodies.

  3. Ordinary people owed loyalty, obedience, and taxes to a wide variety of persons and institutions: the Church, the nobility, and their town (if townsmen), as well as to the king.

B. As Europe approached the year 1500, all this began to change.

  1. A series of new, stronger monarchs arose whose goals were to end baronial rebellions and make themselves more secure and, ultimately, absolute.

2. Inadvertently, these monarchs would establish the modern conception of a nation-state.

II. Renaissance princes may be divided into two groups: the founders of their dynasties and their successors.

A. All across Western Europe, new dynasties emerged from out of the carnage of baronial and civil war.

1. In England, first the Yorkists (1461–1483), then the Tudors under Henry VII (1485–1509), established their dynasties after the Wars of the Roses.

2. In France, the Valois reestablished themselves after the Hundred Years' War under Charles VII (1422–1461) and Louis XI (1461–1483).

3. In the Holy Roman Empire, Habsburg (Hapsburg) power revived under Maximilian I (1493–1519).

4. Spain was united by the 1469 marriage of Isabella of Castile and Leon to Ferdinand of Aragon, who after suppressing ten years of rebellion, became joint rulers of Spain in 1479. Isabella predeceased Ferdinand, who ruled until 1516.

5. Portugal was united under the House of Aviz.

6. In Hungary, Matthias Corvinus (Matthias the Just) ruled strongly from 1458 to 1490.

7. The goal of these rulers was to establish (or, in France and the Holy Roman Empire, to reestablish) their lines and put down baronial opposition.

a. The rulers made strategic marriages to heal wounds within the country and gain friends for it.

b. They ruthlessly suppressed baronial and private armies.

c. They allied with cities for loans and money and were careful to hire educated Renaissance lawyers and merchants, as well as nobles, as counselors and officials.

d. They worked with established assemblies, such as Parliament, the Cortes, and so on.

e. The rulers maintained good relations with the Church, in part by persecuting heretics enthusiastically.

      f. They drove out foreign invaders, consolidated holdings, and imposed religious uniformity.

      g. They reformed their governments and legal systems to be more efficient in order to have more control of the localities, e.g., the Edicts of Montalvo in Spain.

      h. In keeping with the Renaissance, these princes had a healthy respect for education, the arts—and propaganda.

B. These rulers laid the groundwork for a series of powerful successors who inherited and exploited the foundation laid by the previous generation.

  1. The most notable of those successors included:

      a. Henry VIII (1509–1547) and Elizabeth I (1558-1603) in England.

      b. Francis I (1515–1547) and Henry II (1547–1559) in France.

      c. Charles V (1519–1556) in the Holy Roman Empire, who also served as…[see next entry]

      d. Charles I (1506–1556) in Spain, father of Phillip II (1556–1598) of Spain.

  2. Even more than their predecessors, these monarchs had terrific Humanistic educations, e.g., Charles V was tutored by the future Pope Adrian VI, Elizabeth I by famed education reformer Roger Asham, and Francis I by Christophe de Longeuil.

  3. Their policies were a mixture of old and new.

      a. All of these rulers continued the programs of suppression of elite power and heretical groups, strategic marriages, and administrative reforms.

      b. But these rulers also changed policies of consolidation into expansion.

          i. The Holy Roman Emperor and the kings of France, culminating in Charles V and Francis I, vied for control of Italy through the 1520s.

          ii. Henry VIII attempted invasions of Scotland and France in 1513–1515 and 1544–1547.

  iii. Spain expanded overseas in the New World; faced down an Islamic challenge in the Mediterranean by defeating a Turkish fleet at Lepanto in 1571; conquered most of Italy; annexed Portugal when the Portuguese Royal House died out in 1580; and dabbled in the politics of England and France.

c. In terms of religion, these rulers sometimes sought to dominate the Church as well as the state.

  i. The classic example is Henry VIII breaking with Rome and making himself head of the Church of England in 1534.

  ii. In 1516, Francis I used his military power in Italy to secure the right to appoint all bishops and abbots in France.

  iii. Charles V made war on recalcitrant Protestant barons and towns in the War of the Schmalkaldic League. [More about this in Lecture 8.]

  iv. As Charles I of Spain, he gained complete control over Church appointments.

d. Renaissance kings were obsessed with projecting their power through propaganda and by commissioning buildings, poems, paintings, and so on.

  i. Henry VIII confiscated and rebuilt Hampton Court and Whitehall, patronized the great portraitist Hans Holbein, and employed a stable of writers to support his royal supremacy.

  ii. Charles V employed painters like Titian.

  iii. Francis I built the Louvre and the castle and hunting lodge at Chambord, possibly originally laid out by Leonardo da Vinci. He turned Castle Fontainebleau into a major palace, commissioning great architects (e.g., Giacomo da Vignola) and artists of the day (e.g., Rosso Fiorentino, Andrea del Sarto, and Cellini).

4. In reforming their governments, stamping out opposition, and taking control of the arts and even of religion, the princes of the Renaissance redefined loyalty as owed to them alone.

    a. In 1536, Catholic peasants in Northern England rebelled against Henry VIII's break from Rome and were suppressed ruthlessly.

    b. The Jews and Moors of Spain and the nobles of French Brittany all learned the same lesson.

    c. Charles V's failure to stamp out Protestantism at the end of the War of the Schmalkaldic League is the exception that proves the rule: The Holy Roman Empire remained divided in religion and decentralized in authority. The result was a power vacuum in the middle of Europe.

III. Why did other rulers succeed in creating strong nation-states where the Holy Roman Emperor failed?

A. It could be argued that the empire suffered from more religious disunity following the Reformation than did the other regimes noted above.

B. A second factor was money.

C. Rulers needed money to build palaces, commission propaganda, and raise armies to suppress rebellions and project their power abroad.

D. Where were the rulers going to get this money?

    1. They could raise taxes.

        a. But, medieval rulers won support from nobles and the Church by exempting them from taxation.

        b. That left peasants, who did not have any money, and towns, which did.

    2. But overtaxing towns would kill the economies.

    3. Moreover, the need to institutionalize the raising of money had led to the rise of representative assemblies (parliaments, diets, estates, and so on) that might question royal policy.

E. Was there no other source of ready money available to European rulers?

1. The Italian city-states had grown wealthy on trade from the East—leading every major power (except England) to try to control Italy.

2. Henry VIII, having taken over the Church in England, confiscated much of its land: annates (taxes paid to the Pope) in 1534, smaller monasteries in 1536, larger monasteries in 1539, and hospitals and other charitable foundations in 1547. Instead of using those lands to endow the monarchy for centuries, Henry then traded long-term security for quick cash by selling these lands to the nobles and gentry.

3. Beginning with Louis XII, the kings of France sold government offices. While raising cash quickly and cash quickly and stimulating social mobility, this also expanded the size of government and based service on wealth, not merit.

4. The Portuguese prince, Henry the Navigator, had a different idea: He planned to bypass the Italians and go directly to the source, trading with China and India themselves.

Supplementary Reading:

Chambers, chapter 14, sections III–IV.

R. Bonney, *The European Dynastic States, 1494–1660*.

E. F. Rice, Jr., *The Foundations of Early Modern Europe, 1460–1559*.

Questions to Consider:

1. Did the centralizing tendency of Renaissance monarchs contribute to or stifle greater popular participation in the state?

2. Why did Germany fail where other nations succeeded at centralization in the early modern period?

Lecture Five—Transcript
Renaissance Princes—1450–1600

In the last lecture, we learned that as Europe and its inhabitants were emerging from the Middle Ages, they embraced a kind of Humanism that encouraged them to be better educated, more critical of received wisdom, and more practical. Obviously, this struck at the links of the Great Chain of Being. Now you might think that Europe's rulers would fear such a movement. As we'll learn in this lecture, they embraced it. They were the first individuals to be liberated from the Chain. To understand that, we have to understand the medieval background of the kingship.

When we think of medieval kings, I think we tend to think of them as being very powerful; but in fact they weren't absolute. Think of King Arthur, the perfect medieval king in legend; we always think of him as being surrounded by the Knights of the Round Table. If you know the legend, you know that not all of those knights proved loyal.

In fact, a medieval king had to answer to or balance quite a few groups in the Great Chain of Being. First, there was the Church. Remember that the king was subordinate to God and his angels. All medieval commentators agreed that his power came from God and could be revoked. That power was transmitted to him at his coronation. The pope crowns the Holy Roman Emperor; the Bishop of Rheims crowns the King of France; the Archbishop of Canterbury crowns the King of England. In effect, the Church is saying, "You're not a king unless we do this."

The Church also runs other ceremonies; for example the ceremonial homage and fealty by which new vassals were created. And every Sunday, the Church preaches from its pulpits about how great the king is and how people should obey him. Now this implies the king's power could be revoked. During the Middle Ages, emperors and kings had sometimes been excommunicated—in effect deposed, since this was a declaration that they were outside the Church. This could happen over issues like, could a lay ruler tax the Church? Were Churchmen subject to his courts? Could he choose his own bishops? (This became known as the Investiture Controversy.)

In fact, it was a bishop, Archbishop Stephen Langton, who wrote perhaps the most famous and enduring statement limiting the power of a lay ruler: the Magna Carta of 1215. If we recall that popes claimed to be at the top of the Great Chain of Being too, it should be clear that medieval kings had a great challenge in proving their superiority.

Then there was the nobility. Remember that, while medieval kings created and enriched nobles in order to have an army, that meant that they thus created, enriched, and empowered a whole class of people who might rise up to challenge them. In the feudal system, kings and emperors created nobles by making them vassals in the religious ceremonies of homage and fealty. In this process, they endowed them with lands (also known as "fiefs") in order to support mounted knights that the king could call on for his defense. But if you have purchased any of the medieval courses sold by this company, you know that the nobles so created often used their land and wealth to build up independent power bases; hence the modern usage of the terms "feudal" and "fiefdom." They sometimes used their armies not to maintain the king's peace, but to attack local towns or even the king himself. There are lots and lots of examples.

For example, in France, the Hundred Years' War was such a rebellion. It raged from 1337–1456. A series of weak kings were taken advantage of by their vassals, one of whom, the Duke of Normandy, also happened to be the King of England. That didn't stop him from claiming the crown of France as well. He was supported by other powerful French nobles like the Duke of Burgundy and the Duke of Orleans.

At the war's height from 1421–1422, the French king Charles VI was forced to dispossess his own son and sign the succession over to the English King Henry V. When both Charles and Henry died in 1422, both were succeeded by an English infant who became Henry VI.

England, too, had witnessed numerous baronial rebellions in the Middle Ages. In fact, the reason Henry V was king was because his father, the Duke of Lancaster, had rebelled against a previous king, Richard II, and established the Lancastrian line.

Between 1422–1456, the dispossessed crown prince, or *dauphin,* of France, inspired by Joan of Arc, rose up, had himself crowned as Charles VII, and drove the English out. That, in turn, weakened the prestige of the English King Henry VI, inspiring his own barons to rebel against him in the Wars of the Roses (1455–1485). If you want to know more about this, I highly recommend Professor Bucholz's course on English history.

In the Holy Roman Empire, the barons had long operated independently of the emperor. A series of wars and rebellions in the Middle Ages had left the emperor an elective first among about 300 equals. That is, Germany was really made up of 300 individual states, electorates, kingdoms, duchies, margraves, and bishoprics. Basically, the whole thing was a feudal nightmare. The only places where the Hapsburg emperor had any real power were his ancestral lands: Austria and the low countries.

Spain, too, came out of the Middle Ages as really a series of petty kingdoms in which great landowners had immense power. When Ferdinand of Aragon and Lyons married Isabella of Castile in 1469, the nobles, fearing centralization if they succeeded to a united Spanish throne, rebelled for 10 years. Even after that was over, this still left the independent Muslim state of Granada to the south.

To fight the barons, the kings needed soldiers. They needed to hire mercenary armies—soldiers you paid occasionally rather than endowed with land permanently, as with feudalism. Clearly the feudal thing didn't work; hence the rebellions we have talked about. Where are kings going to get the money to do this? Very early on, they figure out that they need to ally with towns and their merchants. Towns are wealthy from trade and they are frequently attacked by the local baron. They are a sort of natural ally in this fight. In return for loans and taxes, kings would give towns military protection and certain rights enshrined in charters, such as the right to hold a market, pass their own laws, and be exempt from some taxes.

Eventually, however, it became too cumbersome to summon the delegations of merchants and nobles to court to explain the king's difficulties on an ad hoc basis; so in the 13th and 14th centuries, European kings began to institutionalize these meetings with both their loyal barons and townsmen. In England, that institution came to be called Parliament. In France, it was the Estates General. In Spain, it was the Cortes, and in the Holy Roman Empire, the Diet. Only in England and Spain did the tradition develop that laws and taxes had to be approved by these bodies.

Let's look at this whole system from below. Imagine you are a medieval peasant. The king or emperor is remote. He's off in

London, Paris, Innsbruck, or Vienna. The local lord or baron is far more powerful in your life. He's probably your landlord. If you are a townsman, you're probably more concerned with your standing in the local guild. Everywhere, the local church is more involved in your everyday life.

In other words, from the point of view of a medieval king, this whole system was an unholy mess. It was nothing like the states we live in today, which tend to assume that our loyalty is absolute. People paid loyalty all right, and attention, but they paid it and taxes to the Church here, the nobility there, and the town if they were townsmen. The king would get his as long as there was time and enough money to go around.

As Europe approached the year 1500, all this began to change. A generation of new stronger monarchs arose. Their goal was to suppress baronial rebellions and subordinate the church and aristocracy. They wanted to make themselves more secure and, indeed, ultimately absolute. They would establish the modern conception of the nation-state with unitary loyalty owed to that state. These were the Renaissance princes.

Actually, I would divide these into two groups: one generation as the founders of the firms, and a second generation of inheritors and exploiters. First, let's look at the founders of the firms. All across Western Europe, new dynasties emerged from out of the carnage of the civil wars that we just talked about. In England, out of the Wars of the Roses emerged first the Yorkists under Edward IV in 1461; and then more permanently, Henry VII established the Tudors in 1485.

In France, the Valois family reestablished themselves after the disasters of the Hundred Years War. First, Charles VII and then, Louis XI ruled France from altogether 1422–1483. In the Holy Roman Empire, the Habsburg power revived under Maximilian I, who ruled from 1493–1519. As we've seen, Spain was united by Ferdinand and Isabella. Isabella predeceased Ferdinand, who ruled until 1516. Even Portugal united under the House of Aviz. In Hungary, Matthias Corvinus ruled strongly from 1458–1490.

All of these rulers had the same goal. They wanted to establish or re-establish their dynasties on a more permanent, stronger footing and reduce baronial opposition. How would they do that? First, they pursued strategic marriages to heal wounds within the country and gain friends abroad. Ferdinand and Isabella married their children into powerful European royal houses. One daughter, Isabella, married into the Portuguese royal house. Another daughter, Juana, married Philip, Duke of Burgundy. A third daughter, Catherine of Aragon, married Prince Arthur Tudor of England. All of these marriages will be important later.

Henry VII of England, descended from the Lancastrians, married Elizabeth of York to unite the two warring houses of the Wars of the Roses. He then married his son Arthur to Catherine of Aragon of Spain. When Arthur died in 1501, Henry fortunately (or perhaps not so fortunately) had another son, another Henry; and as you probably know that didn't work out so well. He married a daughter into the Scottish royal house, and then Henry VII's other daughter Mary was married to Louis XII of France.

Earlier, Charles VII, who you will remember had restored French royal power during and after the Hundred Years' War, had engineered the marriage of Margaret of Anjou into the House of Lancaster. As we have seen, his descendant Louis married an English princess.

Maximilian, the Holy Roman Emperor, married Mary of Burgundy, allowing him to claim one of Europe's richest kingdoms. You can see the almost spider web of entanglement of these royal families, all jockeying for position and all hoping to acquire new territory. Maximilian married his son Philip of Burgundy to Juana, the daughter of Ferdinand and Isabella; thus linking the Habsburgs with Spain. That will be important later. The Habsburgs also married into the ruling house of Hungary. All of these marriages bolstered new or weak lines and gave them powerful friends and increased their holdings.

The second method of the founders of the firms was to suppress baronial private armies, and to do so ruthlessly. In France, Charles VII reduced his barons to obedience after driving the English out. He still faced a powerful Duke of Burgundy, Charles the Bold, whose predecessors had supported the English. In 1474, Louis XI assembled a coalition against Burgundy and killed him in battle three years later.

Louis thus annexed Burgundy, but the low countries went to his daughter Mary, who married Maximilian. (If you're getting a little confused, that's okay.) Louis was known as the "spider" for his ability to weave this sort of web and his patient intrigue. He eventually gathered into that web Anjou, Maine, and Provence, which were all areas that had stood outside French power before.

In England, Henry VII put down a series of rebellions and held nobles in bond; that is, they had to deposit a certain amount of money with him for future good behavior. He banned private armies, virtually ending feudalism in England. He also expanded the powers of the justices of the peace (JPs). These were small landowners who couldn't challenge him. By expanding their power, he took it away from the great nobles.

Maximilian subdued rebellious cities in the Netherlands that had supported France. He also recovered Austria from the king of Hungary, as we'll see later.

Ferdinand and Isabella revoked grants of land and power to nobles. They demolished noble castles. They gained control of noble military orders. You'll notice that these Renaissance princes are very jealous of their own rights, but they are perfectly happy to trample over the rights of others. In fact, I want to be fair here. In Spain's case, they eventually opted for a rather more decentralized government in which local areas were given great autonomy and were ruled for the king and queen by a viceroy.

The third method of these Renaissance princes was to ally with cities for loans and money. They were also careful to hire Humanist educated lawyers and merchants as well as nobles to counsel them.

A fourth method was to work with assemblies. In Spain, Ferdinand and Isabella relied on the Cortes of Castile, composed mainly of merchants, to try criminals and restore order.

Fifth, they maintained good relations with the Church. Who needs trouble here? All of these rulers were enthusiastic persecutors of heretics and religious minorities. They believed that only a subject who worshiped as the king worshiped could be a loyal subject. Most infamously, Ferdinand and Isabella established the dreaded Spanish Inquisition in 1478 to root out *conversos* (converted Jews) and *moriscos* (converted Muslims) who practiced their religion secretly.

They persecuted Moors and Jews ruthlessly. From 1492, 150,000 Jews were expelled, leading to the loss to Spain of many physicians, artists, and government officials. From 1502, Muslims were expelled as well. In 1602, even converted Muslims had to leave. In return, the pope granted to Spanish kings the title of "Most Catholic" and the right to name bishops and abbots in Granada and the New World.

A sixth method of these rulers was to drive out foreign invaders, consolidate holdings, and impose religious uniformity. As we have seen, Charles VII drove the English from France and Henry VII sought to secure his northern border with Scotland. Ferdinand and Isabella drove out the Moors and persecuted the Jews. They also fought to safeguard their possessions in Italy, reformed the army, and established a great diplomatic corps that would come in handy later. Maximilian won the succession to the throne of Bohemia and Hungary by the Treaty of Pressburg in 1491. Remember, I told you that he had married into the Hungarian royal house. He, in effect, became a foreign invader.

A seventh method of these kings was to reform their governments and legal systems to be more efficient, more professional, more in control of the localities, and more responsive to the monarch. Ferdinand and Isabella issued the Edicts of Montalvo, which reduced the size of the Council to make it more flexible; reformed financial agencies; and emphasized promotion by merit, rather than birth. Like Henry VII in England, they relied on small landowners, the *hidalgos*, to police the localities. Henry VII reformed the administration of Crown lands. Both he and the Holy Roman Emperor created new tribunals to determine local disputes. Henry's tribunal is famous as the Court of Star Chamber, which was actually a pretty fair and popular court, in contrast to its reputation.

Finally, in keeping with the Renaissance, these princes had a healthy respect for education, the arts, and propaganda. They employed scholars and artists, and sought to be portrayed in the best possible light while having their enemies portrayed in the worst. For example, supporters of Henry VII actually repainted pictures of his predecessor, the usurped Richard III, to exaggerate his hunchback. He himself commissioned a complimentary history of his reign by Polydore Vergil.

The next generation I want to talk about built upon this foundation. I call them the inheritors and exploiters. Where the pioneers laid the groundwork, their successors grew even more powerful. Here we meet some of the most famous people in European history—names to conjure with. In England, there were Henry VIII and Elizabeth I, who between them dominated that part of the island from 1509–1603 with an intermission in between. In France, there were Francis I and Henry II who ruled from 1515–1559 altogether. In the Holy Roman Empire, it was Charles V, from1519–1556, who also, thanks to the Habsburg marriage of his predecessors, was ruler of Spain as Charles I from 1506–1556, when he was succeeded by his son Phillip II, who ruled until 1598. These are some of the most famous names in European history.

All of them were well trained for the task at hand. Even more than their predecessors, they had terrific Humanistic educations. Charles V was tutored by the future Pope Adrian VI; Elizabeth I by the famed education reformer Roger Asham; and Francis I by Christophe de Longeuil. All spoke several languages, including Latin. The cosmopolitan Charles V used to say, "I speak Spanish to God, Italian to women, French to men, and German to my horse." Henry VIII played the lute and composed. He was an excellent dancer and horseman. He befriended Thomas More and Erasmus (before he killed the former) and he wrote a famous treatise against Martin Luther, for which the Pope named him Defender of the Faith. (Admittedly, that did not turn out very well.) Francis I was a renowned man of letters and book collector. Under his patronage, Guillaume Budé established a great French royal library. Francis was a terrific patron of the arts, as we'll see below. He was also a better wrestler than Henry, which he proved at a summit meeting in 1520.

All of these rulers continued the policies of, first, suppressing elite power. Henry VIII had frequent executions. Charles V launched a war against recalcitrant Protestant barons and towns. They also all engaged in strategic marriages, including Henry VIII with Catherine of Aragon and later Anne of Cleves. He also tried to marry his daughter to Charles V and his son Edward to Mary Queen of Scots. Francis married the daughter of his predecessor, and Phillip II married a host of important European women, including Mary Tudor of England.

All of these rulers suppressed heretical groups. Thus, it was Charles V who summoned Martin Luther to answer charges of heresy before the Diet at Worms in 1521. Similarly, Henry VIII wrote against the ideas of Martin Luther, and later persecuted Lutherans, even as he inadvertently launched a reformation, as we'll see in subsequent lectures. Francis I, after a flirtation with Protestantism, clamped down in 1530. In addition, Philip II imposed the dreaded Spanish Inquisition on the Netherlands and continued it in Spain. Once, when he was reproached for his cruelty, he replied, "If my own son were guilty like you, I should lead him with my own hands to the stake."

All of these rulers engaged in administrative reforms to make their state more efficient. In England, the king's chief minister, Thomas Cromwell, launched a virtual Tudor revolution in government. Under his leadership, Parliament passed the Act in Restraint of Appeals in 1533, which said, "This realm of England is an empire." That didn't mean that England had a lot of territory; it didn't. What it meant was that the English king had the right to exercise imperially—complete control and command within his realms. This is a foundation of the modern nation-state. Cromwell also passed an Act of Union with Wales in 1536 and proclaimed Henry King of Ireland in 1540, though, admittedly, that did not go so well. He reformed Crown finances and the administration in general.

In France, Francis I established an effective inner council and punished rapacious government officials. He reformed government finances, but he also expanded the sale of government offices to raise money.

Charles I's chief minister in Spain, Francisco de los Cobos, established an efficient administration based upon councils coordinated by a Council of State.

In sum, all of these rulers had their methods. Feeling their oats, they also changed policies of consolidation into expansion. Charles V and Francis I fought for control of Italy during the 1520s. Henry VIII attempted multiple invasions of Scotland and France. Spain, of course, expanded overseas in the New World, as we'll see in the next lecture. They also faced down an Islamic challenge in the Mediterranean by defeating a Turkish fleet at Lepanto in 1571; conquered most of Italy; annexed Portugal in 1580 when the Portuguese royal house died out; and dabbled in the politics of England and France.

In terms of religion, these rulers sometimes sought to dominate the Church as well. The classic example, of course, is Henry VIII.

Unable to secure a divorce from Catherine of Aragon from the pope in the 1520s, he declared himself Supreme Head of the Church of England in 1534. Note that he did so because he thought that only a son—a Renaissance prince—could maintain his power. It is, of course, one of the great ironies of history that the successor who did so best was his daughter Elizabeth, who boasted of having "the heart and stomach of a king."

Francis I also increased his power, securing a concordat with the pope in 1516 that gave him the right to appoint all bishops and abbots in France. Charles V made war on Protestant barons in the War of the Schmalkaldic League. We'll talk about that in a later lecture. As Charles I of Spain, he gained complete control over Church appointments. Even the arch-Catholic Phillip II demanded and got papal support for his attempted invasion of England in 1588, even though the pope, Sixtus V, thought the plan to be lunacy.

Renaissance kings were also obsessed with projecting their power through propaganda. They commissioned buildings, poems, and paintings. Henry VIII confiscated and rebuilt Hampton Court and Whitehall, patronized the great portraitist Hans Holbein, and employed a stable of writers to support his royal supremacy. Elizabeth I was more frugal, but still had herself celebrated in elaborate festivals, progresses through the country, and poetry and other written propaganda. Usually, she was good at getting other people to pay for it.

Charles V employed painters like Titian. Francis I built the Louvre and the castle and hunting lodge at Chambord, possibly originally laid out by Leonardo da Vinci. He turned Castle Fontainebleau into a major palace, commissioning some of the greatest artists of the day, such as Fiorentino, Andrea del Sarto, Vignola, and Cellini.

In reforming their governments, stamping out opposition, and taking control of the arts and even of religion, the princes of the Renaissance sought to redirect the loyalty of their subjects and, indeed, were founding the modern conception of the state. Loyalty was owed to them alone; anyone who did not understand would pay a high price.

For example, in 1536 Catholic peasants in northern England rebelled against Henry VIII's break from Rome and they were ruthlessly suppressed. The Jews and Moors of Spain and the nobles of French Brittany all learned the same lesson.

Charles V's failure to stamp out Protestantism; at the end of the War of the Schmalkaldic League is sort of the exception that proves the rule. His best general, Maurice of Saxony, defected to the other side; so Charles was forced to conclude the Peace of Augsburg in 1555, by which Protestant states within the Empire were allowed to remain Protestant.

As a result, the Holy Roman Empire would remain divided in religion and also decentralized in political authority. The Holy Roman Emperor was never successful in establishing the same kind of authority as the other kings we have talked about. That will be crucial.

Why did other rulers succeed in creating strong nation-states where the Holy Roman Emperor failed? One reason hinted at above is obviously religious disunity, but another is money for money makes the world go 'round. After all, if you're going to be one of these kinds of rulers, you need money to build palaces, commission propaganda, and raise armies to overawe nobles, suppress rebellions, and project your power abroad.

That, of course, raises the question, "So, where are you going to get it?" The obvious answer is taxes. But medieval rulers had had to exempt nobles and the Church to gain their support. They didn't want to go back there. That left peasants, but peasants didn't have any money. In France especially, the king taxed the peasantry very hard. That will be important later. You could tax towns; they were cash cows. If you overtaxed them, however, your run the risk that you will kill the goose that laid the golden eggs. Moreover, every time you summon townsmen to Parliament or to the Estates General to ask them for money, you are actually giving more power and memory to that institution. That was fine except that every time Parliament or the Estates General met, the first thing on their minds would be, "Your majesty, how did you spend the money last time?" They might actually refuse to grant you more money, or make the grant contingent upon you redressing some grievance or something. That will never do. This will be a huge story in European history. For now, you need to know that for the princes of the Renaissance, it was an annoyance.

Was there no other source of ready money available to European rulers? We have already seen several examples. There was the Italian example. Remember, the Italian city-states had grown wealthy on trade. We've already seen that every one of the major powers noted above except England tried to control Italy. Why? Because they wanted that trade. Such trade created great wealth. Among other things, it endowed great banking houses. The Medici in Florence allied with the kings of France. The Fuggers worked with Charles V in Augsburg. The Medici became so powerful that they eventually married into the French royal house.

Then there is the English example. Henry VIII, remember, had taken over the Church of England. We'll talk more about that in a subsequent lecture. But among his policies was to confiscate its land. In 1534, he began with annates (taxes paid to the pope). He then confiscated the smaller monasteries in 1536, the larger ones in 1539, and hospitals and other charitable foundations in 1547.

The idea was to increase the king's revenue. Unfortunately, this only tempted Henry to spend more money on wars and palaces. He ended up going so far into debt that he needed quick cash; so he eventually sold this land, which could have endowed the monarchy for centuries, to his gentry and nobles. That made them rich and the English king poor. Stay tuned: that's going to be another important story.

Then there's the French example. Beginning with Louis XII, the French just sold government offices. That raised cash quickly and it stimulated social mobility, but it also expanded the size of government, and it meant that service was based on wealth rather than merit, which, of course, could lead to unsuitable officeholders.

Then finally, there was the Portuguese example. Portugal was a much poorer country than any of the others we have been talking about; but in the 14th century they came up with a brilliant idea. The Portuguese prince, Henry the Navigator, wondered whether you could possibly bypass the Italians, sail to the East, and develop trade with them by going around Africa. There was a great question here: does Africa actually end? Portugal's attempt to answer that question would lead to a rash of state-sponsored exploration, which anybody with a boat wanted to try. It would also lead to the discovery of what was for Europeans a New World.

Lecture Six
The New World & the Old—1400–1650

Scope:

The exploration and exploitation of Africa and Asia by the Portuguese and of the Americas by, first, the Spanish, then, the French and the English changed the economies, cultures, and political makeup of each of these regions forever. Native civilizations were destroyed; native populations were subjugated, enslaved, and transported from place to place; and often, nearly died out. European rulers and merchants gained new sources of wealth, which they used to purchase luxury goods and increase their political and military power.

Outline

I. As the Middle Ages came to an end, the Renaissance princes encountered in the last lecture—well-educated according to Renaissance principles, ambitious, hard-headed, and ruthless—sought to make themselves more powerful and less beholden to the good will of the Church, the aristocracy, or their subjects. To do this, they needed money.

   A. One source of funds was the rich trade with the East.

      1. Europeans were crazy for fabrics, spices, and medicines from China, India, and the Middle East.

      2. Venice, Genoa, Florence, and Milan had grown wealthy on this trade.

      3. But after 1453, when the Ottoman Empire conquered Constantinople, anyone wanting Eastern goods had to go through Muslim merchants.

   B. In the 15th century, the rulers of Portugal began to seek a way around the Muslims and the Italians.

II. Portugal was a relatively poor country ruled by the House of Aviz.

   A. During the reign of King John I (1385–1433), his son, Prince Henry the Navigator, began to explore alternative sources of wealth.

1. In 1419, he founded a college to train seamen.

2. He sent successive expeditions down the West coast of Africa, establishing trading posts and looking for a way to turn East.

B. This led to a century of exploration.

1. In 1415, Portuguese mariners captured Ceuta in Morocco, which later was used to capture Tangier.

2. Portuguese mariners explored the Madeira Islands in 1419, the Azores in 1427, Cape Verde by 1444, and Sierra Leone in 1460.

3. In 1482, they founded a major fort at Elmina, Ghana— arguably the first European settlement in West Africa.

4. By 1488, Bartholomew Diaz reached and rounded the Cape of Good Hope.

5. In 1498, Vasco da Gama rounded the cape, reached India, and returned with ships laden with the wealth of the East.

C. Based on trade with Africa and the East, Portugal became a major seafaring empire.

1. After Columbus laid the foundations for Spanish power in America, the pope worked out the Treaty of Tordesillas in 1494.

   a. Portugal was awarded everything east of a line 370 miles east of the Cape Verde Islands.

   b. This enabled the Portuguese to claim and colonize Brazil.

2. Under Manuel I (1495–1521), the Portuguese become a naval power, conquering a series of trading posts in and about India: Goa in India in 1510; Malacca (now Melaka) in Malaysia in 1511; the Moluccas (now Maluku Islands) in present-day Indonesia by 1514; and the island of Hormuz in the Persian Gulf in 1514–1515.

D. By the mid-16th century, Portugal began to experience decline, in part because of the attempt to keep up with Spain.

1. Spanish kings pressured the Portuguese to expel their Jews and Moors, a mistake that destroyed much of the old Portuguese middle class.

2. In 1536, the King of Portugal introduced the Inquisition.

3. In 1580, the House of Aviz came to an end with the death of Henry I. Phillip II of Spain took over

4. Spain ruled Portugal for 60 years—known in Portuguese history as the "60 Years Captivity"—with revolts in 1634, 1637, and (this one successful) in 1640.

E. The greatest significance of Portuguese exploration is that other European powers began to emulate it.

III. Spain was a poor country, only united under Ferdinand and Isabella at the end of the 15th century.

A. This explains why Ferdinand and Isabella supported Christopher Columbus (Christoforo Columbo in Italian; Christóbal Colón in Spanish) when he approached them with a radical way to reach the fabled East: head West!

1. Most educated Europeans did not believe that the Earth was flat.

2. What this group did not know was how big the Earth was.

3. In fact, Columbus underestimated the distance to Asia.

4. In 1491, the Spanish government agreed to the voyage.

  a. With land spotted by lookout Rodrigo de Triana on the 12th of October 1492, Columbus landed in what is now the Dominican Republic, claiming it for Spain.

  b. He returned to Spain, bringing with him exotic natives, parrots, and gold, and was greeted with honors.

  c. The pope immediately granted Spain the right to the lands discovered by Columbus.

  d. Columbus died in 1502 thinking that he had reached the Indies.

B. The Spanish crown soon figured out that it had not reached the East Indies, but a place far more exotic—and lucrative.

1. In 1513, Vasco de Balboa discovered the Pacific Ocean.

2. In 1519, the one surviving ship from Ferdinand Magellan's circumnavigation arrived in Spain and reported the vastness of the world.

3. In the same year, Hernán Cortés (Hernando Cortéz) landed in Mexico and conquered an advanced Aztec civilization.

4. In 1531, Francisco Pizarro landed in Peru and did the same thing to the Incas.

C. Spain's "discovery" of the "New World" (a totally Eurocentric concept) had momentous consequences for both sides.

1. What were the consequences for the native peoples?

   a. The "Indians" would mostly die, either in futile resistance or from European diseases to which they had no resistance: smallpox, chickenpox, whooping cough, diphtheria, malaria, measles, yellow spotted fever, and even the bubonic plague.

   b. A population of perhaps 50 million in 1492 would sink to 5 million by 1700.

   c. The survivors were enslaved to work the plantations and gold and silver mines of Mexico and Peru.

   d. Some eventually intermarried with their conquerors, producing new peoples.

   e. When the native populations began to die out, both Spain and Portugal began to import slaves culled from Africa. Eventually, some 10 million people were abducted, sold, transported, and worked, often to death, in the New World.

2. What were the effects on Europeans?

   a. Intellectually, the European worldview was challenged significantly by the existence of new and very different civilizations.

   b. Materially, silver, in particular, flooded into Spain via biannual treasure fleets, making the Spanish crown fabulously wealthy and Spain the dominant power in Europe for 150 years.

   c. This wealth bankrolled Charles V's wars to maintain the Holy Roman Empire and Phillip II's to stamp out Protestantism.

   d. But New World silver did nothing for the Spanish people, apart from merchants in Seville.

     e. Moreover, some historians think that the silver flooding into Europe also destabilized the European economy, leading to unprecedented inflation of about 4 percent in the 17th century.

     f. Nevertheless, other countries noted Spain's quick success and wanted on the bandwagon of exploration, colonization, and exploitation.

IV. Unfortunately for France and England, they were too late and too far north to make a quantum leap in wealth or status as a result of American exploration.

   A. In the 1580s, the French began to explore and control Canada, the upper Midwest, and the Mississippi Valley.

     1. Jesuits established numerous missions.

     2. These settlements did not result in tremendous wealth, but they supplied France with furs and pelts and Grand Banks fishing.

     3. France forbade Protestants to settle in Canada, thus eliminating Canada as a social safety valve and limiting the value of the colonies to the whole of French society.

     4. Only in the late 17th century would France aim to exploit its base in North America under the mercantilist policies of Jean-Baptiste Colbert (1619–1683).

   B. The English did not really start to think seriously about the Americas until Elizabeth's reign.

     1. At first, they just wanted to cash in on Spanish trade, hence the early slaving voyages by John Hawkins in the 1560s.

     2. In 1568, Spanish *guardacostas* attacked an English slaving fleet, which led to a covert war between Spain and England, with English privateers like Hawkins, Sir Francis Drake, and Sir Martin Frobisher seeking to intercept and confiscate Spanish fleets or sack Spanish ports in the New World.

     3. The first successful English colony in the Americas was founded at Jamestown in 1607 by a consortium headed by Sir Thomas Smith (Smythe) of the Virginia Company.

       a. The purpose of the venture was to mine gold.

  b. When no gold was found, the colony discovered a marketable commodity in tobacco (despite the prescient opposition of King James, who wrote "A Counterblast to Tobacco" in 1604).

  c. In the 1620s, the colony discovered a cheap source of labor in African slaves.

 4. The colonization of Massachusetts began with the Plymouth settlement on Cape Cod in 1620 on the Virginia Company charter.

 5. In 1629, the Massachusetts Bay Company was chartered to establish a much larger settlement around Boston, absorbing the Plymouth settlement in 1691.

  a. The Massachusetts Bay Company allowed for self-government and its leaders consciously set out to found a Puritan "New Jerusalem"—a "city on a hill"—where Puritan liturgy, morality, and social conventions could be enforced, free from the persecution of the Church of England.

  b. Massachusetts Bay colonists who came for economic opportunity chafed under the intolerant religious regime. Rather, these settlements existed to provide a refuge for those Puritans who could not conform to the Church of England.

 5. Puritan intolerance eventually drove a Salem clergyman named Roger Williams to found Rhode Island as a haven for a wider variety of Protestants, as well as Jews.

 6. In 1632, George Calvert, Lord Baltimore, a Catholic, founded Maryland, which eventually became a haven for Catholics.

 7. In the end, the English colonies of the New World provided limited commercial or military value. These colonies were an increasingly important safety valve for those people who could neither abide nor prosper in Anglican village society. (They provided an alternative to the Poor Law for indigent Englishmen.)

C. The English government also sought to encourage the development of other markets for English products.

 1. The English had only wool to export.

2. Of the several monopolistic trading companies chartered between 1555 and 1600, only the British East India Company (established in 1600)—which was a joint stock company in which profit and loss were shared among all who cared to invest—had the potential to benefit a wider swath of English society.

3. After the Dutch massacred an English trading colony at Amboyna in the Moluccas in 1623, all East India companies—the French, the Dutch, and the English—fought literal trade war for the trade of the Far East.

4. By the late 17th century, they armed their ships as men-of-war, fielded vast armies against each other, and used their armies to intimidate local rulers into acceptance of their trade.

V. The great trading nation in the 17th century was increasingly the Dutch.

 A. In the 1560s, the Dutch began a long insurgency against Spain for their independence, which Spain granted in a truce of 1609, though full independence as a separate country wasn't recognized until the Treaty of Münster in 1648.

 B. The Dutch founded a republic: a confederation of self-governing provinces sending representatives to a legislative body called the States-General, with an executive officer (sometimes elected) called a stadholder (*stadhouder* in Dutch).

 C. Their first important venture was to Java in 1600. Then, there was a series of trading voyages establishing trading posts in Africa—Tasmania and the Cape of Good Hope—and especially in the Far East.

 D. The Dutch East India Company, chartered in 1602, established trading colonies in the Moluccas (or Spice Islands) and in 1619, founded Batavia (now Jakarta) in western Java.

 E. A Dutch West Indian Company established in 1621 sponsored colonies in the West Indies at Curaçao and later St. Martin; North America at New Amsterdam in 1624; and Pernambuco, Brazil in 1630.

F. In 1654, the Portuguese drove the Dutch from Brazil and in 1664, the Dutch lost New Amsterdam to the British, who renamed it New York.

VI. The Holy Roman Empire never engaged in the exploration game and never acquired any major overseas trades or colonies that it could exploit.

    A. Why?

        1. Perhaps, once again, geography is destiny: The Holy Roman Empire was badly placed for either Eastern or Western trade.

        2. Or was it a lack of will? After all, North Germans had always been distinguished sailors.

        3. Was it the close connection with Spain, seeming to absolve the German ruler of the duty to try?

    B. The failure of the Germans to engage in the great game of European imperialism until the 19th century had far-reaching consequences: imperial poverty, powerlessness, and Protestantism.

        1. The Holy Roman Emperor never figured out a financial mechanism to pay his armies beyond taxation and consulting the Diet.

        2. As a partial result, the emperor remained the weakest of the great European rulers, the elected chairman of a board of some 300 kingdoms, duchies, counties, and dioceses.

        3. This will go a long way to explain why the topic of the next lecture—the Protestant Reformation—could happen in only one place: the Holy Roman Empire!

Supplementary Reading:

M. B. Chambers, et al., *Western Experience*, chapter 14, section II.

J. H. Elliott, *The Old World and the New, 1492–1650*.

G. V. Scammell, *The First Imperial Age: European Overseas Expansion, c. 1400–1715*.

Questions to Consider:

1. Why did Spain and Portugal lead in the race for empire in the 15th and 16th centuries?

2. What impulses besides finances drove the first European quest for empire?

Portugese Exploration and Discovery

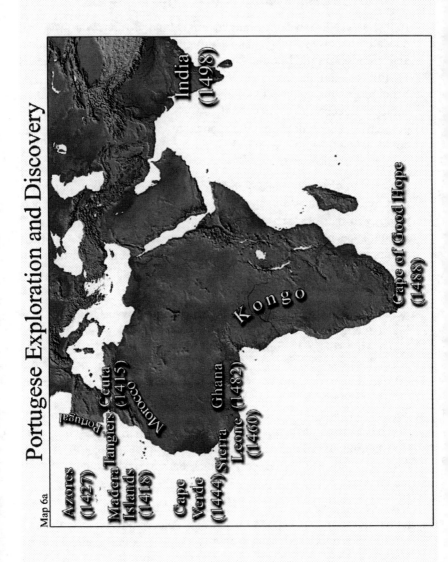

Map 6a

Azores (1427)
Madera (1418)
Tangiers (1415)
Ceuta
Portugal
Morocco
Cape Verde (1444)
Sierra Leone (1460)
Ghana (1482)
Kongo
India (1498)
Cape of Good Hope (1488)

Lecture Six—Transcript
The New World & the Old—1400–1650

In the last lecture, we encountered a new kind of ruler, who was well educated according to Humanist principles, ambitious, hardheaded, and ruthless. As the Middle Ages came to an end, the crowned heads of Europe sought to make themselves more powerful and less beholden to the good will of the Church, the aristocracy, or their subjects generally. They did so by employing armies of propagandists, writers, painters, and composers. Even mapmakers could be useful in projecting their power. When all else failed, they employed soldiers.

But art and war cost money, and therein lay the rub. What good was it to overawe your subjects with fancy palaces and powerful armies when you had to beg them for the money to pay for it all? Renaissance princes knew that excessive taxation might kill their economies, disgruntle their subjects, and raise the importance of legislative and tax-gathering bodies like Parliament and the Estates General.

Renaissance princes, if they were to be truly as powerful as Machiavelli would have them, needed lots of money—no questions asked. One source of funds would have been the rich trade with the East. Europeans were crazy for fabrics, spices, and medicines from China, India, and the Middle East. Everyone knew that Venice, Genoa, Florence, and Milan had grown wealthy on this trade. That's why France and the Holy Roman Emperor tried to conquer Italy, as we have seen. But in 1453, the Ottoman Empire conquered Constantinople, complicating an important trade route to the East. Anyone who wanted eastern goods had to go through Muslim merchants.

Was there no way around the Muslims and the Italians? The answer to that question was supplied from, of all places, Portugal. In the 14th century, Portugal had been a relatively poor country ruled by the House of Aviz. Like Spain, it was partly controlled by the Moors until a series of campaigns of expulsion drove them out. It was frequently threatened to be absorbed by Castile. A powerful Cortes limited the king's power.

Henry the Navigator, the son of King John I who ruled from 1385–1433, began to explore alternative sources of wealth as a way to increase the power of the House of Aviz and reduce that dependence on the Cortes. Beginning in 1419, he founded a college to train seamen. He sent successive expeditions down the west coast of Africa. These expeditions perfected the caravelle, which became the great prototypical ship for exploration during this period of time. They established trade routes. They explored the coast. And always, they were on the lookout for a way to turn east. In other words, the great question for this college was, "Does Africa end?"

This led to a century of exploration, the beginnings of European imperialism, and many fringe benefits for the Portuguese monarchy. Like so: beginning in 1415, Portuguese mariners had already captured Ceuta in Morocco. This became a foothold in Africa; later, it was used to capture Tangiers. By 1419, they had explored the Madeira Islands and, in 1427, the Azores. Both became centers of sugar production, which became a very lucrative trade—people in Europe loved sugar—and also a set of way stations on the way south and on the way west.

Portuguese mariners made it to Cape Verde by 1444 and Sierra Leone in 1460. They founded a major fort at Elmina, Ghana in 1482, establishing relations with King of the Kongo in the interior. That would lead to a brisk trade, first, in gold and, later, in slaves.

Bartholomew Diaz reached the Cape of Good Hope in 1488, and this was the moment when the Portuguese realized you could possibly circle Africa. Ten years later, Vasco de Gama rounded the Cape, reached India, and returned with ships laden with the wealth of the East. His profit was 60 times the cost of the voyage.

The result was a Portuguese seafaring empire based on trade with Africa and the East. After Columbus laid the foundations for Spanish power in the Americas (we'll talk about that in a few minutes), the pope worked out the Treaty of Tordesillas in 1494. As a result of this treaty, Portugal was given free run of everything east of a line, 370 miles east of the Cape Verde Islands.

I have three points to make about this. First, this treaty and the explorations that led up to it would lay the foundations of Portuguese Brazil. Pedro Alvarez de Cabral, hoping to repeat de Gama's success, actually strayed too far west and bumped into Brazil in 1500. My second point is that, as in Africa, the Portuguese would establish trading posts, which would supply wood, red dye, and later, valuable sugar cane to Portugal. This expedition and series of expeditions was based upon new knowledge acquired through science and exploration; but it was also—and this is my third point—based on European arrogance. Were any of the native peoples ever consulted by the pope in drawing this line? Of course not.

Under Manuel I, known as Manuel the Fortunate (he ruled from 1495–1521), Portugal became a great naval power. The Portuguese conquered Goa in India in 1510; Malacca (now Melaka) in Malaysia in 1511; the Moluccas in present day Indonesia by 1514; and the Hormuz Island in the Persian Gulf in 1515. They opened up trade with China and established relations with Ethiopia. In fact, the Portuguese Empire wasn't really a colonizing empire. Lots of Portuguese did not leave their homeland to establish a sort of new Portugal. It was mainly and simply based on trade.

By the mid-16th century, Portugal had begun to experience decline, in part, because of the attempt to keep up with Spain. It became overextended. It had troops and a navy on station around the globe. It was pressured by Spain, among other things, in terms of religion. The Spanish kings wanted the Portuguese to expel their Jews and Moors. The Portuguese reluctantly did this. This was a mistake because it destroyed much of the old Portuguese middle class.

In 1536, the King of Portugal introduced the Inquisition, also following the Spanish example. In 1580, the House of Aviz came to an end with the death of Henry I. There were six claimants to the throne, but the most powerful was Phillip II of Spain, for reasons we are about to learn. He took over and, as a result, Spain ruled Portugal for 60 years. This is known in Portuguese history as the "60 Years of Captivity."

During this period of time, the Portuguese lost the Indian trade to the Dutch. The Dutch occupied Brazil. Eventually, the Portuguese revolted, actually repeatedly, against Spain in 1634, 1637, and finally and successfully, in 1640.

After 1640, a new dynasty, the Braganza, took over and managed to expel the Dutch from Brazil. This is a great and very largely unknown story, but its greatest significance is that other European powers began to emulate the actions of Portugal, most notably, Spain.

As we have seen, Spain was only united under Ferdinand and Isabella at the end of the 15th century. So, of all the great nations of Europe, Spain was in some ways the most recent and untried. Economically, it was much poorer than France or the Holy Roman Empire and it had gotten in late on the Portuguese eastern trade. This helps to explain why the dual monarchs listened when a Genoese sailor named Christoforo Columbo (or Christóbal Colón in Spanish) approached them with a radical idea: that the way to reach the fabled East was to head west.

Now, contrary to popular belief, most educated Europeans did not think the world was flat. The Greeks had proposed a round Earth and sailors knew about the curvature of the Earth. What they did not know was how big the Earth was. The fear wasn't that Columbus would sail off the edge, but that he would just sail, and sail, and sail.

In fact, Columbus's instincts were right, but his math was all wrong. He thought that Asia extended much farther east than it did. He underestimated the circumference of the Earth. He thought that Japan was 2,760 miles west of the Canary Islands. In fact, it's about 12,000 miles. No one in Europe suspected that two vast continents lay in the way.

In 1491, after much wrangling, the Spanish government agreed to the voyage. Here is one of the few places where I almost get to say "and the rest is history." But I'll tell you a little bit about the voyage. Columbus left Spain in early August and left the Canary Islands in early September. That was his last Spanish landfall. His ships carried provisions for a year.

Columbus preferred dead reckoning and his gut experience at sea to celestial navigation. By early October, not having sighted anything, the crew is growing restive. But after midnight on the 12th of October, 1492, a lookout named Rodrigo de Triana spotted land. Rodrigo was supposed to get a nice pension out of this, but Columbus claimed it for himself.

Columbus landed in what is now the Dominican Republic later that day. He raised the royal standard, claiming the island for Ferdinand and Isabella. He traded with Indians, called Tainos, a branch of the Arawaks. He founded a settlement called La Navidad and he returned to Spain accompanied by exotic natives, parrots, and gold.

He was greeted with many honors. He was dubbed the "Admiral of the Ocean Sea." He was given 1,000 doubloons and 17 ships for a return voyage. It was as a result of Columbus's first voyage that the pope had drawn up that Treaty of Tordesillas that we mentioned earlier. If Portugal got all the lands east of the line, Spain got all the lands to the west. Thus the pope divided the New World between Spain and Portugal in 1494.

As you know, Columbus died thinking he had reached the Indies. Even after three more voyages, he was convinced that he had discovered the route to the East, and it was he who dubbed the natives "Indians." But as other sailors came back from the new Spanish claims, the Spanish Crown began to figure out that it hadn't reached the East Indies at all, but something far more exotic and (who knew?) lucrative.

In 1513, Vasco de Balboa discovered the Pacific Ocean. In 1519, the one surviving ship from Magellan's circumnavigation arrived in Spain and reported just how big that ocean was. It took 93 days to cross the Pacific. It was at this point that the Spaniards realized that they could concede the East to Portugal and still have an entire "New World" at their disposal.

At this point, the Spanish ceased to be *exploradors* and became *conquistadors*. In the same year, 1519, Hernán de Cortes conquered an advanced Aztec civilization in Mexico. The Aztecs were unused to guns and especially horses. In 1531, Francisco Pizarro did the same thing to the Incas.

Spain's "discovery" of the "New World" is, of course, a totally Eurocentric concept. From the point of view of the natives of these lands, it was an old world. It was their world. There was nothing to discover. That mutual myopia—the European refusal to see things from the native's point of view and the Native American failure to understand the implications of European expansion—was a recipe for disaster.

I'd like to talk about the effects of the discovery of this "New World" on both the native population and on Europeans. First, the Indians would mostly die, either in futile resistance to men on horseback with guns or from European diseases that they had never encountered before, including smallpox, chickenpox, whooping cough, diphtheria, malaria, measles, yellow and spotted fever, and even the bubonic plague. A population of perhaps 50 million people in 1492 was reduced to five million by 1700. The survivors were enslaved to work the plantations and the gold and silver mines of Mexico and Peru. Some eventually intermarried with their conquerors, producing new peoples.

When the native populations began to die out, both Spain and Portugal began to import slaves culled from Africa. Eventually, some 10 million people were abducted, sold, and transported. About a third died on the voyage. Those who didn't die were exploited in the New World. We'll talk more about the African slave trade in a later lecture. For now, you should understand that Columbus's discovery brought misery to three continents: South America, North America, and Africa.

Now, it is true of course, that the Aztec and Incan civilizations that the Spanish destroyed were also cruel and exploitative, and that most enslaved Africans had been captured in tribal wars or raids by other Africans. In fact, all of these continents were riven by cruel tribal warfare. But European civilization gave African kings an extra incentive for such warfare, and it replaced the Aztec and Incan Empires with something that was even more destructive of humanity and the environment.

What was the effect of all this on Europeans? Intellectually, the European worldview was blown apart. The New World was hitherto unsuspected. It was full of civilizations, some of them quite advanced, that did things differently. It was full of men and women who hadn't heard of Christ or the Christian God, and who arranged themselves in different economic and social patterns—men and women literally in the state of nature (at least from a European point of view), which would cause European philosophers to start to think really hard about what was intrinsic to humanity and what was constructed by culture. More on that later.

Of course, neither the Kings of Spain or Portugal nor their commanders cared a fig for these abstruse questions. To them, the New World was a vast treasure house given to them by the Christian God to exploit. Silver, in particular, flooded into Spain via biannual treasure fleets. Admittedly, these had a distressing tendency to be sunk by Caribbean storms or by English privateers; but enough would get through to make the Spanish Crown fabulously wealthy and Spain the dominant power in Europe for 150 years. That wealth enabled subsequent Spanish monarchs like Charles I and Phillip II to launch more expeditions, raise vast armies and navies, and maintain a vast worldwide empire. In fact, much of Spain's wealth would bankroll Charles V's wars to hold on to the Holy Roman Empire and Phillip II's to stamp out Protestantism, as we'll learn in a later lecture.

Both in the end had disastrous results for the Spanish monarchy. In fact, there's a really good question as to whether all this treasure actually did anything for Spain in the long run. Apart from the merchants of Seville and the king, nobody else seems to have managed to profit out of the treasure from the New World. Some historians think that the silver flooding into Europe also destabilized the European economy, leading to spiraling inflation in the 17th century. By the way, I should explain that "spiraling inflation" was about 4% a year. That may not sound like much to us, but to a world coming out of the Middle Ages, in which prices and wages had been fixed for decades if not centuries, it was disastrous enough.

Finally, the last effect of the Spanish discovery of the New World was that other countries noted Spain's quick rise to power and wealth and wanted to jump on the bandwagon. But in this case, too, geography along with timing was destiny. Unfortunately for the French, the English, and the Dutch, they were just too late and too north to make a quick quantum leap in wealth or status from American exploration. That is, if you sail due west from France, England, or the Netherlands, you don't hit the sunny Caribbean.

In the 1580s, the French began to explore and control Canada, the upper Midwest, and the Mississippi Valley. Americans are quite familiar with French place names commemorating French explorers like de la Salle, Father Marquette, and Cadillac. Father Marquette's name reminds us that much of the impetus here, as with Spain, was religious. Jesuits established numerous missions.

But these settlements did not at first lead to any tremendous wealth. They supplied furs, pelts, and Grand Banks fish to France, and that's about it. In particular, France forbade Protestants from settling in Canada, thus eliminating Canada as a social safety valve and limiting the useful of the colonies to the whole of French society. That will be important later. Only in the late 17th century would France aim to exploit its base in North America under the mercantilist policies of Jean-Baptist Colbert.

Let's turn to England. The first exploratory voyages took place soon after Columbus (1497–1498), but they failed to find a northwest or northeast passage to Asia. The English didn't really start to think seriously about the Americas until Elizabeth's reign. At first, they just wanted to cash in on Spanish trade; hence the early slaving voyages by John Hawkins in the 1560s.

But by the 1560s, the Spanish had built up a colonial and trading infrastructure. In 1568, Spanish *guardacostas* attacked an English slaving fleet. This led to a covert war between Spain and England. English privateers like Hawkins, Sir Francis Drake, and Sir Martin Frobisher sought to intercept and confiscate Spanish fleets or sack Spanish ports in the New World.

In other words, Drake, Hawkins, and Frobisher were terrorists. As with many modern day terrorists, there was even a religious dimension: the English were Protestants and the Spanish were Catholics. And as with modern day terrorists, they were supported by a state that denied their existence. Elizabeth I repeatedly denied to Philip II that she could do anything about Hawkins and Drake. "I don't know what's wrong with these people; I try to control them." In fact, she was secretly funding them and taking a cut of the profits.

This covert war became official in the 1580s when Philip decided to launch the Spanish Armada. By this time, the English saw the advantages to establishing their own colonies in the New World. They could be used as military and naval bases against Spanish colonies, and as trading posts and sources of raw materials. Unlike the French, the English used their colonies as a safety valve for excess population, that is, for people unable to find work or conform in religion; for example Puritans, who didn't accept the moderate theology of the Church of England.

The 1580s saw a series of failed attempts by Elizabethan courtiers to colonize the eastern seaboard, culminating in the "Lost Colony of Roanoke." The first successful English colony in the Americas was founded in 1607 by a consortium headed by Sir Thomas Smith of the Virginia Company. It was established at the headwaters of a river they named the James, after England's new Stuart king. The settlement they called Jamestown.

The purpose of Jamestown was to mine gold. When no gold was found (Virginia doesn't seem to have a lot of gold; I'd be digging under the foundation of The Teaching Company if it did), the earliest colonists proved incapable of growing crops or getting along with the Native American population.

The colony only began to hit its economic stride in the 1610s. It discovered a marketable commodity: tobacco. The smoking of tobacco was just beginning to be popular in England, despite the prescient opposition of King James, who wrote "A Counterblast to Tobacco" in 1604.

In the 1620s, the colony then discovered a cheap source of labor: African slaves. And so the cruel foundations of the plantation economy were laid. If you want to be cynical about it, you could say that the first successful Anglo-Saxon settlement in the New World was founded on cancer, racism, and greed.

The colonization of Massachusetts began with the Plymouth Settlement on Cape Cod in 1620 on the Virginia Company charter. In 1629, the Massachusetts Bay Company was chartered to establish a much larger settlement around Boston, absorbing the Plymouth Settlement, finally, in 1691. Its charter (that is, the Massachusetts Bay Company) allowed for self-government, and its leaders consciously set out to found a Puritan "New Jerusalem"—a "city on a hill" where Puritan liturgy, morality, and social conventions could be enforced, free from the persecution of the Church of England. They encouraged whole Puritan congregations to immigrate. In keeping with Puritan doctrine, they banned other religious groups and Catholic superstitions, such as traditional Christmas celebrations and calendar festivals. Put another way, the Puritans came to America for religious freedom alright, but for themselves, not for anyone else.

Those Massachusetts Bay colonists who came for economic opportunity chafed under the intolerant religious regime. In other words, you would get people who would emigrate to Massachusetts just because they wanted land. They weren't particularly interested in this particular religious orientation. That intolerance eventually drove a Salem clergymen named Roger Williams to found Rhode Island as a haven for a wider variety of Protestants, as well as Jews. In 1632, George Calvert, Lord Baltimore, a Catholic, founded

Maryland. Later in the 17th century, Maryland became a haven for Catholics.

So in the end, the English colonies of the New World actually had very limited commercial or military value. But they were an increasingly important safety valve for those who could neither abide by nor prosper in Anglican village society.

By 1642, some 60,000 people had crossed the Atlantic to found an English society in North America. This was much larger than the French population, and that will be very important in the 17th and 18th centuries as the English and French come to blows over who is going to control this part of the world.

The English government also sought to encourage the development of other markets for English products. There was just one problem here. There's only really one English product during this period of time; it's wool. They chartered a series of monopolistic trading companies to other areas. There's the Muscovy Company, the Spanish Company, the Eastland Company, the Turkey Company (later the Levant Company), the Senegal Adventurers (later the Royal Africa Company), and the East India Company—all chartered between about 1555–1600.

The problem with this should be clear from the names on the list: how many of these regions really are desperate for wool? Sure, Muscovy and the Baltic; but the Levant and India, probably not. Most ended up making their profits out of importing silks, cottons, tea, spices, and medicines from India and the Levant; timber and naval stores from the Baltic; and, in the case of the Royal Africa Company, African human beings shipped to the Americas.

Each of these companies held a royal monopoly and, as in Spain, their real beneficiaries were the king; courtiers who greased the wheels of influence; the merchants who were members; and the ports that did most of the business. In other words, they did nothing to really enrich the country. Only the East India Company had the potential to do so because it was founded as a joint stock company. That is, none of the previous companies were really investment opportunities. By "company," I really mean a guild. In other words, you had to be a member of the Muscovy Company in order to trade with Russia. But in the case of the East India Company, you could buy stock in the company, which mounted its own voyages. And so, as with all joint stock companies, profit and loss were shared. Unfortunately, the late start of the English East India Company led to clashes with the French and especially the Dutch, who had basically gotten to the Indian Ocean first.

In 1623, the Dutch massacred an English trading colony at Amboyna in the Moluccas. From this point on, all East India companies—the French, the Dutch, and the English—fought literal trade war for the trade of the Far East. By the late 17th century, they armed their ships as men-of-war; they fielded vast armies against each other; but they also used those armies to intimidate local rulers into acceptance of their trade.

For the English, this would all pay after 1700. In the meantime, in the 17th century (the 1600s), the great trading nation would increasingly be the Dutch. The Dutch had spent most of the later 16th century fighting Spain for their independence. That is to say, they rebelled in the 1560s and fought a long, in effect, insurgency against Spain that lasted until 1609. It was only in that year that the Spanish called a truce. Full independence of the Netherlands as a separate country wasn't recognized until the Treaty of Münster of 1648.

The Netherlands became a federation of self-governing provinces that sent representatives to a legislative body called the States General. Its executive was an elected officer called a stadholder. In other words, the Dutch founded a republic—the most important republic in early modern Europe.

This republic granted de facto religious toleration to Catholics, various Protestant sects, and Jews. It's a model of toleration. It produced a vibrant urban culture and it was based on a commercial economy. Even before independence, Dutch sailors and traders began to move into the Far East. By the mid-17th century, they dominated its trade.

Their first important venture was to Java in 1600. Remember, I told you they got there just before the English. Then, there was a series of trading voyages establishing trading posts in Africa—Tasmania and the Cape of Good Hope—but especially in the Far East. The Dutch East India Company was chartered in 1602. It established trading colonies in the Moluccas (or Spice Islands) and in 1619, founded Batavia (now Jakarta) in western Java.

As with the Portuguese, this company wasn't really interested in territory. It wanted economically strategic locations and trading posts. A Dutch West Indian Company was later established that established colonies in the West Indies at Curacao and later St. Martin; North America at New Amsterdam in 1624; and Pernambuco, Brazil, in 1630 (the Dutch were moving into Brazil because of Portuguese weakness by then). They also captured Portuguese slaving stations in West Africa.

The tide turned a little bit in the 1650s. In 1654, the Portuguese drove the Dutch from Brazil and in 1664, the Dutch lost New Amsterdam to the British, who renamed it New York. Still, all of this economic activity contributed to the Dutch miracle of the 17th century. For a while, the Netherlands was the wealthiest trading nation on Earth. Amsterdam became the commercial and financial center of Europe. This resulted in the golden age of Dutch art, in part because that art was patronized by wealthy burghers.

So, all of Europe seemed to be racing to catch up with Spain—all except Germany. The Holy Roman Empire never really engaged in the exploration game and never acquired any major overseas trades or colonies that it could exploit. Think about it: you've never heard of the Schmidt expedition.

Why? Perhaps once again, geography is destiny. The Holy Roman Empire was virtually landlocked compared to the Atlantic powers. Certainly, it was badly placed to try for either eastern or western trade. Or was it a lack of will? After all, the North Germans had always been distinguished sailors, so what stopped them here? Was it the fact that the Holy Roman Emperor is a Hapsburg and connected to Spain; so the fact that the Spanish explored the New World sort of gave the Germans a pass?

In any case, the failure of the Germans to engage in the great game of European imperialism until the 19th century had far-reaching consequences. It led to three very crucial "P's," if you will. First, poverty: the Holy Roman Emperor never figured out a financial mechanism to pay his armies beyond taxation and consulting the Diet. In other words, he alone, among the great Renaissance princes, remained poor. Because he remained poor, he remained relatively weak. As a result of this weakness, he remained an elected chairman of a board of some 300 kingdoms, duchies, counties, and dioceses.

This will in turn go a long way to explain why the topic of the next lecture, the Protestant Reformation, could happen in only one place in Europe—the one empire named so ironically "holy" and "Roman."

Lecture Seven
The Protestant Reformation—1500–22

Scope:

German decentralization, the rise of literacy and the development of the printing press in Europe made possible the dissemination of powerful new ideas, in particular the Reformation launched by Martin Luther. Scandalized by the Church's sale of indulgences, Luther came to offer an alternative theology and religious structure to Catholicism. Protestantism, elaborated by such thinkers as Calvin and Zwingli, swept across Europe, leading England, Scotland, Denmark, the Netherlands, and numerous northern German states to repudiate their allegiance to Rome.

Outline

I. Since before the fall of the Roman Empire more than 1,000 years previously, Europe had been officially and primarily Christian.

   A. Declared the official religion of the Roman Empire in 391, Christianity had split into two camps in 1054.

      1. Western Europe acknowledged the Bishop of Rome—later known as the pope—as the Vicar of Christ.

      2. Eastern Europe (Russia and Christians in the Ottoman Empire) acknowledged an orthodox patriarchy based in Constantinople and recognized even by the Ottomans as speaking for its Christians.

      3. Still, the patriarch of Constantinople never had the administrative authority of the pope: the Russian Orthodox Church, under a patriarch in Moscow, had broken away in 1448, and others would break away to form separate Orthodox churches in the 19th century.

   B. Nearly every European state established Christianity as its official religion.

      1. Rulers were crowned by the Church.

      2. Bishops had been, until quite recently, the ruler's chief advisors.

      3. The Church taxed a high proportion of people's income.

      4. The state enforced conformity, by requiring attendance at weekly mass and persecuting Christian heretics.

C. Jews, Muslims, and other minority groups were second-class citizens, even when they were not persecuted and expelled.

   1. From 1295, the Roman Church decreed that Jews should wear badges as a mark of humiliation for their refusal to convert to Christianity.

   2. They were prohibited by successive Church councils from employing Christians or appearing in public on Easter or other Christian holidays.

   3. Because Christians were forbidden from lending money at interest, Jews found a niche as bankers and moneylenders—a niche that only increased their unpopularity in some quarters.

   4. Jews were expelled from England in 1290 and from France in 1306 and again in 1394. In Germany, not a unified country until after the early modern period, the situation varied from place to place.

   5. Medieval Spain had been very tolerant of both Jews and Muslims, but as we have seen, Isabella and Ferdinand harried them out of the country. Many fled to Portugal, but in 1497 Manuel I decided on forced conversions, causing many to leave for Greece and North Africa.

   6. The glorious exception to this really sad picture was Poland.

D. While Church and state generally cooperated in both East and West, there were clashes in the West during the Middle Ages.

   1. Western European kings were increasingly uncomfortable with the Church's claim to have given them their power.

   2. Kings wanted sole jurisdiction in their lands.

   3. Kings resented papal power to tax their subjects.

   4. Kings wanted to appoint bishops because they were also royal vassals and officials.

E. As we saw in Lecture 3, the early modern Church was not in great shape to fight these battles after the French king abducted the papacy to Avignon between 1309 and 1374, and the Great Schism of 1374–1417.

   1. Unity was restored in 1417, when a series of Church councils deposed all three competing popes and elected a fourth, Martin V.

2. After the success of these councils, there was hope that the Church would become more democratic and that conciliarism—the idea that councils should have the power to determine Church policy—would make reform possible by giving priests and lay people a voice in Church governance.

3. Instead, Martin V and his successors concentrated on reviving and strengthening papal power.

4. Too often, the papacy neglected the obligation to be a moral example.

5. Some popes (e.g., Julius II; Alexander VI; Leo X) behaved like great Machiavellian Renaissance princes themselves—which in the long run harmed papal prestige and the sense that popes were spiritual leaders.

F. Most people turned to religion to give their hard lives meaning and consolation. Here, we get into an area of great controversy among historians.

1. Traditionally, the medieval Catholic Church has been portrayed as corrupt and unpopular—but this view is often taken directly from works of literature such as Chaucer's *Canterbury Tales* or the propaganda of Protestant reformers.

2. But recent archival research illustrative of people's actual lives (wills, church records of donations, and clubs) shows a healthier Church.

    a. Most clergy were doing their jobs under difficult conditions.

    b. Most people were orthodox Catholics.

    c. Religious books sold well. The writings of Meister Eckhart and Thomas à Kempis were very popular well beyond Germany. The *devotio moderno* emphasized a practical individual faith that was very popular in the Low Countries.

3. That does not mean that everybody was happy in Christendom.

    a. There was a shortage of priests, who were often poorly educated and sometimes failed to be good moral exemplars.

      b. Church courts monitored personal behavior but had the potential to split communities and breed resentment.

      c. From the 13th century, there was, in many parts of Europe, the Inquisition, which took hearsay evidence, encouraged neighbors to inform on neighbors, and used torture to ferret out people who did not agree with orthodox Catholicism.

          i. Penalties ranged from public humiliation—adulterers were made to stand in the town square in a white sheet holding a taper—to horrible death. Heretics were burnt publicly at the stake in a ceremony that came to be known as an "auto-de- fe"—an "act of faith."

          ii. On the other hand, recent research indicates that most people hauled before the Inquisition were not burnt and that its reputation was worse than its reality.

      d. Church taxes were sent far away to Rome; the perception of greed and worldliness of the Church was widely resented.

      e. Lay people participated minimally in Church ritual.

    4. These problems produced increased anticlericalism and grassroots movements to change the Church.

G. Heresy was the Church's term for anyone who disagreed with the Church.

    1. During the High Middle Ages (1100–1300), there arose mass movements of Western Catholics—sometimes inspired by theologians, sometimes arising on their own—who had problems with their Church, most famously the Albigensians (Albigeois in French), the Lollards, and the Hussites.

    2. In general, these groups wanted:

      a. A de-emphasis of the hierarchy and the authoritarianism of the Church, and an increased role for the laity.

      b. A less greedy, worldly Church with more emphasis on Christ's humility and humanity.

      c. A translation of Scripture into the vernacular.

3. Before the 16th century, kings and lay people rarely joined forces in criticizing the Church: To condone lay questioning of the pope would be to condone questioning of all authority—religious and civil.

H. By the late 15th century, Christian Humanist writers, such as Erasmus, Nicholas de Cusa, Philipp Melanchthon, and Ulrich Zwingli, also sought reform from within the Church.

I. If all three groups (kings, lay people, and reformers) ever came together, real change would be inevitable.

II. The catalyst of the Protestant Reformation was Martin Luther (1483-1546).

A. Martin Luther was a devout Augustinian priest and professor of theology at the University of Wittenberg.
   1. Luther was steeped in the critical method and mentality of Christian Humanism.
   2. He was obsessed with his own sinfulness; his unworthiness of God's mercy.
   3. He was equally appalled at the worldliness and corruption of the Church, especially the Church's practice of selling indulgences, e.g., the sale of indulgences all over Germany by a Dominican priest named Johann Tetzel, who was trying to raise money for the construction of St. Peter's Basilica in Rome.
   4. Luther launched the Reformation by posting 95 theses attacking indulgences on the castle church door at Wittenberg on 31 October 1517.

B. Because it took a while for the Church to respond, Luther and his followers had time to work out the implications of his ideas.
   1. One area of fundamental disagreement between 16th-century Catholics and Protestants was their source of religious truth.
      a. Catholics found religious truth in Scripture, Church tradition, and papal and conciliar decisions.
      b. Protestant reformers found God's will for his people in the Word, that is, Scripture, and its working out by the faithful alone.
      c. From this radical but simple idea came three equally revolutionary planks of Protestantism:

<ol type="i" start="1">
<li>The Bible should be translated into the vernacular, printed using the new technology of the printing press, and made available to the people.</li>
<li>Bibles in hand, there was no need for a corps of professional, sacrosanct clergy (including popes, archbishops, and bishops) to interpret it for the people.</li>
<li>Any piece of religious dogma or practice without scriptural foundation should be rejected or abolished out of hand, including the hierarchy of popes and bishops; elaborate rituals and church decor, including crucifixes, images of saints, and so on; and most of the sacraments.</li>
</ol>

<ol type="a" start="4">
<li>Protestants saw the only hope for reform in secular authority, that is, righteous lay rulers.</li>
</ol>

<ol start="2">
<li>These different attitudes to ministry were paralleled by different attitudes towards salvation.
<ol type="a">
<li>Catholics believed that salvation was won through two mutually supportive means:
<ol type="i">
<li>Faith, that is, belief in God, in the resurrection of Jesus Christ, and in His Church.</li>
<li>The performance of good works, especially the seven sacraments, which forgave sins and produced grace.</li>
</ol>
</li>
<li>Protestants believed that no human being could merit salvation through his or her own efforts; salvation was entirely up to God.
<ol type="i">
<li>Faith alone justified the individual in God's eyes.</li>
<li>Sacraments might or might not be useful in inclining an individual toward God, but they did not automatically result in forgiveness or salvation—that would be telling God what to do.</li>
<li>Indeed, other rituals, the whole apparatus of priests, sacraments, processions, blessings, holy water, the sign of the cross, veneration of images, and so on were, at best, useless and, at worst, mere superstition and idolatry.</li>
</ol>
</li>
</ol>
</li>
</ol>

3. One Swiss Protestant reformer, John Calvin, went further, arguing in *Institutes of the Christian Religion* (1536) that God, who knows all things, has already determined who is saved (the elect) or damned (the reprobate).

III. Unlike previous "heresies," Protestant ideas survived.

   A. Weakened by corruption and perhaps overconfident, the Church did not act decisively.

   1. It excommunicated Martin Luther only in 1521.
   2. It made little response in print, giving Luther and his followers a clear field and time to get their message out.

   B. Luther benefited from two coincidental historical developments.

   1. The invention of the printing press in Germany in the mid-15th century enabled Luther's ideas and translations of the Bible to spread rapidly.
   2. Rising literacy (to about 15–20 percent of the total population in 1600) also allowed for the rapid spread of Luther's ideas.

   C. Luther received government support and protection.

   1. Charles V, the Holy Roman Emperor, opposed Luther's ideas and summoned him to answer a charge of heresy at the Diet of Worms in April 1521.
   2. There, courageously, Luther refused to recant.
   3. The Diet responded by declaring him an outlaw.
   4. If Luther had been living in a more centralized monarchy, such as Spain, France, or even England, his life would have been forfeit.
   5. But Luther lived in Germany, where the central authority of the emperor was weak and the German princes were strong.
   6. Some princes, mostly in the North, agreed with Luther and Frederick the Wise, Elector of Saxony (1463–1525), gave him sanctuary.

IV. Thanks to this support, and because the Holy Roman Emperor—in part because he never explored the New World—was weak and poor, Protestantism spread across Europe to northern

Germany, Bohemia, France, England, Scotland, and Scandinavia.

Supplementary Reading:

M. B. Chambers, et al., *Western Experience*, chapter 12, section V; chapter 13, sections I–III.

D. MacCulloch, *The Reformation: A History*.

J. M. Kittelson, *Luther the Reformer: The Story of the Man and His Career*.

Questions to Consider:

1. Why did Luther succeed where so many earlier critics of the Church had failed?

2. What does the spread of Protestantism say and not say about the state of the Catholic religion in early modern Europe?

Lecture Seven—Transcript
The Protestant Reformation—1500–22

In the last lecture, we saw how Renaissance princes sought financial independence through exploration, colonization, and trade in the Far East and the Americas. We also saw that the European rediscovery of the Americas revolutionized life in both the Old World and the New, decimating native populations but enriching European monarchs, particularly that of Spain.

Toward the end of the lecture, I pointed out that for a variety of reasons—geographical, political, and perhaps even cultural—Germany (the Holy Roman Empire) failed to participate in the land grab. In part because he failed to do so, the emperor would remain more of a feudal lord than a Renaissance prince; more of a first among equals than an absolute monarch. That would have dramatic consequences for the political and religious history of Germany, for a weak emperor would be powerless to stop what is arguably the most important challenge to the Great Chain of Being yet: the Protestant Reformation.

Since before the fall of the Roman Empire over 1,000 years previously, Europe had been officially and primarily Christian. Christianity was declared the official religion of the Roman Empire in 391. European Christianity had split into two camps in 1054. Western Europe acknowledged the Bishop of Rome—the pope—as the Vicar of Christ. Eastern Europe (Russia and also Christians in the Ottoman Empire) acknowledged an orthodox patriarchy based in Constantinople and was recognized even by the Ottomans as speaking for its Christians.

Having said that, the patriarch of Constantinople never had the administrative authority of the pope. The Russian Orthodox Church, under a patriarch in Moscow, had broken away in 1448. Others would break away to form separate orthodox churches in the 19th century.

For the rest of this lecture, we will concentrate on the Western (or Roman) Church, for that is the church at which the Reformation was directed. During the Middle Ages, nearly every Western European state established Christianity as its official religion. Rulers were crowned by the Church. Bishops were often the ruler's chief advisors and administrators. The Church taxed a high proportion of people's income. The State enforced religious conformity by requiring all subjects to attend weekly mass and, in some countries, by tolerating a separate system of Church courts for moral offences like drunkenness and adultery. Toward the end of the period they burned heretics at the stake on behalf of the Church.

During the Middle Ages, Jews, Muslims, and other minority groups suffered discrimination. Before turning to the Church's internal problems, let us examine their situation briefly. From 1295, the Roman Church decreed that Jews should wear badges as a mark of humiliation for their refusal to convert to Christianity. They were prohibited by successive Church councils from employing Christians and appearing in public on Easter or other Christian holidays. But because Christians were forbidden from lending money at interest, Jews found a niche as bankers and moneylenders. Of course, that is a niche that only increased their unpopularity in some quarters. They had also been made scapegoats for the Black Death between 1347–1353. Jews were marginalized in ghettos in places like Venice and other Italian cities. Where they were not marginalized, they were expelled—from England in 1290, and from France in 1306 and again in 1394. In Germany, the situation varied from place to place. Remember, Germany is not a unified country during the Middle Ages or early modern period.

Medieval Spain had been very tolerant of both Jews and Muslims. Jews developed a thriving culture there in the Middle Ages. They were often physicians and tax collectors (but, of course, that too bred popular resentment). Muslims (or Moors as they were called in Spain) were allowed to own property and worship freely. But as we have seen, Isabella and Ferdinand, as part of their state-building process, harried them out of the country. Possibly 100,000 Jews were dispersed, first to Portugal; but then Manuel I decided on forced conversions in 1497, so they left for Greece and North Africa— hence the population there of Sephardic Jews. The Moors were driven out, first to ghettos, then enslaved, and then driven out of the country entirely.

The glorious exception to this really sad picture is Poland, where many Jews found a non-hostile home. There they created vibrant communities. They became scholars, merchants, and physicians.

The justification for other states' mistreatment of the Jews and Muslims was, of course, that in the eyes of European rulers they not only rejected the truth of Christianity and perpetuated damnable error, but just by virtue of disagreeing with the ruler in the matter of religion, they were disloyal.

For the same reasons, the state persecuted Christian heretics. But this begs the question of why there were heretics at the end of the Middle Ages. While Church and state generally worked hand-in-glove in both East and West, as we have seen, there were clashes in the latter during the Middle Ages. Western European kings were increasingly uncomfortable with the Church's claim to have given them their power. Did it not come directly from God? Kings resented papal power and authority. Kings wanted sole jurisdiction in their lands. They didn't want to have to split it with Church courts. For example, they wanted to be able to prosecute clergy for civil crimes, a power which was generally under Church jurisdiction as things stood then.

Kings resented papal power to tax their subjects; they wanted all the money. Kings wanted to appoint bishops since they were also royal vassals and officials. Kings and popes had repeatedly clashed on these issues and, as we have seen, tensions grew worse during the Renaissance as the former seemed to have studied their Machiavelli. After all, the modern nation-state being forged by Renaissance princes could only admit of one loyalty: the state itself. There was no room for a separate, sometimes countervailing, loyalty to the Church. In other words, the multinational corporation that was the Roman Catholic Church had to be subordinated.

Now, as we have also seen, the Church was not in the best shape to fight this fight after the Avignon Papacy and the Great Schism of the 14th century. The Schism (which, if you remember, had resulted in the election of the first two competing popes and then, three competing popes between 1414–1417) had finally been healed when a series of Church councils deposed all three competing popes and elected a fourth, Martin V.

After the success of these councils, there was hope that the Church would become more democratic and that Conciliarism—the idea that councils should have the power to determine Church policy—would make reform possible by giving priests and lay people a voice in Church governance. But Martin V and his successors in the 15th century repudiated the idea of Church councils. They repudiated the idea that Church councils could legislate over the pope's wishes.

They concentrated on reviving and strengthening their power, through military might and magnificent display. Too often, they neglected the obligation to be moral examples.

More specifically, some but not all Renaissance popes dabbled in Italian and European politics, further alienating secular rulers. For example, there was the warrior Pope Julius II (the one who commissioned the Sistine Chapel from Michelangelo) who also raised armies to keep other powers out of Italy at the beginning of the 16th century.

Or, Renaissance popes sometimes concentrated on administrative reform and maximization of revenue, instead of piety and pastoral care. Some violated their vows of chastity and engaged in nepotism. The great example here is Alexander VI, a Borgia pope, who kept a mistress and fathered several children at the end of the 15th century.

Others spent lavishly on papal churches and palaces: the Sistine Chapel and St. Peter's Basilica. The great example here is Leo X, a Medici/Orsini pope, who also ruled towards the beginning of the 16th century. In other words, during the Renaissance, popes behaved like great Machiavellian Renaissance princes themselves. That, in the long run, would harm their prestige and the sense that they were spiritual leaders.

Nor was the great mass of the faithful always happy with their Church on the ground. Most people, of course, turned to religion not to promote their power but to give their hard lives meaning and consolation. Now, here, we get into a great controversy among historians. Traditionally, the Medieval Church has been portrayed as corrupt and unpopular; but this view is often taken directly from works of literature like Chaucer's Canterbury Tales or the propaganda of Protestant reformers.

In recent years, archival research—that is, research into documents illustrative of people's actual lives, such as wills and the church records of donations and clubs (mainly this research has been done in England), seems to show that most clergy were doing their jobs during the late Middle Ages and Renaissance under very difficult conditions. Most people seem to have been orthodox and happy Catholics. Preaching was popular. There was a thriving mysticism. The writings of Meister Eckhart and Thomas a Kempis were very popular beyond Germany, which was their home base. The *devotio moderno* emphasized a practical individual faith that was very popular in the Low Countries. Religious books sold well.

That, of course, does not mean that everybody was happy in Christendom. There was a priest shortage. Too often, priests were absent or foreign. That is to say, the pope might decide that he needed to give somebody a job and he might give your parish to an Italian priest who couldn't speak the language.

Priests were often guilty of being relatively poorly educated. They didn't necessarily know even the truths of their own faith. They, like any other human being, could be hypocritical. Priests might live with women or be drunkards. Now, again, the evidence suggests that most priests were conscientious; but as you know, it takes only a few bad apples to make people remember.

Church courts monitored personal behavior, but, therefore, they had the potential to split communities and breed resentment. How would you like to be tried by your parish priest on a charge of adultery, fornication, drunkenness, blasphemy, or heresy?

Then, from the 13th century, there was, in many parts of Europe, the Inquisition. The Inquisition took hearsay evidence; it encouraged neighbors to inform on neighbors; it used torture to ferret out people who did not agree with orthodox Catholicism. Penalties ranged from public humiliation—adulterers were made to stand in the town square in a white sheet holding a taper—to horrible death. Heretics were burnt publicly at the stake in a ceremony that came to be known as an "auto de fe," an "act of faith." Recent research indicates that most people hauled before the Inquisition were not burnt and that its reputation was actually worse than its reality. But still….

Another source of resentment was that Church taxes were sent far away to Rome. The resultant worldliness of the Church seemed inappropriate to its mission. People who yearned to participate in their church often felt stymied by the minimal popular participation allowed in the Latin Mass. It was said in Latin and behind a rood screen. Some lay people wanted to participate more.

These issues produced two results: first, increased anti-clericalism, a resentment on the part of both kings and people of what they might see as meddlesome or hypocritical clergy; second, the beginnings of grass roots movements to change the Church, which the Church viewed as heresies.

"Heresy" was the Church's term for anyone who disagreed with it. Early in the Middle Ages, heretics were often theologians disagreeing with mainstream opinion about God's nature. But during the high Middle Ages, from about 1100 on, there arose mass movements of Western Catholics—sometimes inspired by theologians, sometimes arising on their own—who had problems with their Church. I refer to, for example, the Albigensians in France and Germany, the Lollards in England, and the Hussites in Bohemia.

In general—and any Medievalist will tell you that I am vastly oversimplifying here—these people and groups wanted similar reforms. First, they wanted to de-emphasize the role of the hierarchy and the authoritarianism of the Church, and increase the role of the laity. They wanted a less greedy, less worldly Church and more of an emphasis on Christ's humility, humanity, and poverty. They thought the Church charged too many fines and fees, and placed too much emphasis on physical plant. They wanted scripture translated into the vernacular, to give people a more active role.

Now, you might think that if kings and lay people combined, they'd have the Church against the wall—and you'd be right. But prior to the 16th century, they rarely combined, despite the fact that each had complaints about the Church. Kings may have resented the power of popes; but with few exceptions, they were not about to condone, let alone mobilize their subjects, in any attack against the Church hierarchy.

Stop and think about it. I may have my disagreements with the pope if I'm the King of England or France, but he is, after all, part of the club. If I condone lay people questioning the pope, I'm condoning my subjects questioning me. Instead, kings and parliaments bolstered the authority of the Church by passing civil laws against heresy and, in fact, they did the dirty work of executing many of the victims of the Inquisition. But if kings and people ever did combine against the Church, their force would, as I have implied, be irresistible.

By the late 15th century, there is a third group of critics that was gaining in importance. We'll call them "Church reformers." You might also call them "Christian Humanists." These were generally Humanist writers, often Churchmen themselves, who clearly saw the problems within the Church. Erasmus, in the *Handbook of the Militant Christian,* urged a simpler and less hierarchical Church. Nicholas de Cusa urged reform of monasteries. In fact, many later Protestant reformers came to their conclusions through Humanist training. Philipp Melanchthon and Ulrich Zwingli are two examples.

At first, most sought reform from within the Church. They did not so much question authority as they wanted it to reform itself. People like Erasmus edited scripture along Humanist lines; they wrote polemics; and they preached. Again, it should be obvious that if all three groups ever came together, change would be inevitable.

This brings me to the story of Martin Luther. It happened in Germany, toward the beginning of the 16th century, starting with one remarkable man. Martin Luther was born in 1483 and he lived until 1546. He was a devout Augustinian priest and a professor of theology at the University of Wittenberg. He was steeped in the method and the mentality of Christian Humanism, which means he was perfectly capable of being critical. But Luther was above all a man obsessed with his own sinfulness—his perceived unworthiness of God's mercy. He was equally appalled at the worldliness and corruption of the Church, especially the Catholic Church's practice of selling indulgences.

To understand indulgences, you have to understand the Catholic doctrine of Purgatory. Catholic theology believed that when we die, the truly saintly go straight to heaven and the truly evil go to hell. But what about us "in-betweeners" who are neither perfectly good nor perfectly bad? Catholic theology posited a sort of middle place, where people would do time for their sins and where those sins could be purged, called Purgatory.

Needless to say, every Catholic wants to spend as little time in Purgatory as possible. Here, the Church's claim to "bind in Heaven" what was "bound on Earth" was crucial. Specifically, the Church believed that it could grant reductions of a specified number of years in Purgatory, called indulgences," in return for good deeds.

The problem arises when we ask just what constitutes a good deed. Would, say, working with the poor be a good deed? I think certainly. I don't have a lot of time to work with the poor. How about if I just give money to the Church so that they can work with the poor? That sounds pretty good. How about if I just give money to the Church because I trust them to know how to spend that money?

It's a very short step from here, taken in the early 16th century, to the notion of selling indulgences. At the time, the Church was trying to pay for the rebuilding of St. Peter's Basilica in Rome. They could make a lot of money by selling indulgences to those who could pay. Famously, Johan Tetzel did a brisk business going all over Germany selling time off in Purgatory.

But this, of course, amounted to selling salvation. After all, in such a system, who gets into heaven first? The wealthy. To Luther, this was an egregious misuse of the Church's power and a fundamental misunderstanding of God's relationship to human beings. To Luther, God was so great and so perfect, and humans were so imperfect and so depraved; how could they do anything to merit heaven? Where the Catholic Church believed that salvation was earned through faith in God and good works, including the performance of the seven sacraments, Luther argued that both faith and salvation alone were gifts from God. It was his decision whether or not to save you.

Luther worked out his position in 95 theses, which he posted on the castle church door (a sort of community bulletin board) at Wittenberg on October 31, 1517. By doing so, he launched the Reformation.

It took a while for the Church to respond. That interval was crucial, for over the next few years, Luther and like-minded followers such as Zwingli, Melanchthon, Martin Bucer, and John Calvin worked out the implications of these ideas. They are perhaps best understood in relation to Catholic ideas; but this is made difficult by two stubborn facts. First, remember that Protestantism was never a single unified faith. Almost from the very beginning, the Protestant reformers are disagreeing with each other. In fact, the second fact is that both faith traditions have changed markedly in 500 years, in many respects becoming more like each other. So, if you yourself are a member of one of these two great traditions, please don't be offended if you don't quite recognize yourself in the following. Remember, we are back in the 16th century.

In addressing what first separated Protestants from Catholics, some professors begin with their respective theologies of salvation; but I see their most fundamental disagreement in their source of religious truth. Catholics found religious truth—God's wish and will for good Christians—in three places: scripture, church tradition, and papal and conciliar decisions.

First, scripture: the Bible is—can we agree?—a complicated document. It is obscure to some readers and contradictory to others. Throughout the Middle Ages, most people couldn't read anyway. The Church, therefore, reserved to itself the interpretation of scripture. That is, scripture should be reserved to trained religious professionals: the pope, Church councils, university theologians, and priests. In theory, they received a careful theological training; but remember what we said about education. They were consecrated beings, rendered semi-sacred by their ordination.

The Church also kept the Bible in Latin, the 4th-century Vulgate, and prohibited vernacular translation. In other words, it maintained a monopoly on this source of knowledge about God.

In terms of tradition, the idea was that what the Church had thought and done for centuries, since this was God's Church, was obviously God's will. If the Church had been doing something for 1,000 years, that meant that it was something that God wanted the Church to do. Finally, the idea that God's truth came through the pope and conciliar decrees—in other words, whatever the Church hierarchy decided—was also God's will.

The basis for these last two, the fundamental reason that Catholics submitted to the papacy and the Church hierarchy, was that they believed that that hierarchy could be traced back in an unbroken apostolic succession to St. Peter, whom they believed Christ had made the first pope. The key passage in the Bible here takes place in Matthew 16, in which Christ turns to silent Peter and says:

> Thou art Peter, and upon this rock I will build my church; and the gates of hell shall not prevail against it. And I will give to thee the keys of the kingdom of heaven. And whatsoever thou shalt bind upon earth, it shall be bound also in heaven; and whatsoever thou shalt loose on earth, it shall be loosed in heaven.

Protestant reformers rejected this wide area of competence for the hierarchy. As a young priest, Martin Luther had visited Rome and been appalled at the materialism and corruption he had witnessed among high-ranking churchmen. They were, in his view, abusing the keys that they had been given. Remember, Luther visited Rome at the height of the Renaissance papacy.

As we have seen, he also found himself at odds with certain practices engaged in by the Church that he couldn't find in scripture; for example the selling of indulgences. Noting the corruption in the Church and the fallibility of human beings generally, Luther concluded that the only sure guide to God's will was to be found in scripture—*sola scriptura*.

From this radical but simple idea came three equally revolutionary planks of Protestantism:

1) The Bible should be made available to the people. It should be translated into the vernacular. It should be printed using the new technology of the printing press. It should be placed into the hands of the faithful. Rising literacy was also important here in the 16th century.

2) Bibles in hand, there was no need for a corps of professional sacrosanct clergy to interpret them. There was no need for popes, archbishops, and bishops to mediate between God and his people. Hence, Luther's idea of a "priesthood of all believers." There would still be ministers, but not with a semi-divine status or the power of Roman Catholic priests.

3) Any piece of religious dogma or practice without scriptural foundation should be rejected or abolished out of hand. From this comes most of the Protestant critique of Catholic practice. The structure of popes and bishops—another reason to get rid of them is that they're not in scripture. The elaborate rituals and church decor, including crucifixes and images of saints, and most of the sacraments. By the way, since the Church hierarchy was obviously unscriptural and corrupt, Protestants saw the only hope for reform in the secular authority; that is, a righteous ruler.

These different attitudes to ministry were paralleled by different attitudes towards salvation. As we've seen, Catholics believed that salvation was won through two mutually supportive means: faith; that is, belief in God and the resurrection of Jesus Christ and his Church; and the performance of good works, especially the seven sacraments, which forgave sins—in three cases directly (baptism, penance, and anointing of the sick)—and produced grace. Grace, earned by human beings in this life, was thought to be necessary for salvation in the next. In addition to the sacraments, the performance of other good works also increased one's store of grace: serving the poor, contributing to the Church, and living a good life generally.

To Luther, this amounted to trying to buy one's way into heaven. Indeed, as we have seen, Martin Luther, tortured by his own sense of sin and convinced of the basic depravity of the human species, believed that human beings were so far below God's perfection that they could not hope to earn or win forgiveness for their sins or salvation in heaven. Sixteenth-century Protestants believed that no human being could merit salvation through his own efforts. Human beings were too depraved and God could not be compelled in any case.

Thus, salvation was entirely up to him. Faith alone justified the individual in his eyes. Sacraments might or might not be useful in inclining an individual towards God, but they didn't automatically result in forgiveness and salvation. That would be telling God what to do. Indeed, other rituals and the whole apparatus of priests, sacraments, processions, blessings, holy water, the sign of the cross, and the veneration of images, were at best, useless and at worst, mere superstition and idolatry.

One Swiss Protestant reformer, John Calvin, went further, arguing in *Institutes of the Christian Religion* of 1536 that, because God knows all things, he already knows—indeed, has determined—the future, and therefore, has known since before the Creation who is saved or damned. Thus, some Protestants embraced predestination. That would lead to much soul searching on their part to determine whether they were of the saved (the elect) or the damned (the reprobate).

Normally, these ideas (Luther's, Calvin's, and the other Protestant reformers) would have gone the way of other radical critiques that the Catholic Church called heresies. After all, how many Albigensians do you know? But Protestant ideas "took" and survived, in part because of three reasons.

First, the Church hesitated. It was weakened by corruption in Rome and, to a lesser extent, outside of it. It was perhaps too big and too worldly, and perhaps too confident to think that it really had to answer Luther. After all, it had defeated all other rivals in the field. Luther was excommunicated only in 1521. By the way, he publicly burnt the Bull of Excommunication. There was little Catholic response in print. That gave Luther and his followers a clear field and time to get their message out.

A second factor in the spread of Protestantism was the rise of literacy and the development of the printing press. Where previous heretical ideas had had to be copied out by hand, Luther benefited from one of the other great innovations that created the modern world: the printing press.

The invention of the printing press with movable type is usually credited to Johannes Gutenberg of Mainz around the year 1450. By 1500, some 6,000 separate works had already been printed in Europe. This meant that Luther's ideas, his tracts, his German translation of the Bible, and the works of other reformers could get out. They could be spread among the masses.

Admittedly, in 1500, only about 5% of the masses could read. But by 1600, that was 20%. This is taking place at a time when literacy is starting to take off. This happened because of Humanistic education and the endowment of more schools, many of them supported by local communities.

You might not think that a 20% literacy rate is terribly good, and that's true; but it does mean that the odds are that you probably know someone who can read. Of course, anybody can be read to.

The third factor in the survival and growth of Protestantism was the support of the German princes. Remember, I told you that if rulers and reformers ever got together, watch out. Early on, Luther got such support, but not from his emperor. Charles V, the Holy Roman Emperor, was decidedly opposed to Luther's ideas and he summoned him to answer a charge of heresy at the Diet of Worms in April of 1521. There, famously and courageously, Luther refused to recant. According to legend, he stood in front of the emperor himself and said, "Here I stand. I can no other. God help me. Amen." The Diet responded by declaring him an outlaw.

Understand this: at this point, if Luther had been in Spain, if he had been in France, or if he had been in England, with their centralizing monarchies interested in making sure that everyone believes the same way, what would have happened? He would have been dragged into the public square. He would have been burnt at the stake. But remember that Luther was living and working in Germany, the Holy

Roman Empire, where the emperor is weak and the German princes are strong. Some support Luther, maybe because they want Church land or maybe because they believe in his ideas. In particular, Frederick the Wise, Elector of Saxony, decides to give him protection. You see, geography really is destiny, and historical events in one part of the world may have a profound influence on another.

Remember that the Holy Roman Emperor is weak because he is poor, and he is poor, in part, because he never explored the New World. Because of that, his princes can defy him; and Martin Luther and other reformers can write. The result would be a revolution in religion. The Protestant Reformation had been launched.

Lecture Eight
The Wars of Religion—1523–1648

Scope:

The Reformation split Europe into opposing camps. Spain, led by Phillip II, spent its immense colonial wealth trying to force Christendom back together. The result was a series of bloodbaths culminating in the Thirty Years' War, the near-bankruptcy of Spain, and the conviction, expressed in the Peace of Westphalia of 1648, that perhaps religion was best not settled at the point of a sword or the barrel of a gun.

Outline

I. How and why did Protestantism spread and take root in some parts of Europe but not in others?

   A. As we have seen, many princes in the Holy Roman Empire, especially in northern Germany, embraced the Reformation.

   1. They did so because of their Humanist educations, religious conviction, greed for Church lands, or a desire to "stick it" to the emperor.

   2. In contrast, such places as Bavaria and Austria, more directly under the emperor's control, stayed Catholic.

   3. The emperor spent the next half century trying to bring the Protestant princes to heel, culminating in the War of the Schmalkaldic League (1546–1552).

   4. But the Peace of Passau (1552), reaffirmed in Augsburg in 1555, granted Lutheran states the free exercise of their religion.

   5. As a result, the emperor remained weak, and Germany remained divided in religion and politics.

   B. Protestantism was embraced by the ambitious monarchs of Sweden and Denmark.

   C. Switzerland was a federation of self-governed city-state republics. Because there was no central control, urban areas, dominated by literate merchants, were able to embrace Protestantism.

1. In 1520, Ulrich (Huldreich) Zwingli persuaded the merchants on the town council in Zürich to embrace Protestantism.
2. In Geneva, John Calvin sought to create a theocracy.
   a. Geneva embraced Protestant liturgical reforms.
   b. The city provided rigorous public religious education for all.
   c. Pastors and other parish officials were elected.
   d. Individual households and personal behavior were closely monitored by a consistory of clergy and lay people.
   e. Notorious sinners were excommunicated and even put to death.
   f. Finally, Calvin founded a university that trained preachers who became especially influential in France and Scotland.

D. Protestant ideas were at first tolerated by the monarchy in France, but after placards attacking the mass were attached to church doors on 18 October 1534 ("Affair of the Placards") the monarchy began a crackdown on Protestants, soon to be known as Huguenots, who fled to Geneva.
   1. The Huguenots returned in the 1550s and drew up a platform based on the Geneva model.
   2. They became especially popular in cities, among merchants, in part because of the Protestant emphasis on literacy.
   3. The attempts of the monarchy and Catholic Church to suppress them led to the French Wars of Religion (1552–1598).
   4. France was increasingly divided into a Huguenot minority led by the Bourbon family (headed by Henry of Bourbon), a Catholic majority led by the Guise family, and the royal house of Valois, which was caught in the middle.
   5. The 1572 murder of Protestant leaders in their beds ("St. Bartholomew's Day Massacre") led to two decades of sporadic civil war and a France too weakened by internal division to play a major role on the international stage.

E. The Low Countries (Netherlands, Flanders, Luxemburg) were ruled directly by Charles V; after 1554, by Philip, eventually known as Phillip II of Spain.

    1. The literate merchant classes embraced Protestantism.

    2. By the mid-16th century, the northern part (Netherlands) was mostly Protestant; the southern part (Flanders—later Belgium), Roman Catholic.

F. In England, Henry VIII, unable to secure a Catholic divorce from his first wife, Catherine of Aragon, declared himself Supreme Head of the Church of England in the 1530s.

    1. From 1547 to 1553, Edward VI's ministers pursued Protestantism aggressively.

    2. Between 1553 and 1558, Mary restored Catholicism and launched a persecution, burning 286 Protestants at the stake.

    3. Elizabeth (1558–1603) instituted the Act of Uniformity (1559), which abolished the authority of the pope and named herself Supreme Governor of the Church of England but retained bishops, vestments, and many old holidays.

        a. Diehard Catholics tried to maintain their faith in secret.

        b. Strict Protestants sought to purify the settlement of Catholic rituals and practices. They became known as Puritans.

        c. Thanks in part to Elizabeth's 45-year reign, most English men and women seem to have accepted the compromise settlement.

G. Scotland, ruled by the House of Stuart, had always been poorer and less centrally governed than England.

    1. After the death of James V in 1547, Scotland was effectively ruled by Mary of Guise as regent for her infant daughter, Mary, Queen of Scots.

    2. By 1557, Mary of Guise began to persecute Protestants.

    3. In 1559, a group of Scottish nobles and lairds (landowners), called the Lords of the Congregation, rebelled against the two Marys, abolished papal jurisdiction and the Mass, and began to establish a Presbyterian Church structure.

    4. The French sent troops to aid Mary of Guise.

5. Elizabeth sent help to the Protestants.
6. In 1560, Mary of Guise died and all parties signed the Treaty of Edinburgh, promising joint rule and religious toleration.
7. In 1567–1568, the Scottish nobility deposed Mary, Queen of Scots in favor of her infant son, who became King James VI (1567–1625).
8. Scotland remained Protestant, eventually embracing a Presbyterian-style church settlement.

II. The Catholic response—the Counter-Reformation—was slow in coming and consisted of three parts.

A. The Council of Trent (1543–1563) convened to respond to the Reformation.
1. The Council of Trent tacitly conceded Luther's point regarding morality and discipline by calling for a moral, well-educated clergy.
2. It rejected, though, the Protestant critique of Church doctrine, reaffirming the authority of the pope and tradition, the sanctity of the priesthood, the seven sacraments, salvation by faith and good works, Purgatory, indulgences, the use of images, and clerical celibacy.

B. The Jesuits were founded by Ignatius of Loyola in 1534 and recognized by the pope in 1540.
1. The Jesuits became leaders in Humanistic education, immediately developing a following with ruling elites.
2. They went as missionaries to China, Japan, the coast of Africa, Canada, and South America.
3. They also went to European countries, either as advisors to Catholic princes or to minister to Catholic minorities in Protestant countries.
4. In both cases, the Jesuits involved themselves in political plots, often supported by the power and wealth of the Spanish Empire.

C. The Spanish Crusade, led by Philip II, was an attempt to stamp out Protestant heretics wherever he found them.

III. The Wars of Religion reached their height thanks to the efforts of Philip II.

    A. Phase I lasted from 1567 to 1608.

        1. The Revolt of the Netherlands began in the 1560s after Philip II imposed the Inquisition, backed by the Spanish army.

        2. In 1574, Antwerp was sacked (known as the Spanish Fury), and the port never fully recovered.

        3. After the Dutch received assistance from Elizabeth I in 1585, Philip decided to send the Spanish Armada against England in 1588.

            a. The defeat of the armada was a tremendous propaganda victory and confidence-booster for England.

            b. Despite the loss of thousands of men and about 60 ships, the disaster of the armada did not seriously weaken Spain.

            c. This defeat was only the beginning of a war that would last another 17 years, spread to three continents and two oceans, and drain the treasuries of England, Spain—and France.

        4. In 1589, Henry III, the last Valois king of France, was assassinated.

            a. The next in line for his throne was the Protestant leader of the Huguenots, Henry of Bourbon.

            b. He was opposed by the Catholic League and Philip II.

            c. By 1598, Henry IV, supported by Elizabeth, had defeated his enemies in France.

                i. He appeased Catholics by becoming one.

                ii. He reassured Huguenots by granting a toleration via the Edict of Nantes (1598).

        5. By 1605, both Philip II and Elizabeth were dead and the Spanish monarchy had declared bankruptcy three times.

            a. Peace with England came at the Treaty of London in 1605.

            b. Spain recognized the Dutch Republic in 1608.

    B. Phase II comprised the Thirty Years' War (1618–1648).

        1. The war began when the Protestants of Bohemia revolted from the Holy Roman Emperor (a Habsburg related to the king of Spain), threw the Emperor's representatives out the window ("Defenestration of Prague"), and asked the Elector Palatine, a small prince on the Rhine, to be their king in 1618.

2. The Holy Roman Empire and Spain responded by seizing Bohemia and the Palatine.

3. The result was a general European war over religion and the balance of power.

    a. The Catholic side included Spain, the Holy Roman Empire, and Bavaria.

    b. The Protestant side included Saxony and other north German states, Sweden, the Netherlands, and France.

4. For 30 years, armies crisscrossed Central Europe, leaving devastation in their wake.

5. Finally, the Peace of Westphalia in 1648 enshrined the position "*Cuius regio, eius religio*," that is, the religion of the state is the religion of the ruler.

C. The Wars of Religion had significant consequences.

1. Germany would remain weak and divided well into the 19th century.

2. Spain, saddled with debts from more than a century of trying to fight heretics on all fronts, began a long, slow decline.

3. England stayed out of it and, after a period of instability, would emerge a major player at the end of the 17th century.

4. France, having achieved a degree of dynastic stability, would become the leading power in Europe.

5. Europeans finally agreed to live and let live (more or less) on the issue of religion.

6. With such an intensely rational settlement in place, it is no accident that the remainder of the 17th century would be regarded as the age of reason.

Supplementary Reading:

M. B. Chambers, et al., *Western Experience*, chapter 13, section IV; chapter 15, sections I–II.

G. Mattingly, *The Armada*.

G. Parker, *The Thirty Years' War.*

Questions to Consider:

1. Did the Catholic Church's refusal to make doctrinal concessions to Luther strengthen or weaken the Counter-Reformation?

2. In reality, was Phillip II the aggressor or the defender in the first wave of the Wars of Religion?

Lecture Eight—Transcript
The Wars of Religion—1523–1648

As we have seen, during the 16th century, questions of religion were intimately wound up with questions of politics, both local and global. In this lecture, we will see how early modern rulers confronted the Reformation, sometimes using it as an excuse to increase their power and sometimes feeling personally driven to promote it or eradicate it. As a result, as so often in history, a religious impulse—an argument about how best to worship God—would produce hatred, bloodshed, misery, and destruction.

In the last lecture, we sought to explain how it was that the Reformation originated and survived. In this lecture, our first question is, "How did it spread and take root in some parts of Europe but not in others?" Each country's situation is different. Let us, therefore, take a sort of Cook's Tour of Protestant Europe.

As we have seen, many princes in the Holy Roman Empire, especially in northern Germany, embraced the Reformation. They did so because they had Humanist educations, or out of religious conviction, or maybe they wanted Church lands. Maybe they resented the emperor. Maybe they were German nationalists and resented the pope. And some did so because their merchants and peasants wanted them to do so. In contrast, places like Bavaria and Austria, which were more directly under the emperor's control, stayed Catholic.

What was the emperor's response? As we have seen, the emperor's initial attempt to get Luther to recant had failed. Charles condemned Luther, but he was preoccupied with his wars in Italy against France, and also with a resurgent Ottoman Empire that in 1529 laid siege to Vienna. If royal finances can affect religion, so can the international situation.

In 1524, everybody in Germany was diverted by the Peasants' War. Peasants saw Luther's call for a priesthood of all believers as a general attack on hierarchy, and so they attacked their landlords; they plundered monasteries; they went on tax strike; and they demanded autonomy for their villages and the ability to name their own priests. Luther began by trying to mediate, but eventually he decided that the peasants had simply gone beyond the pale. He wrote a famous pamphlet called *Against the Murdering, Thieving Hordes of*

Peasants. I guess the idea is pretty clear. The peasants' rebellion was ruthlessly put down by the German princes: over 100,000 peasants were killed.

Two years later, at the Diet of Speyer, Lutheran princes were granted the right to practice their religion; but three years after that, another diet at Speyer reversed this toleration. The Lutheran princes who protested this became known as "Protestants."

In 1530–1531, the Protestant princes banded together for their own protection to form something called the Schmalkaldic League. Pressed by the Turks, in 1532 Charles granted them some privileges in the Peace of Nuremberg. In other words, he had to deal with the Turks; he couldn't deal with his own princes. But he was only biding his time.

In 1546, after concluding peace with the French and the Turks, he launched the War of the Schmalkaldic League in which, after initial success, he was eventually defeated. He was forced to agree to the Peace of Passau of 1552, reaffirmed at Augsburg in 1555, granting Lutheran states the free exercise of their religion.

The consequences of Augsburg were immense. First, Charles V, by some measures the greatest monarch in Christendom, worn out with war and controversy, announced his intention to abdicate in 1556, retiring to a monastery two years later. Germany remained divided in religion and politics. The idea of a united Christendom under a Holy Roman Emperor had been repudiated forever.

Now, in fact, Lutheranism had taken root elsewhere already. For example, the ambitious kings of both Sweden and Denmark had embraced it in the 1520s and 1530s. The same was also true of much of Switzerland.

Switzerland was a federation of self-governed city-state republics whose armies had defeated every attempt by the Holy Roman Emperor to subdue them. Here's another area where there's no central control. Basically, rural areas remained Catholic, but urban areas, dominated by literate merchants, embraced Protestantism and moral reform. This happened in Zurich; it happened in Basel; and most famously, it happened in Geneva.

In the latter, the dominating figure was John Calvin, a French Protestant forced to flee his native country. Spurred on by Calvin's preaching, Geneva sought to become the Bible's shining city on the hill, a theocracy—in practice, a combination of democracy and strict restriction of freedom.

First, the Geneva city council reformed the liturgy and included congregational singing of psalms, which was very much a hallmark of Protestantism at this time. It also decreed public education for all and rigorous religious instruction of children. Pastors were elected, as were other parish officials. It also decreed the close monitoring of individual households and personal behavior by a consistory of clergy and lay people. Dancing, card playing, and gambling were forbidden in Calvin's Geneva. Its illegitimacy rates were famously low. That was true, in part, because notorious sinners were excommunicated and even put to death.

Finally, Calvin founded a university to train preachers who became especially influential in France and Scotland. Let's talk a little bit about France. Protestant ideas were at first tolerated by the monarchy there, but on the morning of October 18, 1534, Parisians awoke to find that upon going to church, a series of placards attacking the Mass had been attached to their church doors. The Affair of the Placards led to a royal crackdown. French Protestants fled to Geneva, where they were trained under Calvin. They returned in the 1550s and, in 1559, representatives of 66 reformed churches drew up a platform based on the Geneva model. These French Protestants became known as Huguenots.

Protestantism proved to be especially popular among the nobility (about a third converted) and in the cities among merchants. Of course, if you haven't figured out by now, Protestantism, with its emphasis on literacy, always did best in cities and among the aristocracy and middle classes.

Royal attempts to suppress Protestantism would lead to the French Wars of Religion. Allow me to explain. France was increasingly divided into a Huguenot minority led by the Bourbon family, which was, in turn, headed by Henry of Bourbon. The Catholic majority was represented by the Catholic League led by the Guise family. The royal house of Valois was caught in the middle.

In 1559, Henry II suffered a sudden accidental death in a tournament. This guy stupidly forgot to put his visor down and he was basically impaled on a lance. France was thereafter ruled in quick succession by weak, sickly boy kings: Frances II who ruled 1559–1560; Charles IX, 1560–1574; and Henry III, 1574–1589.

The real power in France was the Queen Regent, Catherine de' Medici. At first, she tried to maintain a toleration, which was periodically upset by assassinations of prominent figures on both sides. In 1572, under pressure from the Catholic faction, she authorized the St. Bartholomew's Day Massacre. Protestant leaders were murdered in their beds. Parisian mobs took this as a signal to murder 3,000 of their fellow townsmen and 10,000 more Protestants died in the countryside. The pope responded by ordering church bells rung throughout Christendom.

The result of the St. Bartholomew's Day Massacre was disastrous for France: decades of on-again, off-again civil war; atrocities on both sides; priests, ministers and sometimes whole congregations massacred. France, weakened by internal division, would cease to play a major role on the international stage for almost 20 years.

Let me now go north to the Low Countries (Netherlands, Flanders, and Luxemburg). These were ruled directly by Charles V and after 1554, by his son Philip, eventually Phillip II of Spain. Protestantism was early embraced by the literate merchant classes. If you remember, the Netherlands is famous for its commercial power. Charles V ordered the burning of Lutheran books and imposed the Inquisition in 1522, which was not entirely successfully. By the mid-16th century, the Low Countries had split. The northern part—the Netherlands—was mostly Protestant. The southern part—Flanders (later Belgium)—was Roman Catholic.

Moving across the Channel to England: England was staunchly Catholic at the beginning of Henry VIII's reign, but medieval English kings had a long history of clashing with popes. In the mid-1520s, Henry VIII, heretofore a committed Catholic, began to seek a divorce from his first wife, Catherine of Aragon. Catherine had given birth to one living child, a girl named Mary, in 1514, and had not been pregnant for years.

Henry was convinced that only a male could rule England. Remember that the Wars of the Roses were a living memory for many. He was further convinced that his marriage had been cursed by God because he had married his brother's widow. It did not help that he had fallen for Anne Boleyn, a young witty Protestant lady-in-waiting to Catherine. The pope, Clement VII, refused the divorce, not because the Church did not believe in divorce. It had usually granted divorce for important people in the past; but that's the key. Catherine was the aunt of Charles V, and Charles was a more important ruler. Moreover, to grant the divorce would be to repudiate the actions of a previous pope, Julius II, in granting a special dispensation for Henry to marry his brother's widow. To repudiate that would call into question lots of papal powers.

So Henry VIII, stymied in Rome, but abetted by a compliant Parliament in London, abolished the authority of the pope in England and declared himself Supreme Head of the Church of England in 1534. He more or less granted his own divorce and married Anne.

But that didn't mean that he was a Protestant. In fact, Henry liked the ceremony and the hierarchy of the Catholic Church. He actually wanted to be Catholic; he just didn't want to listen to the pope. You could argue that he was the first American Catholic.

But realizing that Catholics would never be completely loyal—and they might always undo his royal supremacy—on his deathbed in 1547, he named Protestant tutors for his son by yet another wife, Edward VI. Edward VI's ministers pursued Protestantism aggressively: they outlawed the Mass; they repealed the heresy statutes; they commissioned an English Book of Common Prayer.

Edward died in 1553 and he was succeeded by his older sister who was a Catholic, Mary. Mary and her Parliament tried to return England to Rome. They restored the spiritual authority of the pope, the Mass, elaborate vestments, images, devotions, and the heresy laws. Mary Tudor launched a program of persecution, burning 286 men, women, and adolescents at the stake; hence her nickname: "Bloody Mary." Mary's Catholic restoration might nevertheless have succeeded, but she failed to produce an heir and she died in November 1558.

Henry's last remaining daughter, Elizabeth, needed to pacify a divided nation, so she sought compromise. In the settlement of 1559, once again Parliament abolished the authority of the pope and named Elizabeth Supreme Governor of the Church of England (conservatives would never accept a female "Head"). Parliament also restored the Protestant Book of Common Prayer, but it retained bishops, vestments, and many old Catholic ceremonies and holidays.

I like to say that the Church of England thinks and writes Protestant but looks and feels Catholic.

Admittedly, die-hard Catholics tried to maintain their faith in secret, aided by missionary priests sent from Rome. Strict Protestants tried to purify the settlement of Catholic rituals. They became known as Puritans. But, thanks in part to Elizabeth's long 45-year reign, most English men and women seem to have accepted the compromise settlement. England entered the 17th century a Protestant country, but with a rather milder form of Protestantism. Groups on either extreme who wanted to change it, and were willing to engage in political activity and even violence to accomplish that. (If you want to know more, I can recommend an excellent course in English history by Professor Robert Bucholz.)

Let us now move north to Scotland. Scotland was ruled by the House of Stuart. This country had always been poorer, less centrally governed, and its monarchy less powerful than England. After the death of James V in 1547, Scotland was effectively ruled by a regent, Mary of Guise, for her infant daughter Mary, Queen of Scots. (I'm sorry there are so many Marys in this lecture.)

By 1557, Mary of Guise was alarmed by the violence that Protestant preachers trained in Geneva, such as John Knox, were inciting against Catholicism. So she began to persecute them. In response, a group of Scottish nobles and lairds (small landowners) banded together, swearing to defend a Protestant "Congregation of God."

In 1559, the lords of the Congregation rebelled against the two Marys and abolished papal jurisdiction and the Mass. Both the French and the English sent troops, but in June 1560, Mary of Guise died, weakening the Catholic side. In July, all parties signed a truce, the Treaty of Edinburgh, which seemed to be a compromise that would allow religious toleration.

But in 1567, after experiencing several years of Mary Queen of Scots' rule, much of the Scottish nobility rose. Some of this was Protestant lords seeing their chance, but Mary had also grown unpopular due to a series of marital disasters. I don't really have time to go into it. She had married the unstable Henry Lord Darnley and then run off with his murderer, James Hepburn, Earl of Bothwell.

Over the course of 1567–1568, the Scottish aristocracy deposed her in favor of her infant son, who became King James VI. James would rule Scotland until 1625 very successfully. Mary was forced to flee to England to seek the protection of her cousin Elizabeth, where she would be a focus for Catholic plots for the next 20 years. Scotland would remain Protestant, eventually embracing a Presbyterian style of Church settlement.

So, within half-a-century of Luther's Halloween prank, half of Europe had turned Protestant. Which raises the issue, what were the Catholics doing all this time? As we have seen, the Catholic response could be summed up in one word: slow. At first, the Church refused to take Luther's criticisms too seriously. After all, he was hardly the first. Popes rejected the call by many Churchmen, including Luther, that there should be a general Church council to work out these issues. They worried that such a council would attack the power of the pope. They failed to launch much of a Catholic propaganda effort. They sought obedience, not discussion.

Eventually, the Church was forced to confront the break-up of Christendom and the loss of over half of Europe. It did so in three ways. First, the Council of Trent was finally called in 1543. It was convened to respond to the Reformation. Representatives from every Christian country came, and everything was on the table. This Church council lasted 20 years, in part, because it was interrupted by war and politics, but also because its members realized that they would probably only get one shot. Indeed, the decisions made at Trent would shape the Church until the Second Vatican Council of the 1960s.

Tacitly, they conceded that Luther had been right about morality and discipline. They urged bishops to go live in their dioceses and they reaffirmed the need for a moral and well-educated clergy. But they rejected the Protestant critique of Church doctrine. They reaffirmed the authority of the pope and tradition; the need to interpret scripture within the Catholic tradition; the sanctity of the priesthood; all seven sacraments; salvation by faith and good works; Purgatory; even indulgences; the use of images; and clerical celibacy.

Finally, and less tangibly, the Council of Trent gave Catholic Churchmen a sense of cohesion—a crusading vigor to match the Protestant reformers. In other words, reconciliation was impossible; the battle was joined.

The most famous Catholic soldiers in that battle would be the Jesuits. The Society of Jesus was founded by Ignatius of Loyola in 1534. He was a Spanish soldier wounded in battle. While recovering from those wounds, he experienced a series of intense visions, and became convinced that God was calling him to found a community of religious men who would defend Roman Catholicism with the fervor and discipline of soldiers.

In 1540, his new order was recognized by the pope and sent all around the world. The Jesuits went to China, Japan, the coast of Africa, Canada, and South America, producing lots of ethnographic information (the *Jesuit Relations*), and establishing footholds for Catholicism. The Jesuits were also leaders in Humanistic education. They immediately developed a following with ruling elites who sent their children to their schools.

They were also sent to European countries. If Catholic, they became advisors and confessors to princes. In Protestant countries, they were sent ostensibly to defend and preserve Catholicism. But in both cases they often found themselves involved in political intrigue and plots—in England famously against Queen Elizabeth. In 1581, it was made high treason to be a priest in England. Over 250 Catholics, many of them Jesuit priests, were executed. Why? What were these plots? Why were Protestant leaders so fearful of Jesuits? Because they had the power and wealth of the Spanish Empire behind them.

That brings me to the third response to the Reformation: the Spanish Crusade. Spain, as you know, had long had a special relationship with the Roman Catholic Church. Its ruler's official title was "His Catholic Majesty." Ferdinand and Isabella had persecuted Jews and Moors, embraced the Inquisition, and authorized the forcible conversion of native peoples throughout their empires.

Their successors, Charles I (who was also Charles V of the Holy Roman Empire) and especially Phillip II, who would use the immense power of Spain to attempt to turn back the Protestant tide. Philip II in particular was determined to use Spanish wealth and power in a great crusade against Protestantism.

That crusade began in the 1560s with the revolt of the Netherlands. What happened was that in 1566, the Dutch Calvinists began attacking Catholic churches and destroying statues and stained glass as graven images. This practice is known as iconoclasm. In 1567,

Philip responded by sending the Inquisition and the Spanish army under the Duke of Alba. Over 1,000 Dutch Calvinists were executed. This produced open rebellion led by William of Orange, also known as William the Silent.

The rebellion seesawed back and forth for decades. In 1574, Philip's poorly paid troops sacked Antwerp in what became known as the Spanish Fury. They slaughtered 7,000 and the port never fully recovered. By the mid 1580s, the Dutch were desperate. William the Silent was assassinated and a new army under Alexander Farnese, Duke of Parma, was taking town after town. The Dutch begged for assistance from the only major Protestant monarch in the neighborhood, Elizabeth I, who, with much reluctance, sent 6,000 troops. She had been secretly supplying the Dutch in fact for years. She had also secretly promoted privateers such as Drake, Hawkins, and Frobisher, who had terrorized Spanish colonies and shipping.

So, in this equation, Spain was, by modern American standards, perfectly within its rights when, in July 1588, it launched the Spanish Armada against what it considered to be a terrorist nation: England. Contrary to popular belief, Philip probably didn't want to actually rule England. What he wanted was to solve his piracy and insurgency problems, and he wanted a toleration for English Catholics.

Pope Sixtus V, who rather admired Elizabeth, thought the Armada a foolish venture, but he granted his banner reluctantly. In fact, he was right. The Spanish Armada consisted of 130 ships, the largest ocean fleet assembled since ancient times. It carried up to 19,000 soldiers (there's some debate about the number). But the ships were slow and outgunned.

The English, on the other hand, had about 50 faster, better-gunned warships in the Royal Navy. Since the English ships were faster, they were able to stand at long range (about 300 yards) and pound the Armada; but the latter held its formation as it proceeded up the English Channel in late July 1588.

When the Armada pulled into Calais on July 27, the English sent in fire-ships—nothing more than old ships that are piled high with stuff that burns—causing the Spanish to flee in chaos. This allowed the English gunfire to pick them off one by one. At this point, the invasion was over.

When the Spanish attempted to return to Spain by sailing north around Scotland and down the west coast of Ireland, they were battered by storms. About half of the Spanish Armada made it back to Spain safely.

The defeat of the Spanish Armada was a tremendous propaganda victory and confidence booster for the English. The storms that wrecked the Spanish Armada were dubbed a "Protestant Wind." The English came to see themselves as a new Israel—a "chosen nation."

But despite the loss of thousands of men and about 60 ships, the Armada defeat did not seriously weaken Spain. Spain was too big and too powerful. Thus this was only the beginning of the war. It would last another 17 years. It would spread to three continents and two oceans and it would drain the treasuries of both England and Spain.

It would also drag in France. In 1589, a crazed Dominican seminarian assassinated Henry III, the last Valois King of France, because he wasn't Catholic enough. Ironically, the next in line for the throne was the Protestant leader of the Huguenots, Henry of Bourbon (I told you the Dominican was crazed). Needless to say, Henry was opposed by the Catholic league and their best friend, His Most Catholic Majesty, Philip II. Henry, desperate, called on Elizabeth.

Now Western Europe had erupted into an all-out Protestant-Catholic fight—or, if you will, it was Spain against the world. It turns out you can't actually beat the whole world. By 1598, Henry IV had defeated his enemies in France. He appeased Catholics by becoming one, famously uttering the Machiavellian line, "Paris is worth a Mass." He reassured Huguenots by granting a toleration, the Edict of Nantes of 1598. In theory, Protestants and Catholics would live side by side in France. In the end, that didn't work out so well. We'll talk about it later.

By 1605, both Philip II and Elizabeth were dead and the Spanish monarchy had declared bankruptcy three times. As a result, both sides sued for peace, resulting in the Treaty of London of that year. In 1609, Spain finally called a truce with the Dutch, who established a republic; it was Protestant, but as we have seen, tolerant.

What had Spain achieved out of its glorious anti-Protestant crusade? In fact, not a single country had switched sides during this entire time. Protestant countries remained Protestant and Catholic countries remained Catholic. On the one hand, Spain had received for her troubles exhaustion and impoverishment. Yet the Spaniards were not about to give up.

Phase two of the Wars of Religion would begin in 1618 with the Thirty Years' War, which would, of course, obviously last until 1648. In the long term, the causes of the Thirty Years' War were continued religious tension in Europe. In the short term, the Holy Roman Emperor wanted to roll back the privileges of the Protestants in Bohemia. These are Habsburgs, so he's related to the kings of Spain.

When he sent representatives in Prague in 1618, the civic leaders of Prague threw them out the window. This became known as the "defenestration of Prague"—*fenêtre / finestra* being a word in both French and Italian for a "window." The Bohemian Protestants then abjured their loyalty to the Holy Roman Emperor and asked a Protestant, the Elector Palatine (he was a small prince on the Rhine) to be their king.

The Elector Palatine ruled the Protestant kingdom of Bohemia for just one year. That's because the Holy Roman Emperor and the King of Spain responded by defeating the Czechs at the Battle of the White Mountain, seizing Bohemia and the Palatinate on the Rhine, which in effect, spread the Thirty Years' War.

The result was a general European war. The Catholic side consisted of Spain, the Holy Roman Empire (in particular in the Habsburg ancestral lands of Austria), and Bavaria. The Protestant side included Saxony and other northern German states (technically part of the Empire, but exercising their independence), Sweden, the Netherlands, and France.

France is key here. It's true that the Thirty Years' War was a war about religion, but note that France is a Catholic country and, yet, it is supporting the Protestant side. That tells us that the Thirty Years' War was also about balance of power. Louis XIII's chief minister, Cardinal Richelieu, saw an opportunity to seize European control from Spain—to seize dominance from Spain—and to make France the greatest power in Europe.

It took a while. The Thirty Years' War raged for 30 years. Catholic and Protestant armies crisscrossed Central Europe, sacking towns, raping inhabitants, and leaving devastation in their wake—all, remember, in the name of how best to worship God. Neither side was really strong enough to crush the other. Finally, both sides agreed to peace talks.

The war was concluded by the Peace of Westphalia of 1648, which enshrined this position: "*Cuius regio, eius religio.*" In other words, whatever the ruler decides is the religion of the state is the religion of the state. In other words, the great powers of Europe had finally agreed that some of them would be Catholic and some of them would be Protestant. Spain also finally recognized Dutch independence in the Treaty of Münster of 1648. Remember, the previous agreement had been a truce. Still, the Spanish wouldn't entirely give up. They didn't settle with France until the Treaty of the Pyrenees in 1659.

The consequences of the Thirty Years' War and this peace settlement are immense. First, the devastation of Central Europe: some parts of Germany lost a third of their population. Germany itself would remain a disunited, divided country well into the 19th century. Failing to win the Thirty Years' War is in another sense yet another nail in the coffin of the power of the Holy Roman Emperor. Indeed, the emperor would never again drive European politics.

Neither would Spain. Spain was exhausted. Spain was chronically in debt after over a century of trying to fight evildoers on all fronts. Spain became a rotting hulk.

On the other hand, England stayed out of it, and that was very smart. As we shall see, England had its own problems, but would emerge a major player at end of 17th century.

And then there was France. With immense agricultural wealth, the French had subsidized other people's armies to fight on other people's soil. They had achieved a degree of dynastic stability by 1648. France, in fact, would be to the later 17th century what Spain had been to the 16th.

Finally, the Thirty Years' War and Peace of Westphalia discredited religious wars. Europeans, drowning in blood, had finally been forced to agree to live and let live. Religion would continue to divide them and would play a part in foreign policy for another century, but never again would they kill each other primarily over religion.

This is very significant. Europeans had been obsessed with forcing everyone to conform and had engaged in murderous adventures over how best to worship God in a way that strikes us as, well, medieval. The notion that different European countries can be Protestant and Catholic and live together strikes me as being very, very modern and intensely rational. It is no accident that the 17th century would be known as the Age of Reason.

Lecture Nine
Rational & Scientific Revolutions—1450–1650

Scope:

Beginning with Copernicus in the 15th century, European thinkers, such as Galileo, Kepler, Bacon, and Newton, questioned received views of how the world worked and pioneered the scientific method in the process. The resultant discoveries and intellectual tools promoted confidence in the ability of human beings to understand and even master the physical world through reason and technology and encouraged philosophers, such as Thomas Hobbes and John Locke, to apply the same methods to politics and society.

Outline

I.   To understand the significance of the scientific discoveries of the 16th and 17th centuries, we must go back to the Great Chain of Being and the astronomical theory at its heart, the theory of the Ptolemaic Universe.

   A. In 1500, most people believed that the Earth was the unmoving center of the Universe.
       1. Expanding outward in concentric spheres were the Moon, Sun, planets, and stars orbiting in perfect circles, because the sphere is the most perfect shape.
       2. The outermost sphere, or *primum mobile*, was inhabited by God himself.
       3. The closer one got to God's realm, the more perfect the sphere.

   B. Europeans embraced this model for three reasons:
       1. It matched their experience, their observations, and common sense.
       2. It was handed down from the scientific writings of the ancients.
       3. It fit biblical revelation.

   C. In fact, this universe did not fit careful observation because the planets sometimes appeared to stop, reverse course, then reverse again and continue.

II. The new worldview sought to reconcile observation not with Scripture but with observation and reason.

    A. Nicholas Copernicus (1473–1543) made the radical suggestion in 1543 that the Sun was at the center of a solar system in which the Earth was third.

    B. Galileo Galilei (1564–1642), a professor at the University of Padua, also questioned old Aristotelian assumptions about the movement of bodies, both heavenly and terrestrial.

        1. Galileo was the first major astronomer to turn the newly invented telescope to the heavens, and he discovered some alarming facts.

            a. The surface of the Moon is pitted, cratered, and irregular.

            b. The surface of the Sun is marked by spots.

            c. The planet Jupiter has moons of its own—implying that it was a model for a solar system and the Earth's relationship to the Moon.

            d. Venus has phases.

            e. There were many more stars than previously thought.

        2. None of this new information fit the Great Chain of Being.

        3. In 1532, Galileo published his findings in *Dialogues on the Two Chief Systems of the World*.

        4. Within a year, Church authorities threatened Galileo with excommunication and torture and forced him to abjure his book.

        5. The Church could silence Galileo, but as with Luther a century earlier, the printing press spread his ideas among university scholars, especially in Protestant countries.

    C. The Protestant Johannes Kepler (1571–1630) refined the Copernican system by proposing that the planets did not circle the Sun but revolved elliptically.

III. Even more important than what was discovered about the cosmos was how it was discovered—using the new *scientific method*.

    A. Copernicus, Galileo, and Kepler did not follow traditional scholastic methods in devising their new worldview.

1. Medieval schoolmen worked deductively, assuming a first principle, and then constructing theories to fit it.
2. Copernicus, Galileo, and Kepler did not assume a first principle.
3. Instead, they used inductive methods, making no prior assumptions.
   a. These men collected facts and gathered observations of nature itself.
   b. Out of these thousands of facts, they devised theories.
   c. These theories were translated into mathematics, suggesting that nature was rational and predictable.
   d. Theories could be modified or discarded as new observations were made.
   e. These men were pioneering the scientific method, missing only one element.

B. Sir Francis Bacon (1561–1626) proposed the next and final step in the method: experimentation, that is, testing the theory.

C. Armed with the scientific method, 17th-century Europeans produced a Scientific Revolution, an explosion of new knowledge.
   1. In France, Blaise Pascal invented an adding machine; Rene Descartes made advances in optics; and both famously advanced mathematics.
   2. In the Netherlands, Anton von Leeuwenhoek (1632–1723) perfected the microscope; Christian Huygens (1629–1695) wrote a seminal treatise on light; and Dutch universities, not bound by Catholic taboos regarding the dissection of dead bodies, became famous for medical training.
   3. In England, the physician William Harvey (1578–1657) discovered the circulation of the blood; the chemist Robert Boyle (1627–1691) formulated the law of pressure and volume ($pv = nrt$); and Edmund Halley (1656–1742), an astronomer, successfully predicted the orbits of heavenly bodies, especially the return of comets.

D. Sir Isaac Newton (1642–1727) put it all together.

1. As an undergraduate at Cambridge, he posited the idea of gravity.
2. From this simple proposition came Newton's three laws of motion.
   a. Every body at rest or in movement remains so unless and until a force is applied to it.
   b. The change in motion is proportional to the force exerted.
   c. Every action produces an opposite reaction.
3. To demonstrate how motion works, and to explain and predict how the Universe works, Newton developed the calculus (simultaneously with Leibniz in Germany).
4. Newton published his findings in 1687 in *Mathematical Principles of Natural Philosophy*, better known as the *Principia*.
   a. This book and the work that lay behind it caught the imaginations of Newton's contemporaries.
   b. The implication of the *Principia* was that God's universe ran according to natural laws that were unchanging, rational, mathematical, and discoverable using the scientific method.

E. This discovery was a revolution.
   1. Humans can discover nature's—God's—secrets; they were no longer mysterious but rational.
   2. If humans can discover nature's laws, they can discover nature's remedies.
      a. They can cure disease.
      b. They can increase the food supply.
      c. They can divert mighty bodies of water.
      d. They can build ever greater buildings.
      e. They could, perhaps, one day, fly.
   3. Clearly, if humans could grasp these powers, then they would be less in the thrall of God.
      a. Newton and his colleagues were not atheists.
      b. Rather, they were, in a sense, more self-reliant.

IV. The rational and empirical philosophers of the 17th century tried to apply the new method to the truths of religion, philosophy, social relations, and so on.

A. Conservatives were appalled.

1. Blaise Pascal (1623–1662), the great French mathematician, feared that the new science would lead to skepticism and atheism.

2. Others—such as Bishop Bossuet (1627–1704) in France, King James VI in Scotland, and Robert Filmer (c.1588–1653) in England—mostly retreated into reassertions of the Great Chain

B. Thomas Hobbes (1588–1679) applied the scientific method to political society in *Leviathan* (1651).

1. Hobbes considered himself a scientist and, thus, rejected explanations for human behavior derived from the Bible, Greek philosophy, or medieval Scholasticism.

2. Instead, like Galileo or Newton surveying the heavens, Hobbes observed people, coming to the following conclusions:

a. Humans are creatures dominated by passions, appetites, and physical needs.

b. They will satisfy those passions, appetites, and needs at the expense of their fellow men and women.

c. Therefore, humans in the state of nature—prior to their enacting government or society—are in a constant state of war.

d. Hobbes's solution is for human beings to form government by contract, giving full, irrevocable power to some strong, absolute ruler.

e. Hobbes understands the reluctance to do this.

i. The ruler may turn into a tyrant, with no recourse.

ii. But Hobbes would argue that the state of nature would be far worse.

f. To break the contract would lead to chaos.

3. God does not enter into Hobbes's equation: Power originates with the people, not the Supreme Being.

C. John Locke (1632–1704) went one step further in his greatest works, *Essay Concerning Human Understanding* and *Two Treatises of Government*, both published in 1690.

1. Locke had been private secretary to the Whig politician Anthony Ashley-Cooper, Earl of Shaftesbury (1621–1683) in the 1670s and 1680s.

2. Like Hobbes, Locke claimed to be a scientist, an observer of men.
3. But unlike Hobbes—or traditional Christian theology—he did not believe in the natural depravity of men.
   a. Rather, in the *Essay Concerning Human Understanding*, Locke argued that human beings are born neither good nor bad but more or less as blank slates: *tabula rasa*.
   b. He believed that environment was more important than any pre-programmed human nature (today we might say genetics) in shaping human character.
4. Locke believed, further, that human beings are naturally rational and that reason, if left alone, would lead to decent moral behavior, even Christianity.
5. In the *Treatises of Government*, Locke rejects a biblical basis for government.
6. He agrees with Hobbes that the authority for government comes from the people in the form of a contract.
7. Locke argues, though, that human beings get out of the state of nature by making two contracts:
   a. The first to form civil society.
   b. The second to form government.
8. Locke believes that human beings form government to protect their lives, liberty, and property.
9. If any government fails to do that, the people retain a right to rescind the contract with their rulers and, in effect, depose them.
10. Chaos would not ensue because the people have not dissolved the contract of civil society.
11. This bold idea contradicts the Great Chain of Being and would be used to justify revolutions in Britain in 1688, in America in 1776, in France in 1789, and in South America in the 19th century.

Supplementary Reading:

M. B. Chambers, et al., *Western Experience*, chapter 16.

S. Shapin, *The Scientific Revolution*.

Questions to Consider:

1. Why was the new science so dangerous?
2. How scientific is the thought of Hobbes and Locke?

Lecture Nine—Transcript
Rational & Scientific Revolutions—1450–1650

Throughout the last lecture, we saw Europeans engage in an orgy of killing, all in the name of God and, maybe, geopolitics. By 1648, they had come to accept that Christendom was forever torn asunder and that Protestants and Catholics would continue to walk the planet, eyeing each other warily, perhaps, but no longer hell-bent on exterminating each other. I would argue that that realization and accommodation were entirely rational, humanistic, and modern: maybe it's better to just agree to disagree, rather than kill each other. I would argue further that rationality and humanism—here, meaning a value for human life—were gaining ground in Europe as it entered the modern world, and that this was part of a major cultural shift born of Renaissance Humanism that would revolutionize how humans saw the world and themselves. In the period after 1500 and accelerating after 1600, Europeans were beginning to apply reason and their powers of observation less to questions about God, which seemed now too complex to resolve—hence the Peace of Westphalia—and more to the natural world in which they lived. The result was the rational and scientific revolutions.

At first glance, the resultant scientific discoveries were neutral or harmless. What does it matter whether the Earth revolves around the sun or vice versa? But, in fact, the answers to these questions would change how humans thought not just about nature, but about God and about themselves. In short, they too would rend the Great Chain of Being.

To understand why, we have to go back to the Chain and the astronomical theory at its heart, the Ptolemaic Universe. The Ptolemaic Universe, you will recall, meant that in 1500 most people believed—along with Ptolemy, a 2nd-century Egyptian astronomer, and based on Aristotle, a 4th-century B.C.E Greek philosopher—that the Earth was the unmoving center of the universe. Expanding outward in concentric rings or spheres were the moon, the sun, the planets, and the stars, orbiting in perfect spheres or circles, because a sphere is the most perfect shape. The outermost sphere, or *primum mobile*, was inhabited by God himself. The whole structure was traversed by angels. The closer one got to God's realm, the more perfect the sphere. So the moon was supposed to be less hilly and rugged than earth, and the planets and stars more perfect still.

Europeans embraced this model for three reasons. First, it matched their experience, their observations, and their common sense. After all, if you go outside and you look up, it does appear that the sun and the moon are circling us. Second, it was handed down from the ancients. As you may recall, medieval Europeans thought that the Greeks and the Romans were smarter than they were, that God had revealed knowledge to them.

Third, it fit revelation. That is, this universe fit their biblical Christian worldview. In fact, you could argue that this system, or its acceptance by medieval Christians, was deduced from scripture. That is, if the God of the Bible had created a universe—that's the assumption—this would be its logical arrangement, rather than being induced from observation.

Now, the reason I say that this system was based more on deduction—assume a fact, then extrapolate from it—then induction—that is, gather facts, then generate a theory—was that, in spite of what I said above about common sense, in fact, this universe did not really fit careful observation. If you observe the heavenly bodies over a period of time, as the ancient and medieval astronomers did, then you will know that sometimes the planets in particular don't progress in a stately fashion across the sky. Instead, they appear to stop, reverse course, then reverse again, and continue on their way.

Now, this made no sense; so, Ptolemy invented epicycles—sort of loop-de-loops in the middle of orbits. The more medieval scholars looked heavenward, the more epicycles they needed if they didn't want to toss out their worldview. This may seem silly today, but the alternative was to dismantle the universe. That's just what a Polish astronomer named Nicholas Copernicus did in 1543.

In 1543, Copernicus publishes *On the Revolutions of the Heavenly Bodies*. In this book, he made the radical suggestion that perhaps the Earth is not the center of the universe. He posited a sun-centered system—a solar system in which the Earth was third. This would explain why some planets appeared to be going forwards and others in reverse. We were all racing around the sun at different rates.

Now, in fact, this theory too had been known to the ancient Greeks. But it was to early modern Europeans a shocking suggestion. How could common sense and the naked eye be wrong? How could 2,000

170   ©2006 The Teaching Company Limited Partnership

years of received opinion, Aristotle, and Ptolemy be wrong? How could the Earth not be the center of the universe? Not be the battleground of good and evil? Could the Great Chain of Being be wrong? Why would humans be third? Is man just another creature? Was the Bible itself wrong? Almost no one in Europe wanted to go there.

There were other reasons for rejecting Copernicus, in fact. Scientists are not will-o'-the-wisps. They need to live with a new theory for a while before abandoning the old one. In fact, the math still didn't work out. It turned out that even Copernicus needed epicycles. Knowing nothing of gravity, he made the mistake of assuming that the planets orbit in perfect circles at the same rate of speed. Only later, when Johannes Kepler would propose elliptical orbits, and Isaac Newton explained them with gravity, would Copernicus's system make sense.

Fortunately for Copernicus, he didn't have to worry about these problems. He had the good sense to die the year after publication. The trouble he avoided was inherited by Galileo Galilei. Galileo was a professor at the University of Padua. He was a distinguished physicist. As a young professor, he took on an old Aristotelian theory by demonstrating that the rate of fall of a body is constant regardless of its weight. Aristotle thought that the heavier a body, the faster it would fall.

More importantly for our purposes, Galileo was the first major astronomer to turn the newly invented telescope to the heavens. Beginning in 1609, he discovered some alarming facts. It turns out that the surface of the moon is pitted, cratered, and irregular. The surface of the sun is marked by spots. The planet Jupiter has moons of its own, implying that it was a model for a solar system. Venus has phases. There were many more stars than previously thought. In fact, Galileo discovered and mapped a great deal of the density, at least, of the Milky Way. None of this fit the Great Chain of Being. The bodies closest to God should be more perfect than the Earth. They shouldn't have phases, moons, or craters. But this universe was messier and more complicated than that system imagined.

Galileo published his findings gradually in the 1610s and 1620s. He was attacked by churchmen and other professors, and some of his work was banned. In 1614, Galileo responded with an open letter asserting the Bible's irrelevance for scientific knowledge—that it should be reinterpreted in the light of new discoveries. That was revolutionary.

In 1616, Cardinal Robert Bellarmine of the Society of Jesus, the leading Catholic theologian of his day, told Galileo to shut up. He forbad Galileo from arguing that the Earth moved. In 1632, Galileo tried, at considerable risk, to get around the ban by publishing his *Dialogues on the Two Chief Systems of the World*. It's written in the form of a dialogue between two characters, one supporting Ptolemy's theory and the other supporting Copernicus. The idea between the dialogue form is that Galileo doesn't have to come out and say which one is right; but the data very clearly point in the direction of Copernicus.

The Church originally licensed the book, but within a year, Galileo was summoned before the Inquisition on "grave suspicion of heresy." He was threatened with excommunication and tortured. In 1633, he was forced to abjure his book, which was publicly burnt. He was sentenced to life in prison, which was soon commuted to house arrest. The sentence was to be read publicly in every university. Still, there is a legend that as Galileo was being led away, he muttered under his breath, "*E pur si muove*" ("It still moves"), referring to the Earth.

The Church could silence Galileo and they could ban his books, but as with Luther a century earlier, thanks to the printing press, thanks to rising literacy, and thanks to better communications and transportation, his ideas circulated among university scholars, especially in Protestant countries.

One of those scholars was a German astronomer in the service of the Holy Roman Emperor, Rudolf II, named Johannes Kepler. As a Protestant, Kepler was not bound by the Church's prohibitions. Kepler could make everything fit, in fact, by proposing that the planets didn't circle the sun, but revolved elliptically. From 1618–1621, he published *The Epitome of Copernican Astronomy*, encapsulating his findings. In 1625, he published the *Rudolfine Tables* (you don't have to be a great scientist to get something like that named after you; you just have to pay for it), which provided precise mathematical tables that could be used to predict the orbits of the heavenly bodies. The math now fit, but this was even more destructive of the Great Chain: ellipses aren't perfect the way circles and spheres are.

Even more important than what was discovered here about the cosmos was how it was discovered. Copernicus, Galileo, and Kepler did not follow traditional scholastic methods in devising their new worldview. Medieval scholastics worked deductively. They assumed a first principle—say, that the cosmos must conform to the Bible—and then they worked out from there.

Copernicus, Galileo, and Kepler did not assume a first principle and then ignore or twist what didn't fit. Instead, they used inductive methods. They made no *a priori* assumption. They collected facts and gathered observations of nature. Remember that Renaissance Humanistic interest in nature. They used the telescope. In fact, Aristotle would have liked this. Out of these thousands of facts, a portrait of nature emerged, and from that, a theory that was capable of being translated into mathematics, as Kepler had done in his tables. The implication is that nature is rational, regular, and predictable. The result was then modified as new observations were made. It is never an article of faith, whatever the Church might say. These men were pioneering the scientific method, but they missed only one element.

That element was to be supplied by an English government lawyer and official, who proposed the next step: Sir Francis Bacon, later Lord Verulam. In a series of speculative philosophical works—*The Advancement of Learning* in 1605, *The Novum Organum* in 1620 (a take-off on Aristotle's original *Organum*), and the *New Atlantis* of a later year (1627)—Bacon argued for a) no *a priori* assumptions. "If a man will begin with certainties," he said, "he shall end in doubts; but if he will be content to begin with doubts, he shall end in certainties." Then b) he argued for the primacy of empirical observation, leading to c) a theory (always provisional), expressed d) in mathematics. This was, so far, the same method used by Copernicus and Galileo.

Bacon added one last step: experimentation. You had to test the theory. The theory must always be falsifiable. This, by the way, is why creation science and intelligent design, however valid they might be in their own terms, can't be science: because you can't design an experiment to test them. Sir Francis had just articulated the scientific method, one of the most powerful tools for the achievement of truth in the arsenal of civilization. For the first time since perhaps the Greeks, it was no longer enough of an explanation to say, "Well, God willed it." Bacon argued that the method should be applied not just to study of the physical world, but to all human knowledge.

Indeed, armed with the new method, 17th century Europeans produced a scientific revolution—an explosion of new knowledge. In France, Blaise Pascal invented the adding machine; Rene Descartes made advances in optics; and both most famously advanced mathematics. Pascal devised Pascal's theorem and, with Fermat, the theory of probability; Descartes systematized the study of curves and devised that alphabetical system for unknown variables (variable a, b, c, x, y, z, etc.) and the system of superscripts for powers.

In the Netherlands, Anton von Leeuwenhoek perfected the microscope. Christian Huygens wrote a famous treatise on light. Dutch universities, not bound by Catholic taboos regarding the dissection of dead bodies, became famous for their medical training.

In England, the physician William Harvey discovered the circulation of blood. The chemist Robert Boyle discovered the law of pressure and volume ($pv = nrt$) and wrote it up in a work whose title sums up the attitude of the entire age: *The Skeptical Chemist*. Edmund Halley, an astronomer based at my old Oxford College, New College, coordinated his observations of the heavens with mathematical formulae to predict the orbits of heavenly bodies and the return of comets; hence Halley's Comet.

But the greatest of them all and the man who epitomized and revealed the potential of the scientific revolution was, of course, Isaac Newton. Isaac Newton put it all together. As an undergraduate at Cambridge, he came to be influenced by the works of Galileo. It was here that he had perhaps his greatest achievement: the positing of the idea of gravity.

If Galileo was correct that objects in motion stay in straight-line motion unless restrained, why don't the planets fly off into space? Newton posited that there must be an attractive force between objects based on weight—that's gravity. That is, the same force that causes an apple to fall to Earth causes the planets to stay in their orbits.

From this simple proposition came Newton's three laws of motion. 1) Every body at rest or in movement remains so unless or until a force is applied to it. 2) The change in motion is proportional to the force exerted. 3) Every action produces an opposite reaction. To demonstrate how motion works and to explain and predict how the universe works, Newton developed the calculus, simultaneously with Leibniz in Germany.

In short, Newton used Bacon's method: observe phenomena, posit a theory, and express it mathematically. But what was his experiment? (I suppose the apple, although there's no evidence the apple actually ever really happened or existed.) In a way, it was the motions of the heavenly bodies themselves—that is, every time they ended up where Newton said they would be—that confirms his theory. Three centuries later, the space program verifies Isaac Newton every time something lands or rendezvous with a heavenly body successfully.

Newton published his findings in 1687 in *The Mathematical Principles of Natural Philosophy*, better known as *The Principia*. This book and the work that lay behind it caught the imaginations of European contemporaries because it was a complete world system to replace Ptolemy's. It explained how the universe worked to everyone's satisfaction. In the words of Alexander Pope: "Nature and Nature's laws lay hid in night / God said: "Let Newton be!" and all was light."

The implication of the *Principia* was that God's universe ran according to natural laws. They were unchanging; they were rational; they were mathematical; they were discoverable using the scientific method. This is a revolution. It implied that humans could discover nature's secrets—God's secrets. These were no longer mysterious.

If humans could discover nature's laws, they could discover nature's remedies. They could perhaps cure disease, increase the food supply, divert mighty bodies of water, build ever greater buildings, and perhaps one day fly. Clearly, if humans could grasp these powers, then prayers and rituals were no longer your only recourse to change or avert your fate.

God was, in fact, no longer necessary to explain the daily running of the universe. Perhaps he was not concerned at the fall of every sparrow. Perhaps God was more of a celestial watchmaker who designed the universe, wound it up, and set it going. This philosophy is known as Deism and would be very popular in the 18th century.

Please understand that neither Newton nor his contemporaries were atheists. The age saw a continual flood of religious treatises, devotional works, and arguments. Newton himself wrote many religious works, including a commentary on the Book of Revelation. But human beings now had a much more powerful tool for understanding their surroundings in the scientific method. Many 17th century philosophers would try to apply it to human beings themselves.

After all, if the free, unhindered human mind could discover the laws of nature via the scientific method, why could it not also discover the truth in religion, philosophy, social relations, etc.? Why couldn't accepted truths about human nature, and divine nature for that matter, be subjected to the cold hard light of observation, reason, and experimentation?

Thus, Rene Descartes attempted to apply induction and reason to human philosophy. He rejected not only *a priori* assumptions, but anything for which there was no rational proof. The only certainty was that thought implied existence: "I think, therefore I am."

Conservatives were appalled by this. Blaise Pascal, the great French mathematician, was deeply troubled by the inroads of science and mathematical reasoning into what he called, "The empty cold spaces of the universe." In the *Pensees*, notes for a great religious work he never lived to write, he argued that man remained corruptible and imperfect; therefore, his reason was unreliable. Man is merely a thinking reed. As Pascal wrote, "The heart has reasons that reason knows not of." Pascal feared that the new science would lead to skepticism and atheism.

Other conservatives—Bishop Bossuet in France, King James VI in Scotland, and Robert Filmer in England—mostly retreated into reassertions of the Great Chain. According to King James, "The state of monarchy is the supremest thing upon earth, for kings are...God's lieutenants upon earth and sit upon God's throne." But this formula didn't seem to work any more. Humanism, the Reformation, the Wars of Religion, and even the discovery of the New World raised disturbing questions as to where kings got their power, and whether a bad king or one who worshiped God differently should be obeyed. During the Wars of Religion, both Catholic and Protestant theologians began to argue that a heretic king could be deposed. The pope absolved Catholics of their allegiance to Elizabeth and both sides used assassination as a weapon.

So, in the new, scientific, secular, modern Europe, philosophers were increasingly called on to construct new justifications for the state. At least two sought to do so using the scientific method. Thomas Hobbes was arguably the most original thinker of the 17th century. His great work, written during a civil war in England, when everyone was debating the origins of legitimate government, is *Leviathan*, published in 1651.

Hobbes considered himself a scientist. Therefore, he rejected explanations for human behavior derived from the Bible, Greek philosophy, and medieval scholasticism. Instead, like Galileo or Newton surveying the heavens, he just observed people. He came to the following conclusions: man is a creature dominated by passions, appetites, and physical needs—far more animal than angel. He will satisfy those passions and appetites and those needs at the expense of his fellow men and women. Therefore, men in the state of nature prior to their enacting government or society are in a constant state of war. They are like atoms crashing into each other, constantly fighting for food, shelter, and power. Note how the discovery of the New World forced European philosophers to think about human beings in this mythical state—what would happen to human beings if they weren't in civilization?

According to Hobbes, the only alternative to the state of nature is for people to form a contract with some strong man to which they give full irrevocable power over their lives, their liberty, and their property—a single absolute ruler. Now, Hobbes understands that we don't really want to do this; the ruler may turn into a tyrant. But he would argue that the state of nature would be far worse. To break the contract would lead to chaos.

So, science seems to lead to the same conclusion as religion: the best form of government is monarchy. But note that in this monarchy, God doesn't enter into the equation. Power originates with the people, not the Supreme Being. That is revolutionary.

John Locke went one step further. If Hobbes is the most original thinker of the 17th century, Locke is probably the most influential, not only in Britain, but in 18th century France and in 18th century America. Arguably, he's the great philosopher behind the

Declaration of Independence. Perhaps one reason for Locke's success is that he worked for real practical politicians. He worked for the Whig politician Anthony Ashley-Cooper, Earl of Shaftesbury. In the 1670s and 1680s, he was his private secretary. So Locke didn't spend a whole lot of time in the ivory tower. In fact, in the 1680s, he actually has to flee England because of his political opinions. So he knew real experience. He published his two greatest works in 1690: *The Essay Concerning Human Understanding* and the *Two Treatises of Government*.

To understand Locke's political philosophy, you have to understand his philosophy of knowledge and being, his epistemology; so we'll start with the *Essay*. Like Hobbes, Locke claimed to be a scientist— an observer of men. But unlike Hobbes or traditional Christian theology, he did not believe in the natural depravity or rapaciousness of men. Rather, Locke believed that human beings are born neither good nor bad, but more or less as blank slates: *tabula rasa*. That is, he believed that environment was more important than any pre-programmed human nature—today we might say genetics—in shaping human character. Note what that implies about the Great Chain of Being: maybe you weren't programmed to be a peasant. Maybe with the right training, you'd make a fine king. Locke would probably have rejected that, but it's implied in his philosophy.

Locke believed further that human beings are naturally rational and that reason, if left alone, would lead to decent moral behavior, even Christianity. In the *Treatises of Government*, Locke rejects a Biblical basis for government, as well as the idea that kings are a species of father. He agrees with Hobbes that authority for government comes from the people in the form of a contract. But he argues that human beings get out of the state of nature by actually making two contracts. The first contract is with each other to form civil society. The second is with a ruler to form government. This business of two contracts explains Locke theory on resistance. Locke believes that human beings form government to protect their lives, their liberty, and their property. If any government fails to do that, the people retain a right to rescind the contract with their rulers and, in effect, depose them. Chaos would not ensue because they have not dissolved the contract of civil society.

This bold idea contradicts the Great Chain of Being. You can depose your ruler. It would be used to justify revolutions in Britain in 1688, in America in 1776, in France in 1789, and in South America in the 19th century. It will infuse our Declaration of Independence.

In 1701, Locke published his important *Letter on Toleration*, which provides a philosophical basis for arguing that toleration is the most rational position for Christians to take with each other.

Thus, John Locke, Isaac Newton, and friends have pursued Renaissance Humanism with its emphasis on human concerns and rationality to its logical conclusion: humans are rational and by and large good. They are capable of understanding the universe and of changing it to suit themselves without God's help. They are capable of establishing societies, establishing governments, and even dissolving the latter and starting over again—again without God's help.

This does not mean that Newton, Locke, et al., were atheists. They were just more self-reliant, more confident, and more tolerant of different points of view than their medieval counterparts. Their lifetimes would see the beginnings of a new way of thinking as human beings came to believe that they could master their environment.

The late 17th century would see—and I will end with these two developments—first, the first consistently successful surgical operation: cutting for stone. Samuel Pepys underwent this painful procedure in 1658, and he always thanked God on the anniversary that he had survived it; but the point is that he and lots of other people survived it. The other thing about the late 17th century is that you get the first insurance companies.

What do these two seemingly disparate developments have in common? They both mark a refusal to accept fate—a refusal to accept God's will. "I'm going to have this surgery. I'm going to change my fate. I'm going to be cured." In the case of insurance, what does insurance actually say? It says terrible things can happen to you—what insurance companies still to this day still call "acts of God." What we will do is we will rebuild your house. We will rebuild your life. We will not let the "act of God" stop you.

This confidence in human abilities and sense of entitlement to a good life—life, liberty, property, or, as Jefferson would have put it later, "the pursuit of happiness"—and this refusal to abide by the decrees of nature, of kings, and of God—this is all profoundly modern.

But as we have seen, not everyone shared these views. The 17th century would see the forces of conservatism; churches and monarchs mount a dramatic rearguard action. The result would become the "crisis of the 17th century." In the next lecture, we turn to that crisis, and two solutions that will set the tone for politics in Europe for hundreds of years: French Absolutism and, in subsequent lectures, English Constitutionalism.

Lecture Ten
French Absolutism—1589–1715

Scope:

Following the disasters of the Wars of Religion, the monarchies of Europe experienced a crisis of authority. The French response, foreshadowed by Henry IV and Cardinal Richelieu and perfected by Louis XIV, was an absolutism that made the king a virtual god on Earth. This solution was imitated in Spain, Austria, Prussia, and Russia. The major continental exception was the Protestant Netherlands, which, under William of Orange, fought almost single-handedly to thwart Louis' plans to inherit the Spanish throne and achieve European domination.

Outline

I. The disaster of the Thirty Years' War shook the foundations of government all across Europe in what historians call the crisis of the 17th century.

    A. The expense of the Thirty Years' War had exhausted the treasuries of the great European monarchies.

    B. The nobility in France, England, Spain, and elsewhere resented the centralizing tendencies of the post-Renaissance monarchs.

        1. Nobles saw an opportunity in the king's financial exhaustion and the people's resentment of these wars to try to get some power back.

        2. They did so through government office and rebellion.

    C. The nobles were sometimes joined by merchants who resented high taxes and the disruption of trade that accompanied these wars.

    D. They were also sometimes joined by the peasantry.

        1. Peasants were the primary victims of the wars because of the destruction of farmland.

        2. Peasants were also the primary sponsors of war through taxes.

    E. In the next two lectures, we will concentrate on two countries that responded very differently to the crisis of the

17th century, providing contrasting models of government for the rest of Europe.

1. France embraced a conservative attempt to revive a modified Great Chain via *royal absolutism* (in effect, a Hobbesian solution).
2. England came to embrace a more liberal, contractual arrangement known as *constitutional monarchy* (the Lockean solution).

II. France had suffered terribly during the first wave of the Wars of Religion.

  A. France emerged from these troubles under the leadership of Henry of Bourbon, who founded the Bourbon line and became Henry IV in 1589.

   1. Henry IV (1589–1610) was an effective military leader and ruler.

      a. He promulgated the Edict of Nantes, granting toleration to Protestants (Huguenots) in 1598.
      b. Working with his financial minister, Maximilien de Béthune, Duc de Sully (1560–1641), Henry IV pursued the following goals:
         i. To limit the power of the nobles.
         ii. To end religious and blood feuds.
         iii. To limit the power of regional assemblies, called *parlements*.
         iv. To build up an extensive local bureaucracy.
         v. To centralize the economy.
      c. These measures were unpopular with many noble and Catholic families.

   2. Henry IV was assassinated by a Catholic sympathizer in 1610.

  B. Louis XIII (1610–1643) was not nearly as impressive—or popular—as his father.

   1. During the minority of Louis, from 1610–1618, his mother, Marie de' Medici served as regent.
   2. As an adult, he left real power in the hands of Armand, Cardinal Richelieu (1585–1642).
   3. Richelieu continued Henry IV's policies.

      a. He reduced the power of the nobles and local parlements, imprisoning political opponents.

      b. He continued to centralize the economy, encouraging the exploration and colonization of the Americas.

      c. He pursued an aggressive anti-Habsburg foreign policy by entering the Thirty Years' War on the Protestant side.

C. By the time of Louis and Richelieu's deaths in 1642–1643, France was the most powerful nation in Europe; noble power seemed broken, but the royal treasury was bare and the country groaned under high taxes.

III. The *Fronde* (1643–1651), the "slingshot," was the result of these policies.

    A. Louis XIV (1643–1715) ascended the French throne at age four.

      1. Real power lay in the hands of his mother, Anne of Austria, and her advisor, Cardinal Jules Mazarin (1602–1661).

      2. The nobles of France saw their chance.

    B. The *Fronde* began at court in 1649 with the wives of imprisoned nobles demanding their release.

      1. Their cause was taken up by the *Parlement* of Paris, then the people of Paris.

      2. Much of the nobility and some towns joined the cause.

      3. In 1651, Paris fell to the rebels, and Louis was forced to abandon his palace at the Louvre.

    C. The *Frondeur* state ruled France in Louis' name in 1651–1652.

      1. The Frondeur state was inefficient and corrupt.

      2. In 1652, Louis and Mazarin returned to power by popular demand.

IV. Louis XIV was determined that he would never again be forced into submission by his nobles or anyone else in France. Following Mazarin's death in 1661, he began to revive the Great Chain of Being and to perfect the absolutist state of his grandfather, Henry IV, and Cardinal Richelieu by pursuing five principles that I have dubbed Louis XIV's five rules of absolutism.

   A. The king must be godlike.
   1. Louis had been raised to believe that he was God's lieutenant, wielding God's power.
   2. Louis began a program to disseminate this image throughout France.
      a. He established royal academies of art, music, literature and rhetoric, drama, science, and medals.
      b. He legislated that the French style in art was to be Classical, harking back to the Golden Age of Greece and Rome.
         i. Louis was portrayed everywhere as Apollo, the Greek god of the Sun.
         ii. When not portrayed as a Greek god, he was portrayed as the Sun itself: the center of the solar system and the source of all life.
      c. Louis maintained strict censorship of the arts to ensure that the message was never diluted.
   3. The epitome of this program was the magnificent palace that Louis set about building at Versailles.
   4. The king's daily routine emphasized his exalted station.

   B. The king must be in control.
   1. Louis was tireless, working long days, reading reports, and drafting diplomatic correspondence himself.
   2. He assembled a corps of professional secretaries and administrators drawn not from the nobility but from the ranks of professional men.
   3. Louis never called the Estates General.
   4. In the localities, he established trained professional bureaucrats called *intendants*.

   C. The king must be wealthy. When Louis declared himself of age, the country's finances were a mess, largely from more than 40 years of war. But Louis had two advantages in restoring those finances.

1. He was advised by a financial genius named Jean-Baptiste Colbert (1619–1683), who continued the Bourbon program of centralizing the economy and perfected a policy of mercantilism.
2. Louis was able to tax at will, without the interference of a legislature.
    a. In the short run, this paid for Versailles, armies of bureaucrats and soldiers, and a great navy.
    b. In the long run, though, it hampered mercantile initiative and would eventually impoverish the peasantry.

D. The king must impose religious conformity on his subjects.
1. France had been bitterly divided in religion between Roman Catholics and Huguenots.
2. Though Louis virtually controlled the Church in France, Huguenots were outside of his spiritual power thanks to the toleration granted by his grandfather in the Edict of Nantes.
3. In 1685, Louis revoked the Edict of Nantes.
    a. Thousands fled to Germany, the Netherlands, England, and North America.
    b. This action, too, hurt the French economy in the long run.

E. The king must have an army, if only to back up the other four rules of absolutism.
1. Louis launched a series of reforms of the military, resulting in the most professional fighting force in Europe.
2. Louis used that army on his neighbors in an attempt to position himself to be the next king of Spain.
    a. In the 17th century, Spain still ruled a vast empire.
    b. Spain had overextended itself in the 16th and early 17th centuries and was now the sick man of Europe, a rotting hulk of an empire.
    c. Louis, who was related to the Spanish royal house, wanted to absorb that empire after the death of its sickly, childless ruler, Carlos II (1665–1700), known as El Hechizado ("the bewitched").

3. Louis was opposed in this undertaking by the Netherlands.

    a. The Protestant Dutch Republic had the motivation and the wealth to stand against Louis' dreams of European monarchy.

    b. The Dutch stadholder, William of Orange, was deeply aware of the consequences for Protestant Europe if Louis combined the Spanish Empire with French military might.

    c. This led to a series of wars in which Louis XIV conquered numerous small states along the Rhine and Dutch border—Franche-Comté, Luxemburg, Lorraine, Orange, and the Spanish Netherlands (roughly modern-day Belgium)—in an attempt to encircle the Netherlands.

    d. By the late 1680s, Louis was planning the *coup de grâce*—another war to wipe the Dutch off the map.

V. But at this point, Louis began to face a much greater challenge from England.

Supplementary Reading:

M. B. Chambers, et al., *Western Experience*, chapter 15, sections V–VI; chapter 17, section I.

R. N. Hatton, *Europe in the Age of Louis XIV*.

S. Schama, *An Embarrassment of Riches: An Interpretation of Dutch Culture in the Golden Age*.

Questions to Consider:

1. What would have been the consequences of a French takeover of the Spanish Empire?

2. Why was the Netherlands able to mount a credible challenge to the ambitions of Louis XIV?

Lecture Ten—Transcript
French Absolutism—1589–1715

If the 17th century was the Age of Reason, that had a lot to do with widespread revulsion at the effects of the Wars of Religion, and, in particular, the violence and bloodshed of the Thirty Years' War. The disaster of the Thirty Years' War shook the foundations of government all across Europe. Historians call this the "crisis of the 17th century."

The widespread crisis experienced by European monarchies had many sources. First, financial: the sheer cost of the war. It wounded economies that had already been hurt by the inflation at the beginning of the 17th century. It exhausted royal treasuries.

Then there was aristocratic dissatisfaction. The nobility in France, England, Spain, etc., had resented the growth of the state and the centralizing tendencies of the post-Renaissance monarchs. This is the other side—the flipside—to Lecture Five. They used the opportunity of royal financial exhaustion and resentment of these wars to try to get some power back through government office and through rebellion.

Then the merchants were dissatisfied. They objected to the high taxes needed to pay for the wars, the disruption of trade, and the neglect of exploration, colonies, and markets. Sometimes even the peasantry joined in. They were the primary victims of these wars: much farmland was laid waste; many peasants were killed; and they were the primary payers for it through taxes.

We are not going to try to sort out the crisis for every state in Europe. Rather, we are going to concentrate on two states, for they provided models of government that, it could be argued, have served the West ever since: France, which embraced a conservative attempt to revive a modified Great Chain of Being via royal Absolutism, a sort of Hobbesian solution; and England, which came to embrace a more liberal, constitutional arrangement known as "constitutional monarchy"—the Lockean solution.

In this lecture we will discuss France. Now, you will recall that France had suffered terribly during the first wave of the Wars of Religion: massacres, assassinations, terrible religious hatreds, and violence. France had emerged from these troubles under the leadership of Henry of Bourbon, who founded the Bourbon line and became Henry IV in 1589.

Henry IV was famous for his bravery, his approachability, and his practicality. He was an effective military leader, but also something of a compromise candidate. Remember that he was raised a Protestant but had converted to Roman Catholicism. To reassure Protestants, he promulgated the Edict of Nantes, granting toleration to Huguenots in 1598.

With his financial minister, Maximilian de Bethune, Duc de Sully, he sought to limit the power of the nobles, to end religious and blood feuds, and to limit the power of regional assemblies, called *parlements,* the most powerful of which was at Paris. He began to build up an extensive local bureaucracy. He raised money to pay for it by selling offices. He centralized the economy. He established government monopolies on gunpowder, mines, and salt. He built a canal system linking Atlantic and Mediterranean ports. He established the royal *corvée*, a draft of peasants, to work on the French roads during the summer. He also reduced taxes on those peasants.

All of these things were good for the king, good for the French economy, and good for France in general; but they also gave just about everybody in France a reason to grumble. In 1610, he was assassinated by a Catholic sympathizer.

Louis XIII, his son, was not nearly so impressive. He was raised in an extremely sheltered environment, and he basically let other people run his government. From 1624, he left real power in the hands of his chief minister, Armand Jean du Plessis, Duc de Richelieu, better known to history and readers of Alexander Dumas as Cardinal Richelieu.

Richelieu continued Henry IV's policies. He reduced the power of the nobles and the local *parlements*. He imprisoned powerful political enemies. He attacked and captured the Huguenot stronghold of La Rochelle in 1628—so he had no love for Protestants. He kept a tight reign on the Catholic Church in France and he centralized the economy, encouraging exploration and colonization of the Americas. He also, as we saw in a previous lecture, pursued an aggressive anti-Habsburg foreign policy by entering the Thirty Years' War on the Protestant side. By the time of Louis and Richelieu's deaths in 1643,

France was the most powerful nation in Europe. Noble power seemed broken, but so was the royal treasury. The country groaned under excessive taxation.

Louis XIV ascended the French throne at the age of four; so the real power was in the hands of his mother, Anne of Austria, and Jules, Cardinal Mazarin, a student of Richelieu's. The nobles of France, heretofore beaten down by a strong Bourbon monarchy, saw their chance. Their resentment exploded in a rebellion known as the Fronde. By the way, let me say that if you're going to name a rebellion, this is a terrific one. The *Fronde* means "the slingshot."

The Fronde began at court with the wives of imprisoned nobles demanding their release. Their cause was taken up by the *Parlement* of Paris and then joined by the people of Paris. Eventually, they were also joined by much of the nobility and some of the towns who'd been groaning under that taxation.

In 1648, Paris revolted. In 1649, the Prince de Condé, France's greatest general in the Thirty Years' War, restored order, but then embraced the Fronde himself. In 1651, Paris fell to the rebels and Louis was forced to flee the Louvre, the principal royal residence. This would remain a bitter childhood memory. He would never forget the night that he had to be smuggled out of his own palace.

The Frondeur State ruled France for about two years in Louis's name, but not terribly well. It was inefficient and corrupt. Remember that the French had always had a strong belief in the sanctity of monarchy. It dated back to the Middle Ages—a belief that French kings had been careful to cultivate. The failures of the Frondeur State seemed to reaffirm the Great Chain of Being: break it and you will be punished. In 1652, Louis and Mazarin were returned to power by popular demand.

Louis would never forget the humiliation of being forced to sneak out of his own palace. He was determined that he would never again be forced into submission by his own nobles or anyone else in France. For a decade, Mazarin tutored the young king in the ways of kingship. But following Mazarin's death in 1661, he declared himself of age. He announced that he would rule without the aid of a chief minister and immediately began to perfect the absolutist state that his grandfather, Henry IV, and Cardinal Richelieu had begun to erect.

I would argue that there were five main features to that state, and I call them "Louis XIV's Five Rules of Absolutism." You understand, of course, that Louis never sat down and wrote out five rules. This is Bucholz talking.

The "Five Rules of Absolutism" are as follows: 1) The king must be godlike. 2) The king must be in control. 3) The king must be wealthy. 4) The king must enforce religious conformity. 5) The king must have an army.

First, the king must be godlike: Louis had been raised to believe that he was unlike other men. As king, he was God's lieutenant, wielding his power. As Louis, the son of kings, he had been chosen by God for this role. He embodied God's power on earth; that is, he was the physical body that represented both God and France.

But, of course, Louis's subjects had forgotten all that, or else they wouldn't have gone on the Fronde; so he began a program to redefine his image. He established royal academies of art, of music, of literature and rhetoric, of drama, of science, and of medals. He trained and supported numerous artists and scholars generously. In return, their job was to create art that glorified Louis XIV in buildings, in statues, in paintings, in opera, in scientific discoveries dedicated to him, and in medals continually struck for his many victories.

He legislated that the French style in art was to be Classical, harking back to the golden age of Greece and Rome. If Ronald Reagan harked back to the cowboy in American life, Louis was looking for an image of greatness and he found it in the Roman emperors and Alexander the Great. If you read the plays of Racine and Corneille, you'll see this.

Everywhere, he was portrayed as Apollo or painted with the symbols of Apollo, with a lyre and a laurel. Apollo was, of course, the Greek god of the sun. Louis chose the sun as his symbol because the sun is the center of the solar system (he's a Copernican) and the source of all life itself. When you saw the sun on the side of a building; when you saw the sun depicted on a medal; when you saw the sun in the sky, you were supposed to think of *le Roi Soleil* (the Sun King).

He maintained strict censorship of the arts to ensure that the message was never diluted. What if you violated the rules? What if you criticized the king or the absolutist state? That's what we have the Bastille for.

Versailles was the epitome of this program of magnificence. Originally, Versailles was a royal hunting lodge located about 15 miles outside of Paris. That's the first key: outside of Paris. Louis had no love for Paris. He spent one half of the French royal revenue—think about that. What if the president of the United States went to Congress and said, "I want to take half of the government revenue and I want to spend it on a new house."

He spent it on 30,000 workmen who worked 20 years to build thousands of rooms and extensive gardens. Versailles's sheer size was a monument to Louis and the wealth of France. But its size was also a political strategy. You know the phrase: "Keep your friends close. Keep your enemies closer." Versailles was big enough to house all the nobility of France, keeping them under Louis's watchful eye, away from Paris and away from the countryside, where they could plot against him.

Of course, Versailles's gates, entrance halls, dining halls, and boudoir were all decorated with portraits of the Louis. There were tapestries and paintings of his great achievements. The great hall of mirrors celebrated his battles and, of course, everywhere you looked—everywhere—was the sun.

Just to make sure that everyone got the hint, at the center of the palace was not a throne room, not a Cabinet room, and certainly not a hall where the Estates General could meet. There was, instead, the king's bedchamber. Make no mistake: Louis was the beating heart of France.

The king's daily routine emphasized this. Upon rising (the *levee*), there was an elaborate dressing ritual in which different noblemen held particular articles of the king's clothing. This was a chance for them to have the king's ear to ask for a favor, a pension, a job, or some land. It served the king by allowing him to watch his nobles and by breaking them into subservience. Imagine holding the king's shirt was a job to be fought over jealously. It was considered more honorable than any military or civil command. Of course, if you spend all your day angling to hold the king's shirt, you weren't plotting rebellion.

Morning mass followed the *levee* in the Chapel Royal. It was attended by the king and his court. According to one observer (and I haven't been able to verify this with more), Louis alone faced the altar. The courtiers faced Louis because he was their conduit to God.

There then might follow long Cabinet meetings in the mid-morning—lots of business. Louis often skipped lunch. One of the themes of this lecture was that he was a very hard worker. The afternoon was spent hunting, riding, and shooting. These were viewed as kingly and aristocratic sports, like presidents jogging today.

The evening was spent watching an opera, or at a play, or gambling, though Louis often skipped this frivolity because he had business to do. Late, perhaps at 10 p.m., there was a supper in state, which means that Louis was served by cupbearers, carvers, and servers on bended knee. There was live music. No one else dined with him. Spectators stood about to watch "God on Earth" eat.

He then retired with the spectacle of *couchée*. A candle was held for him as he entered the bedchamber. He had assistance undressing. Then, he got into bed. When everyone had gone, he probably got out of his ceremonial bed and snuck off to a smaller bedchamber to sleep or to spend the night with one of his mistresses.

When I explain all this to my undergraduate students, they usually react in shock and horror at the sheer egotism seemingly on display here. But Louis would have said that this wasn't egotism at all. It had nothing to with him. It was a promotion of the monarchy and in a sense a promotion of France.

Imagine what it must have been to be Louis. Think of the sheer strain to always be on public display. One historian has suggested that Louis XIV probably never had a hot meal because there was all that ceremony to bring in the meat, etc. Everything was a ritual.

It wasn't all done for Louis's comfort. He would have said it was done for the good of France. After all, the king embodied France. That means he was, in a sense, France itself. He was "God on Earth." How would you treat God if he came to dinner? How would you treat France, or Great Britain, or the United States, if they were embodied in a single person, at their rising in the morning? How do we treat our flag? It is, after all, a mere piece of cloth and yet, we revere it in some ways as Frenchmen revered their king.

In the worldview of the 17th century, this all made sense. But it was also politically astute following the Fronde. It elevated the monarch. It made him untouchable. It reduced the nobility to servants and supplicants. It lets them hold his shirt, but it gives them no real power. There was no Richelieu or Condé for Louis.

So who did have real power in France? Why, Louis, of course. Remember rule number two: the king must be in control. Louis said, "The position of sovereign can be properly filled only by the sovereign himself." He also said, "*L'etat c'est moi*": "I am the state."

Louis was tireless, working very long days reading reports and drafting diplomatic correspondence himself. He often missed the entertainments that I mentioned before. But he couldn't do everything himself, so he assembled a corps of professional secretaries and administrators drawn not from the nobility, but from the ranks of professional men: lawyers, bankers, and merchants. His successive finance ministers, Nicolas Fouquet and Jean-Baptiste Colbert, are good examples.

The reason he was interested in these people was 1) They knew how to get things done. 2) They had financial resources, which could help the Crown. He was constantly borrowing money from these guys. But 3) they were not so powerful individually that they could become a center of resistance. The king could make them; he could always break them.

The king never had to call the Estates General and that was another way of conserving his power. In the localities, he established trained professional bureaucrats called *intendants* (intendants) who collected taxes, acted as judges, and recruited his army. This frequently allowed him to bypass traditional institutions like the local nobles or the *parlements*.

Recently, historians have cautioned us against going too far with this interpretation. Even Louis understood that he had to rule with consent and that he couldn't just ride roughshod over these institutions and nobles. So there was a sort of break on his power, but push never really came to shove because he knew how far to push it.

How did the king pay for this vast bureaucracy? Remember number three: the king must be wealthy. When Louis declared himself of age, the country's finances were a mess, largely from over 40 years of war. Fortunately, Louis had two aces up his sleeve.

First, a financial genius named Jean-Baptiste Colbert who continued the Bourbon program of centralizing the economy. In fact, he is often thought to have perfected the idea of mercantilism—the idea that the economy should be run by the state to maximize national wealth. Colbert protected French trade and raised more money for the king with high tariffs on foreign goods—high customs rates. He encouraged, even created, French industries with government loans and privileges. Many of them were tied to war but others of them were tied to the luxury trade at Versailles. Colbert funded the French shipbuilding industry and practically founded the perfume and silk industries. He set standards of workmanship that were subject to government inspection. He supported exploration and colonization of French possessions in the New World, especially Canada. The idea was that these would provide raw materials, and also markets for French goods. He attacked noble privilege and tried to get them to pay taxes, with moderate success. He increased taxes on the French peasants, in particular a poll tax called the *taille*.

This brings us to Louis's second economic weapon. Louis XIV could tax at will. Unlike the King of England, who had to get Parliament's permission to impose or raise a tax, Louis could just order it. He had so effectively reduced the power of local institutions that there was little resistance.

Now in the short run, this is terrific for him. It builds Versailles. It funds all those operas, plays, paintings, statues, armies of bureaucrats, armies of soldiers, and navies of ships. But in the long run for France, it's terrible. It hampers mercantile initiative—everything has to be approved by the government. It hit the peasants hard and it combined with the relative lack of taxation on the nobles and Church to increase the gulf between rich and poor.

Louis' legacy on religion was similarly advantageous in the short run and destructive in the long run. The next rule of Absolutism is that the king must impose religious conformity on his subjects. Remember that France remained bitterly divided in religion between Roman Catholics and Calvinist Protestants called Huguenots. Catholicism remained the official religion of the state. Huguenots had been granted toleration by Louis's grandfather in 1598. But this did not sit well for Louis. Louis had been raised a Catholic. He had been raised to believe that God was the source of his power and that the only loyal subjects were those who believed as he believed. Only Catholics could be loyal subjects of the Sun King.

For Louis, Roman Catholicism fit Absolutism like a glove. It emphasized hierarchy, ritual, and obedience. How could supposedly loyal subjects choose to worship and interpret their Bible differently from their king? Though Louis virtually controlled the Catholic Church in France, he couldn't control the Huguenots; so in 1685 Louis revoked the Edict of Nantes. Huguenots were given a choice: convert, depart, or go to prison.

Thousands fled to Germany, the Netherlands, England, and North America. In fact, this was a major blunder. Huguenots were among France's most industrious citizens: they were merchants, craftsmen, and artists. They would enrich the economies and cultures of France's enemies.

The revocation of the Edict of Nantes was also a public relations disaster, for it confirmed for many Europeans the sinister reputation of international Catholicism and of Louis XIV. That reputation was born in war. As you'll remember, the fifth rule of Absolutism is, "The king must have an army."

One way of thinking of this was that this was a guarantee of all the other four. If you weren't impressed by Versailles, if you weren't overawed by Louis's officials, if you didn't pay your taxes, if you didn't worship as the king bid, or if you didn't obey like a good Catholic Frenchman, Louis could always sick the army on you.

To that end, Louis launched a series of military reforms involving extensive study of fortifications and sieges. The French became the greatest builders of forts in the world. He promoted officers on merit, not just because they were noble. He standardized the enlistment at four years. He provided good and regular pay—here the idea that the king is wealthy is crucial. He offered better logistical support for the bureaucracy and regular inspections by *intendants*. Finally, he expanded the army to 300,000 men, the largest army in Europe at the time. It was also Europe's greatest.

Because after the Fronde, most Frenchmen yearned for peace and quiet, Louis almost never had to use his army on his people, which meant that he could use it on his neighbors. As with his financial and religious policies, Louis's foreign policy would increase his power and prestige in the short run, but bring misery to his people in the long run.

The road to ruin for Louis XIV lay, as it had for Philip II, through Spain. Remember Spain? In the 17th century, Spain still ruled a vast empire that included the Spanish Netherlands (roughly modern Belgium), southern Italy, most of Central and South America, and the Philippines. But, as that list implies, Spain had overextended itself in the 16th and early 17th centuries. The Protestant Netherlands had been lost in 1609 and Portugal in 1640. As we have seen, Spain's involvement in the Wars of Religion, culminating in the Thirty Years' War had left its treasury deeply in debt and its military forces weak. By the 1670s, Spain was the sick man of Europe, a rotting hulk of an empire.

Louis planned to raid the deathbed. He wanted to wear the crown of Spain as well as that of France. Now that may seem crazy—a pipe dream—but God seemed be playing into Louis's hands given the Spanish throne's current occupant. First, Louis had a claim to the throne because in 1659–1660, in one of his last acts of statesmanship, Mazarin had engineered the Treaty of the Pyrenees, ending the conflict with Spain that begun in the Thirty Years' War. The capstone of the treaty was Louis's marriage to a Spanish princess, Marie Therese. That wouldn't have mattered, of course, if the King of Spain had had heirs. But since 1665, Spain had been ruled by the sickly and mentally incompetent Carlos II (*Carlos Segundo*).

Carlos was something of a walking medical experiment, for he was the product of centuries of Habsburg interbreeding. Remember the Habsburgs? Remember how many territories they ruled in the early modern period? The way they did that was by marrying into various royal houses and then marrying into each other's royal houses. This kept the Holy Roman Empire, Spain, and lots of other places in the family, but it was hell on the family gene pool.

Carlos was the end result. Among the highlights of his medical history, he was unable to stand unaided until his fourth year. He took seven years to learn how to walk. His jaw was deformed, which made the simple act of chewing food an ordeal. He was mentally impaired and almost certainly impotent.

We have seen that monarchs were thought to embody the nation over which they ruled. Carlos, known as *El Hechizado* ("the bewitched") certainly embodied what his nation had become. Because Carlos was obviously not going to produce an heir, the Spanish throne and empire would be up for grabs when he died. Louis's position, bolstered by his marriage to a Spanish princess, was simple: "Why not Louis?"

The result would be the greatest empire the world had ever seen. He took his first step toward that goal in 1667 when his armies swept into the Spanish Netherlands (roughly modern day Belgium, not to be confused with the Dutch Republic, which was independent to the north; we'll get to them in a minute). Thereafter, Louis took an avid interest in Carlos's health, sending ambassador after ambassador to inquire, "And how does his Catholic Majesty feel today? How does he look? We're very concerned for him, you know."

Louis's plan was that as soon as Carlos shuffled off to his heavenly reward, the French army would sweep across the Pyrenees and capture Madrid. But Carlos clung to his dismal existence year after year, and there was yet another problem with the plan: the Dutch.

Obviously, Louis's dream was Europe's worst nightmare. The Catholic Habsburg Holy Roman Emperors feared it. The Anglican English feared it, and the Protestant Netherlands and northern German princes feared it. If Louis could combine French military power with the wealth of the New World, he would be unstoppable, and international Protestantism would be in jeopardy. International trade would become a French monopoly.

But the rest of Europe was not really in a position to do much about it. The Holy Roman Empire was preoccupied with Muslim Ottoman invaders to the east, whom Louis, cynically and actively encouraged to attack his fellow Catholic prince. In other words, here you have Louis, a Catholic making a big deal about being a Catholic, and he's encouraging a Muslim empire to attack Catholic Austria—talk about *Realpolitik*. England had its own crisis in the 17th century, as we'll see in the next lecture. It was wracked by a Civil War from 1642–1660. The German princes were militarily weak. Louis gradually gobbled them up in a series of border wars in the 1670s and 1680s.

Only the Netherlands had the wealth and the resolve to stand against Louis's dreams of European monarchy. In the 1670s and 1680s, the

Dutch leader (or stadholder) was William of Orange. This is the great-grandson of William the Silent. He rallied his people and the European powers against Louis.

William is interesting. Like Louis, William had had a formative childhood memory. He lost his ancestral homeland, Orange, to a French invasion. He remembered as a small boy having to flee before French armies, this time when the Dutch Republic itself was attacked in 1672. As an adult, he saw clearly the danger of Louis's ambitions; that the Dutch were the only major republican and Protestant continental state west of the Rhine; that they would need friends—a grand alliance—to maintain a balance of power to contain Louis XIV. William's life mission began to be to create that grand alliance against the Bourbon Catholic domination of Europe. That is why, for Louis, the road to Madrid lay through Amsterdam.

Louis knew that if he ever invaded Spain itself, he would face a Dutch invasion on his northern border. And so the Sun King spent the 1670s and 1680s conquering the many small states along the Rhine and Dutch border: Franche-Comté, Luxemburg, Lorraine, Orange (which we've mentioned before), and the Spanish Netherlands. He didn't actually need Orange; he just wanted to stick it to William. The point was to encircle the Netherlands and cut it off from potential Protestant allies like Hanover; Brandenburg, Prussia; Denmark; and other German princes. By the late 1680s, Louis was planning his *coup de grâce*—a final war to wipe the Dutch off the map. In the words of his finance minister, Jean-Baptist Colbert, "It is impossible that his Majesty should tolerate any longer the insolence and arrogance of that nation."

By 1688, Louis XIV was on the verge of becoming the virtual emperor of the Western World. But the Dutch were about to get a great ally, one that would bring the Sun King not only to the bargaining table, but metaphorically to his knees. Unexpectedly, and for reasons that will take two whole lectures to explain, the Dutch would find that ally in England.

Lecture Eleven
English Constitutionalism—1603–49

Scope:

The English response to the crisis of the 17th century was far less neat than the French. The Stuart monarchs of England struggled with Parliament and their own foibles and extravagancies over taxation, religion, and foreign policy. The result was the British Civil Wars, which culminated in the trial and execution of King Charles I in 1649.

Outline

I. Nearly every problem faced by the English monarchy in the 17th century can be traced back to the 16th century and the reign of Henry VIII.

   A. A century before Louis XIV, Henry had sought to strengthen the English monarchy against a repeat of the Wars of the Roses.

   B. But in making himself head of Church and state, in relying on Parliament to do so, and in spending recklessly on repeated wars, Henry left a series of problems for his successors.

   C. Instead of anticipating Louis XIV's five rules of absolutism, Henry created five problems that prevented absolutism: the problems of royal personality, of control and sovereignty, of royal finance, of religion, and of foreign policy.

   1. The problem of royal personality: Because Henry, like Louis, was larger than life; he set the bar impossibly high for his children and subsequent monarchs.

   a. Edward was a sickly adolescent who died shy of his 18th birthday.

   b. Mary and Elizabeth were women.

   c. In short, his successors did not conform to the expectations of the Great Chain of Being.

   2. The problem of control and sovereignty: Henry VIII clearly wanted to be a more powerful sovereign.

    a. To throw the pope out of England, Henry had to rely on parliamentary legislation.

        i. Parliament already had the right to approve or disapprove of taxes.

        ii. From now on, it would also claim the right to debate and legislate religion.

    b. Each of Henry's successors also went through Parliament to get their religious settlements: Edward VI to establish Protestantism, Mary to re-establish Catholicism, and Elizabeth I in 1559 to establish the Anglican compromise.

    c. Empowering Parliament raises a question in England that would never be raised in France: Who was truly sovereign, the king or Parliament?

3. The problem of royal finance: As mentioned, Parliament had the right to approve or disapprove of taxes.

    a. For centuries, the English king could tax his subjects only with Parliament's permission.

    b. Henry loved to spend money on wars and over 60 palaces.

    c. Henry's great minister, Thomas Cromwell, secured him a windfall when the two dissolved all the Catholic monasteries in England.

    d. This should have brought the Crown £90,000 additional a year, but Henry wanted quick cash for his wars and sold off the monastic lands, thus impoverishing the Crown in the long run while enriching the landed gentry (the lower aristocracy) of England.

4. The problem of religion: Henry wrenched England from Rome but refused to bring it to the Protestant side as represented at the Peace of Augsburg (1555).

    a. He was congenitally attracted to Catholicism but only really supported by Protestants.

    b. His son, Edward VI, imposed a stricter Protestantism during his six-year reign.

    c. His daughter, Mary, reestablished Roman Catholicism during her five-year reign.

     d. Henry's last daughter, Elizabeth, promoted a compromise: a Church of England that was more or less Protestant in doctrine but Catholic in ritual and hierarchy.

     e. This left extremists on each side—diehard Catholics and Puritans—hoping to force the country to their own views on religion.

   5. The problem of foreign policy: Henry VIII died leaving England alienated from Spain, embroiled in war with Scotland and France, and financially exhausted.

     a. Edward lost the war in Scotland.

     b. Mary lost a second war with France.

     c. Elizabeth staved off the Spanish War as long as she could but spent the last 15 years of her reign fighting it.

     d. Through it all, England struggled against richer, more powerful countries, wondering whether it should retreat behind its watery walls or embrace a major role in Europe.

II. Because Elizabeth died the Virgin Queen in 1603, she was succeeded by her next Protestant heir, King James VI (1603–1625) of Scotland.

  A. By contemporary standards, James was not godlike (the problem of royal personality).

   1. James's Scottish heritage was difficult to stomach for his English subjects.

   2. James's informal, unconventional personal behavior contrasted with the Tudors.

  B. James was not in control (the problem of control and sovereignty).

   1. James rarely got along with Parliament.

   2. Because he could not afford an efficient bureaucracy, James relied on the goodwill of unpaid aristocrats to watch the country for him.

  C. James was not wealthy (the problem of royal finance).

   1. The English administration was corrupt and inefficient.

   2. James spent money he did not have on buildings, masques, parties, and royal favorites.

3. His debts rose from £300,000 in 1603 to £1,000,000 by 1621.

D. James did not control the religion of the country (the problem of religion), or, rather, his three countries.

    1. England was mostly Anglican.

        a. But Puritans wanted an even more Protestant settlement, like Scotland's Presbyterianism.

        b. Catholics were a tiny but hated minority by 1603, constantly feared because of such events as the attempted invasion of the Spanish Armada in 1588 or the failed Gunpowder Plot to blow up the king and Houses of Parliament in 1605.

    2. Scotland was mostly Presbyterian, with some Catholics in the Highlands.

    3. Ireland was mostly Catholic, but land and power had been taken over by Scots and English Protestants.

    4. James dealt well with this mess largely by not dealing with it.

E. James did not have an army (the problem of foreign policy) because he did not have any money.

    1. This was fine with James because, unusually for a king, he sought to be a *rex pacificus*, a peaceful king who would heal the religious and diplomatic rifts that tore Europe.

    2. This peace policy was unpopular, especially with Puritans, who wanted an aggressive Protestant foreign policy and a role in the Thirty Years' War.

III. Charles I (1625–1649) appeared, on the surface of things, to be an improvement on his father.

A. He was more dignified but also more rigid.

    1. Charles expected instantaneous obedience.

    2. He refused to compromise or explain the reasons for his actions.

B. Charles was no better at dealing with Parliament than his father had been.

    1. Despite needing money desperately, he prorogued (suspended) Parliament repeatedly.

    2. He finally tried to dissolve Parliament for good in 1629.

    3. He ruled without Parliament for 11 years.

C. Charles was no wealthier than his father but just as extravagant.

  1. Charles assembled the most magnificent art collection in Europe.

  2. But after dissolving Parliament in 1629, Charles had to live within his means.

   a. He trimmed expenses, launching a major retrenchment of government called "Thorough."

   b. He maximized revenue through dubiously legal taxes.

  3. These measures were unpopular, and England began to go on a tax strike in 1638.

D. In religion, Charles was a High Church Anglican but also an inflexible man who wanted every one of his subjects to worship as he did.

  1. He promoted High Church bishops who wanted more hierarchy and ceremony and less Puritanism.

  2. He persecuted Puritans for failing to conform to Anglican ritual.

  3. Worse, Charles was married to the Catholic princess Henrietta Maria (1609–1669) of France.

  4. All of these issues led Charles's subjects to wonder whether the king was a secret Catholic.

  5. He upset his Scottish subjects in 1637 when he tried to force an Anglican-style prayer book on Presbyterian Scotland.

  6. This led to the Bishops' Wars, which began in 1637 and lasted to 1642. [In 1641, Irish Catholics took advantage of the distraction to rebel against their Protestant landlords.]

  7. By 1642, the English Parliament came to believe that it, not Charles, represented the interests of the nation and that royal policy had to be stopped.

  8. That conviction led to the English Civil War of 1642–1646.

E. Charles had no regular army with which to fight these British civil wars (1637–1660).

  1. He relied on wealthy aristocrats and local militias (nicknamed Cavaliers) for his army.

2. In response, after much to-ing and fro-ing, Parliament raised a professional force, the New Model Army (nicknamed Roundheads, for the ordinary people who lacked courtier hair).

3. The New Model Army defeated the king in 1646.

IV. When King Charles would not negotiate in good faith, Parliament tried and convicted him on a charge of high treason in 1649.

A. When the king questioned the court's legitimacy at trial, Parliament responded that it represented the interests of the people.

B. The king was publicly executed on 30 January 1649.

C. For the first time in English history, the English people had judicially and publicly murdered their king.

D. Within weeks, the Rump Parliament abolished the monarchy and the House of Lords and proclaimed England a republic.

E. Would England now settle down and the English people accept rule by the Rump, the gentry, and the army in a truncated Chain of Being?

F. Or would England demand that the revolution go farther and embrace such radical notions as democracy and religious toleration?

Supplementary Reading:

M. B. Chambers, et al., *Western Experience*, chapter 15, section IV.

M. Kishlansky, *A Monarchy Transformed: Britain, 1603–1714*, chapters 1–7.

Questions to Consider:

1. To what extent were the British Civil Wars the fault of the Tudors, the fault of the Stuarts, or a result of long-term structural problems within the British state(s)?

2. Was the trial and execution of Charles I legal? Just? Deserved?

Lecture Eleven—Transcript
English Constitutionalism—1603–49

In our last lecture we saw that France, or at least King Louis XIV, reacted to the crisis of the 17th century by embracing royal Absolutism, a system in which the king explicitly claimed his power from God and wielded it as a god would do. Louis used the power and wealth of France to threaten the freedom of all Western Europeans by angling for control of the Spanish Empire. Spain itself had grown weak and defeatist due to crushing debts from its century-long *jihad* against Protestantism and rule by the imbecile Carlos II (*Carlos Segundo*).

The other great Habsburg empire to the east, the Holy Roman Empire, was unable to challenge Louis because it was occupied with attacks by the Ottoman Empire (often encouraged by Louis), and the German princes were too weak to credibly oppose him. Only the Dutch under William of Orange stood against the Sun King; but despite a century of Dutch commercial success, it seemed only a matter of time before they and European Protestantism were overwhelmed. As the 1680s drew to a close, that time seemed very near.

The Netherlands' one hope—the one unanswered question in European diplomacy—was, "What would England do?" That question would have seemed absurd to the Sun King, for England had spent most of 17th century being wracked by civil wars, rebellion, economic depression, religious strife, and, of course, English weather. If Spain was the sick man of Europe, England was its resident lunatic. So how could events in England possibly derail the "Sun King Express?" That is what the next lecture will be about.

In this one, I have to explain why England did not seem to be very much of a threat to Louis; why England was perceived as the least stable state in Europe; why England chose a very different path from Louis's Absolutism; and why, in fact, 17th century England violated every rule of Absolutism and still got away with it.

To explain that, I'm afraid that I have to go back into the mists of time, a century before that of Louis XIV, to possibly the one European monarch who could claim an ego to match the Sun King. I mean, of course, Henry VIII.

In print and in another course for this company, I have argued that nearly every problem faced by the English monarchy in the 17th century can be traced back to the 16th century and the reign of Henry VIII. Put another way, if English kings failed to invent, and later broke, the five rules of Absolutism, it was because Henry had made it so difficult for them.

You will recall that a century before Louis XIV was even a gleam in Anne of Austria's eye (there is some doubt as to whether his purported father Louis XIII was capable of "gleaming"), Henry had sought to strengthen the English monarchy against a repeat of the War of the Roses. In a sense, the problem facing Henry in the 16th century was not all that different from that that would face Louis in the 17th after the Fronde.

But in making himself Head of Church and State, in breaking from the Church, in relying on Parliament to do so, in marrying multiple wives, and in spending recklessly on repeated wars, Henry VIII left a series of problems for his successors. That is, instead of creating five rules of Absolutism, he created five problems that prevented it. They are 1) the problem of royal personality; 2) the problem of royal control and sovereignty; 3) the problem of royal finances; 4) the problem of religion; and 5) the problem of foreign policy. If you're paying attention, it should be obvious that those are the very obverse of Louis's solutions.

First, the problem of royal personality. Henry, like Louis, was larger than life. He had no problem claiming to be "God on Earth;" but having made the claim, he set the bar impossibly high for his children and subsequent monarchs. His son, Edward, was a sickly adolescent boy who died shy of his 18th birthday. Mary and Elizabeth were women. None of this conforms with the Great Chain of Being.

As far as the problem of control and sovereignty is concerned, Henry VIII clearly wanted to be a more powerful sovereign. But to throw the pope out of England, he had relied on parliamentary legislation. The Act in Restraint of Appeals of 1533 forbad appeals of cases such as divorce to Rome. The Act of Supremacy of 1534 is what made him Supreme Head of the Church of England. Basically, Henry didn't want to go it alone. Breaking from the Catholic Church was such a scary and momentous thing to do that even Henry felt that he needed friends.

Now, Parliament already had the right to approve or disapprove of taxes. But now Henry had given them the right to debate and legislate religion as well. So, each of Henry's successors went through Parliament to get their religious settlements: Edward VI to establish Protestantism; Mary, to reestablish Catholicism; and Elizabeth I in 1559, to establish the Anglican compromise.

Fine. They got the religious settlements they wanted; but empowering a body like Parliament in this way raised a question in England that would never be raised in France: Who is truly sovereign? King or Parliament?

Then there's the problem of royal finances. For centuries, the English king could only tax his subjects with Parliament's permission—permission that they sometimes refused. They even refused Henry VIII. Worse, Henry, like Louis a century later, loved to spend money. He owned over 60 palaces. He patronized artists and writers. He built magnificent naval ships. You can still see the Mary Rose at Portsmouth, or what's left of it.

He fought a series of wars against France, Scotland, and the Holy Roman Empire. The first of these wars drained the royal finances. The last, against France and Scotland simultaneously, cost over £3 million on an annual revenue of maybe £100,000.

Henry's great minister, Thomas Cromwell, secured him a windfall when they dissolved the Catholic monasteries in England. Cromwell's plan was, "I know my king likes to spend money. I'm going to find a way to endow the monarchy permanently."

This should have brought the Crown £90,000 additional a year; but Henry wanted quick cash for his wars, and so he sold off the monastic lands. That had two long-term effects. It enriched the gentry (the sort of lower aristocracy of England) and made them more important. But it also drained the royal treasury in the long run. For the future, English kings would be relatively impoverished. As a result, the Tudor monarchy was chronically short of funds, and never free to pursue its wildest ambitions.

Then there was the problem of religion. You know this already. Henry wrenched England from Rome, but he refused to bring it to Augsburg. That is, he was congenitally attracted to Catholicism, yet he was only really supported by Protestants. That left confusion in its wake. After oscillating between Protestantism and Catholicism under Edward and Mary, England finally opted, under Elizabeth, for a compromise: the Church of England was Protestant in doctrine and Catholic in ritual and hierarchy, leaving extremists on each side with the hope that they could eventually win—die-hard Catholics and Puritan Protestants.

Then there was the problem of foreign policy. Henry VIII died leaving England alienated from Spain and the Holy Roman Empire because of how he treated the pope and Catherine of Aragon; embroiled in war with both Scotland and France; financially exhausted; and incapable of maintaining the large armies and navies needed to win.

Edward lost the war in Scotland. Mary lost a second war in France. Elizabeth staved off the Spanish War as long as she possibly could, but spent the last 15 years of her reign fighting it.

Through it all, England struggled against richer, more powerful countries to find its place. Should England retreat behind its watery walls or embrace a major role in Europe? Compare this with the decisiveness of Louis XIV a century later.

All of these problems help to explain why, contrary to popular belief, Queen Elizabeth died relatively unpopular. Her subjects grumbled about her imperious manner, a continuing war, high taxation, and religion. Since she died a virgin queen, this event brought a new family to the throne of England: the Scottish House of Stuart. Lots of people anticipated the new family in 1603 with great hope. Nobody knew it at the time, but they would do even worse.

James I of England had actually ruled Scotland as James VI since his mother's abdication, when he was an infant, in 1568. But James was a very different fish from Henry VIII. As we saw in an earlier lecture, James liked to trumpet that kings were practically gods on earth. He was one of the major proponents of the notion that kings ruled by Divine Right. To that extent, Louis XIV would have found him very congenial.

But the problem with this is that, by contemporary standards, James was not very godlike. That brings us back to the problem of royal personality. It was not James's fault, of course, that he didn't look much like a god or that he had spindly legs in an age when a shapely calf became a man. Those legs supported an ungainly body crowned by an overly large head. That head housed a tongue that was itself too large for his mouth, causing a pronounced lisp. The lisp exacerbated a stutter and a thick Scots accent.

All this might be overlooked in our day and age, or even celebrated in the name of diversity, but not in James's day. It is an unfortunate comment on human nature that appearance really does matter. In this case, the contrast with the Tudors' regal bearing didn't play to James's advantage. It didn't help that English people hated the Scots. They fought the Scots for centuries and thought of their northern neighbors as rude impoverished brigands.

It did not help that James came south accompanied by an entourage of what were called the "hungry Scots," that is, Scottish courtiers who were thought to see England as a vast treasure house to plunder.

Above all, James's personal behavior contrasted with the Tudors. He was a remarkably informal man—affable, with a poor head for drink. This put people at ease and it brought them to court, but it also reduced their fear. It meant that he wasn't nearly so good at keeping people off balance as the Tudors had been.

James hated crowds. Queen Elizabeth loved to go out amongst the crowds on her progresses. He rarely did so. Once, when told that a group of his loving subjects had gathered to express their love for him, he replied with characteristic earthiness, "God's wounds! I will put down my breaches and show them my arse."

In his later years, he grew lazy, neglecting business to hunt or spend time with the favorites. Then there was the matter of those favorites. James was married to Anne of Denmark. They had several children. He clearly preferred, however, the company of handsome young men, on whom he lavished offices, titles, lands, and affection—often public affection. Thus, one Puritan gentleman reported his shock after observing the king with his favorites, "Kissing them after so lascivious a mode in public [as] ...prompted many to imagine some things done in the tiring house that exceed my expression." There is some debate among historians as to whether James was a practicing homosexual. In a sense, it doesn't matter. The king's physical affection for his favorites contrasted sharply with the bluff masculinity of the Tudors (even the female Tudors, if you stop and think about it).

In conclusion, it should be obvious that many of the king's personality traits would have been perfectly acceptable in our own day; but in the context of his times and office, James's manner was problematic. It clearly offended his more conservative contemporaries, who were used to the Tudors. This made it more difficult for him to overawe Parliament, as they would have done, by his appearance and by his behavior. That was a problem because English kings needed Parliament because, unlike French kings, they were not in control.

This brings us to the problem of control and sovereignty. Unlike the King of France, James had to deal with Parliament, with which he rarely got along. He once complained to the Spanish ambassador that he didn't understand how his predecessors ever allowed such an institution to even be thought of. This is like President Kennedy complaining to Anatoli Dobrynin about Congress, because the guy he's complaining to—the Spanish ambassador—is, of course, one of England's great enemies.

James couldn't afford an efficient bureaucracy. He relied on the goodwill of his aristocrats. So the king is not in control; nor was he wealthy (the problem of royal finances). English administration was corrupt and inefficient. James spent money on buildings (the Banqueting House at Whitehall, Greenwich Palace), masques and parties, and favorites. His debts rose from £300,000 at his succession in 1603 to £600,000 by 1608, and £1,000,000 by 1621.

Nor did James control the religion of the country (the problem of religion). The first problem is that the Stuarts didn't rule one country; they ruled three countries. Remember that when James became the King of England, he was also the King of Scotland. By becoming King of England, he also became King of Ireland as well.

England, as we have seen, was mostly Anglican. But, as we have also seen, the Puritans wanted an even more Protestant settlement, such as Scotland's Presbyterianism, with less ritual and ceremony, and less hierarchy (no bishops). Catholics were a tiny minority by 1603, but they were hated, thanks to the persecutions of Bloody Mary; the attempted Spanish Armada invasion in 1588; and the Gunpowder Plot of 1605, in which Catholic hotheads had tried to blow up the king in the House of Lords.

The English also feared invasion from Catholic Ireland. Scotland was mostly Presbyterian, sort of in the same direction and inclination of Protestantism as the Puritans. There were some Catholics in the Highlands. Ireland was mostly Catholic; but land and power had been stripped from Catholics and rested now with a small minority of Scots and English Protestants. All of these groups hated each other. The result was a religious mess.

James actually dealt with the mess pretty well. He wasn't a zealot. He was content to let sleeping dogs lie—he didn't poke them; he didn't try to make anybody conform; and that was wise.

Finally, and one reason it's wise, is that James did not have an army, which brings us to the problem of foreign policy. He didn't have an army, of course, because he didn't have any money. This was okay with James, in a way, because, unlike Henry before or Louis afterwards, James never figured himself for a great warrior prince. Rather, James sought to be a *"Rex Pacificus,"* a peaceful king who would heal the religious and diplomatic rifts that tore Europe.

Immediately upon his accession—remember, the War with the Spanish Armada was still raging at the end of Elizabeth's reign—James worked out a treaty, the Treaty of London, with Spain in 1605. He kept England out of the Thirty Years' War and thus, out of some of the most terrible bloodshed of the 17th century.

This seems entirely admirable now, but, at the time, it led Englishmen to wonder what was wrong with James. Why didn't he pursue a red-blooded, anti-Catholic, anti-Spanish, anti-French foreign policy? Isn't that what English kings were for?

So somewhat ironically, James's peace policy, which kept his country out of the disasters of the Thirty Years' War and which might have won him a Nobel Prize today, caused Englishmen to find him less godlike. Henry VIII they liked. He spent the whole country into debt and he started all these wars he couldn't finish. James, they're not so sure about.

In 1625, James died and was succeeded by his only surviving son, who became Charles, now known as Charles I. Charles appeared, on the surface of things, to be a definite improvement on his father. First, he was more dignified, so you get godlike points. The problem of royal personality looks to be solved; except that Charles was a zealot who expected instantaneous obedience and who refused to compromise or explain the reasons for his actions.

Nor was he better than his father at dealing with Parliament, which means that he wasn't in control. Despite needing money desperately, Charles repeatedly sent Parliament home whenever they questioned his policies. He finally tried to dissolve them for good in 1629 and he ended up ruling without Parliament for 11 years.

But because Parliament voted the taxes, what did he do for money? Charles was no wealthier than his dad, and he was just as extravagant. He liked to spend money on his magnificent art collection—the best art collection in Europe. He patronized Rubens. He brought Van Dyck to England, who painted a great lot of royal portraits, which are quite beautiful.

But after 1629 (his dissolution of Parliament), he had to trim expenses. This ended up being a major retrenchment of government called "Thorough"—that was actually the name of the program.

He also sought to maximize revenue. From henceforward, Charles's government was funded through forced loans. A royal official would turn up and say, "You're loaning the king some money. Thank you very much." Customs impositions meant that he raised the rates charged on duty on goods coming into the country without asking Parliament's permission. Feudal dues: Charles's lawyers looked through the books for any old law they could find whereby they could charge you. For example, if the king knighted his son, they could charge you for doing that. Finally, ship money: a tax that had been levied on port cities to support the Royal Navy, which Charles extended to inland cities, which never saw a ship. The result was terribly unpopular. These taxes were dubiously legal and the country went on tax strike by 1638.

But Charles's most unpopular policies came in the area of religion. Charles was an Anglican, but unlike his dad, Charles was also an inflexible man who wanted every one of his subjects to worship just the way he did. This is very much the way Louis XIV would think a generation later; but remember that Louis XIV wasn't ruling three countries with very different religious make-ups.

Charles promoted High Church bishops who persecuted Puritans for failing to conform to middle of the road, or High Church, Anglican practice. Worse, for diplomatic reasons, he was married to a

Catholic, Princess Henrietta Maria of France. That meant that the court was full of Catholics. It also raised the question of how the children would be raised. All of these elements led his subjects to wonder: what kind of a Protestant is this guy? Maybe he's secretly a Catholic. He upset his Scottish subjects in 1637 when he tried to force an Anglican-style High Church prayer book on Presbyterian Scotland. Scotland erupted into open rebellion known as the Bishop's Wars, which began in 1637 and lasted to 1642.

By 1642, Parliament came to believe that it represented the interests of the people better than the king did. Now, in fact, it really represented the aristocracy and merchants who voted for it; but it was the principle that counts here. They also came to believe that royal policy was increasingly harmful to those interests—that is, the interests of the people—and that the king had to be stopped. This idea that the king might not embody the welfare of the country, that he might have to obey a higher law than his own—that is, his responsibility to the people—and that he might have to answer to his subjects, is revolutionary. But in order to prove their point, Parliament ended up having to fight the king. The result was the First English Civil War, which lasted from 1642–1646.

Now remember, we haven't talked about one more thing Charles doesn't have: he doesn't have an army. He was too poor. So he had to rely on wealthy aristocrats and local militias, who, in part because they were so dashing, were known as "cavaliers." He also tried to get an army from Ireland. That wasn't very popular in anti-Catholic England.

After lots of to-ing and fro-ing, Parliament, too, raised an army—a professional army that they called the New Model Army. It was commanded by Thomas Fairfax and its leading cavalry commander was named Oliver Cromwell (remember that name). The nickname for the New Model Army was the "roundheads" because it employed lots of ordinary people—common people—who normally did not have long hair the way that courtiers did. They worked for a living, and so they couldn't afford to be dressing their hair all the time.

The New Model Army defeated the king in 1646. That doesn't mean you've won. You still have a king. You still have to work out a settlement with him. There ensued years of negotiation and broken agreements, because, quite frankly, Charles I had no intention of "treaty-ing" with rebels.

Finally, when King Charles would not negotiate in good faith—remember, he's rigid—Parliament put him on trial on a charge of high treason in January 1649. But this raises a problem. High treason? High treason against what? Treason was normally a crime against the king. The law was the king's law. How could Charles be guilty of treason against himself? How could he be guilty of violating his own law?

Parliament's solution was to charge the king with violating not statute law, but a more fundamental unwritten law, hinted at in his coronation oath—his responsibility to his subjects:

> Whereas it is notorious that Charles Stuart, the now King of England,...hath had a wicked design totally to subvert the ancient and fundamental laws and liberties of this nation, and in their trade to introduce arbitrary and tyrannical government, and that ...he hath prosecuted it with fire and sword, levied and maintained a cruel war in the land against the Parliament and kingdom, whereby the country hath been miserably wasted, the public treasure exhausted, trade decayed, thousands of people murdered, and infinite other mischiefs committed....

Put simply, the king was charged with committing treason not against himself, but against the English Constitution and the English people. This is a revolutionary idea: that a ruler's chief responsibility is not to God and not to himself, but to the people over whom he rules. Even more revolutionary is the idea that if he failed in that duty, he could be held accountable by a court and jury not of his peers, but of his subjects. Unlike the Fronde, this is a revolution with an intellectual underpinning, which anticipated Locke by 50 years.

In fact, the king refused to plead to the charge. He didn't recognize this court, so you won't be surprised that the verdict was a foregone conclusion: guilty. The sentence was given on January 27 and, as in all treason trials, it was death.

At this point, Charles demanded to speak, but the court refused to hear him. In the meantime, Oliver Cromwell used every means of persuasion he had to secure 59 signers to the most notorious death warrant in English history. The king was taken to St. James's Palace while a scaffold was built at Whitehall. The night before his death, he burnt his papers, he said goodbye to his youngest children, and he urged them never to compromise with the rebels. You see, Charles may have lost the war and he may be about to lose his life, but he wanted to make sure that there was a monarchy left to be preserved after his death. It's the only piece of foresight and prescience he ever experienced.

On the morning of his death, he and his attendants took some time over his appearance. He actually joked with his groom of the bedchamber to take care of his hair and his head, "Though it has not long to stand on my shoulders, take all the care you can of my head." He also asked about the weather. He wanted to know the temperature. When told it was cold, he put on two shirts. He didn't want to shiver because he didn't want anyone to think he was afraid.

Finally, a Parliamentary guard took him and at 1:30 p.m., he was escorted through the Banqueting House at Whitehall. The Banqueting House was one of those expensive building projects that had led the English to their taxpayer revolt. It's today the only part of Whitehall Palace that still stands. You too can walk Charles I's route.

He walked through a window against which the scaffold had been built. At the end of his walk, facing west, he saw the scaffold draped in black, at the center of which was the block. Beyond the block were rows of Parliamentary soldiers in red coats, and beyond them and below them, a crowd of ordinary Londoners—the very people in whose name this action was about to be carried out.

The king emerged into the gray January light and asked to speak, but dogged with ill luck to the last, his voice failed him. Had the crowd been able to hear that voice, they would have heard him make an argument that, "A subject and a sovereign are clean different things." To kill him was to kill God's authority and so, to kill law and order in the state. Therefore he, not Parliament, represented the true interests of his subjects. He ended by claiming that he was the "martyr of the people."

He then turned to his faithful Bishop of London, William Juxon, who had accompanied him to the scaffold. He looked him squarely in the eye and he said, "Remember!" Poor Juxon spent the rest of his life trying to figure out exactly what it was he was supposed to remember. Was it the execution? Who could forget what happened next?

The king turned back to the block and said to Juxon that his executioner sent him, "From a corruptible...to an incorruptible crown." He then knelt. He said a silent prayer and extended his hands. This was the predetermined signal that he was ready. The axe fell. The henchman then raised the severed head of the king for all to see. According to one eyewitness, "At the instant when the blow was given, there was such a deep universal groan amongst the thousands of people...as I never heard before and desire never to hear again."

And well might they have groaned. For the first time in English history, the English people had judicially and publicly murdered their king. Such an action went against the Great Chain of Being and a thousand years of sermons, ceremonies, traditions, and propaganda. Remember, they hadn't just killed him in battle or in rebellion. They had done it through legal means.

For a thousand years, Europeans had been taught that their king was virtually "God on Earth," the "Father of the Nation," sacrosanct and inviolable like a Roman tribune. Now he and those habits of mind had been violated. Within weeks, the Rump Parliament abolished the monarchy and abolished the House of Lords. England was now, for the first and only time in its history, a republic.

But it was not yet a democracy. The civil wars, the execution of the king, and the establishment of that republic had been worked out by and in the interests of a very small oligarchy of landed gentry and urban merchants.

The next question was, "Would England now settle down?" Would the English people, in whose name the civil wars had been fought and the king executed, now accept rule by a small group of parliamentary gentry and the army, as they had once accepted rule by the Stuarts? Or would they demand that the revolution go farther and embrace such radical notions as democracy and religious toleration?

On a deeper level, what did these events mean? Had the English people and their representatives committed a heinous act, murdering not only a king, but law and order and justice? Or had they taken the first steps toward freedom and modernity?

Lecture Twelve
English Constitutionalism—1649–89

Scope:

After the execution of the king, the English people experimented with a republic called the Commonwealth ruled by Parliament, followed by a protectorate ruled by Oliver Cromwell, before inviting the return of the Stuart monarchy in 1660. The restored Stuarts, Charles II and James II, sought to emulate Louis XIV by pursuing absolutism, but the power of Parliament over royal finances and the English people's rejection of Catholicism thwarted their plans. Finally, in 1688, the Protestant William of Orange invaded England and, with the support of the English people, overthrew King James II. The "Glorious Revolution" of 1688–1689 made England a Protestant constitutional monarchy and set the pattern for an alternative, more democratic form of government in Europe and the Americas.

Outline

I. The Commonwealth (1649–1653): Immediately upon the execution of the king, Parliament declared England a republic.

    A. Like the *Frondeur* aristocracy of France, the members of Parliament, landowners, and merchants who engineered this revolution now wanted it to stop, with themselves at the top of the social hierarchy.

        1. But in killing the king, they had provided an opportunity and an example for ordinary people to break more links in the Great Chain of Being.

        2. Many ordinary people, including the soldiers of the New Model Army, no longer wanted to be ruled by someone else.

        3. In particular, a group arose in the army called the Levelers who wanted religious toleration, law reform, and universal manhood suffrage.

        4. One participant in the New Model Army's debates over England's post-war constitution, Colonel Thomas Rainsborough, propounded the Leveler notion of

contract and consent bubbling up from the people themselves— half a century before Locke.

B. Other groups took advantage of the end of censorship to explore religious possibilities.

   1. The Baptists or "Dippers," believed that baptism, and the choice of faith it implied, should be delayed until adulthood, when one could make a rational choice.

   2. The Seekers actually went from congregation to congregation seeking a permanent home.

   3. The Diggers, led by Gerard Winstanley (c. 1609–1660), believed that Christ wanted property to be shared in common.

   4. The Ranters believed that nothing was a sin unless one conceived it to be a sin.

   5. The Quakers, led by George Fox (1624–1691), believed that all people contained God's inner light in equal measure, implying that a peasant was as good as a lord, a woman as good as a man.

   6. The Muggletonians believed that Lodowick Muggleton (1609–1698), a tailor from the West Country, was the last prophet named in the Revelation.

   7. Most disturbing of all, though, to those who loved order were the Fifth Monarchy Men.

      a. They believed that the Bible had foretold five great monarchies on Earth.

      b. Four had already fallen: Babylon, Persia, Greece, and Rome.

      c. Given that the fifth was to be the kingdom of King Jesus, the Commonwealth was only an interim arrangement, to be brought into conformity with Mosaic Law.

C. Religious toleration and a free press had produced religious and political diversity—or, to contemporary eyes, chaos.

   1. The ruling elite was horrified by the sects and began to think better of the experiment with religious toleration and freedom of speech.

   2. This would doom rule by the Commonwealth and, eventually, the revolution.

D. In the end, the Parliament that ruled the Commonwealth was too radical for conservative country gentlemen and too conservative for Levellers and sectaries.

    1. In 1653, the army, upset at being sent to Ireland to pacify Catholics (which they did with enthusiasm) without being paid, sent Parliament home.

    2. After a number of experiments, the army named its current commander, Oliver Cromwell, Lord Protector (1653–1658) of England, Scotland, and Ireland.

II. Cromwell briefly pursued Louis' policies, even before Louis himself did so.

  A. He assumed many of the trappings of godlike kingship without being king.

  B. Cromwell was a strong, decisive leader and tireless worker.

    1. He divided England into 11 military districts, each ruled by a major general, not unlike the French *intendants*.

    2. The generals were supposed to maintain law and order, keep an eye on Anglicans and Royalists, and suppress rebellion, riot, blasphemy, swearing, drunkenness, gambling, fornication, adultery, indecent fashions, alehouses, playhouses, Sunday sports, and Christmas celebrations.

    3. The generals were terribly unpopular.

    4. Parliament's complaints about money also gave Cromwell fits.

  C. Cromwell, an "independent Puritan," granted religious toleration for all Protestant sects and readmitted the Jews into England—which he saw as part of the Second Coming.

  D. Cromwell pursued an aggressive, Protestant foreign policy.

    1. He crushed rebellions in Ireland and Scotland, in the former case, ruthlessly.

    2. He won a trade war with the Dutch.

    3. He captured Jamaica from the Spanish.

  E. Cromwell was the first solvent ruler of England since Henry VII but at tremendous cost.

    1. The Protectorate's excise tax on beer and other commodities hurt the poor.

2. Cromwell confiscated the lands of Royalists, Anglicans, and Catholics.
3. This activity yielded an annual revenue of £2 million, far more than Charles I had to play with, but at the cost of much grumbling and resentment.

F. Oliver Cromwell died in 1658.

III. As in France, after more than a year of instability, the English ruling elite decided to restore the Stuart monarchy in the person of Charles I's son, Charles II, to the throne of his father. In many ways, Charles II (ruled 1660–1685) and his brother James II (ruled 1685–1688) were reruns of their father and grandfather.

A. Neither Charles II nor James II was godlike.
1. Charles II was witty, affable, and a great conversationalist.
   a. He could, also, be quite undignified.
   b. Having been made cynical by his father's fate, he gave himself over to pleasure in the company of his mistresses, who included the beautiful and ambitious Countess of Castlemaine (who converted to Catholicism), the Duchess of Portsmouth named Louise-Renée de Kéroualle (French and Catholic), and "pretty, witty" Nell Gwynne (Protestant).
2. James II, who succeeded Charles II in 1685, was more dignified, a military man who had shown courage under fire.
   a. He was also less witty, more of a plodder.
   b. Worse in the eyes of his subjects, James II was a Roman Catholic.

B. Neither Charles nor James was in control, unlike their cousin, Louis XIV.
1. Though Charles was lazy, James was a hard worker like Louis XIV.
2. Unlike Louis, they did not have an efficient local bureaucracy at their disposal.
3. Above all, though restored to the throne of their father, the brothers still had to deal with a powerful and sometimes uncooperative Parliament.

C. Neither Charles nor James was wealthy, at least at first.

1. At the restoration, Charles II was voted revenue that was supposed to yield £1,200,000 a year.
   a. But the taxes voted with it did not always yield that amount.
   b. Worse, like his father and grandfather, Charles loved to spend money on art, architecture, his mistresses, and their numerous offspring.
2. Parliament was unwilling to finance these hobbies.
3. In 1685, James was luckier: Because a group of Whigs revolted soon after his accession, Parliament voted him more than £2 million in revenue.

D. Neither Charles nor James could enforce conformity, in part because they did not entirely conform to the Church of England themselves.
1. Both Charles and James were attracted to Catholicism and religious toleration, but Charles was too smart and knew his people too well to do much about it.
2. James was not smart.
   a. As Duke of York, he openly worshipped as a Catholic in the 1670s.
   b. As king, he tried to convince Parliament to legalize Catholicism.
   c. This action was very unpopular, but people put up with it because they assumed that when James died, he would be succeeded by his Protestant daughter Mary, married to William of Orange, the Protestant champion.
   d. But in 1688, James's second wife, Mary Beatrice of Modena, gave birth to a son, who would clearly be raised Catholic, supersede the female Mary, and continue his father's policies.

IV. The Glorious Revolution (1688–1689): At this point, William of Orange decided to invade England, landing in the south on 5 November 1688.

A. James II fled to France on 11 December 1688.

B. After much debate, Parliament, on 13 February 1689, asked William and Mary to take the Crown as William III (1689–1702) and Mary II (1689–1694).

C. These actions began to solve most of the problems plaguing English monarchs since the reign of Henry VIII in a very different way from Louis XIV's solution.

1. The problem of sovereignty: Clearly, the king was not a god because Parliament had chosen him; in effect, Parliament was sovereign.

2. The problem of control: The English king remained powerful, but his financial and diplomatic situation would dictate that he could no longer rule without Parliament.

3. The problem of finance: The revolution would lead to a series of wars with France that would force the Crown and Parliament to finally solve the Crown's money problems by tapping into the growing wealth of the English economy.

4. The problem of religion: Clearly, England would not be Catholic.

    a. England would remain Anglican officially.

    b. Parliament would grant toleration to Puritans, though, because they had supported the revolution.

5. The problem of foreign policy: William's accession would bring the British kingdoms into his fight against France. In fact, the ensuing Nine Years' War would be the first of seven colossal conflicts pitting Britain against France between 1688 and 1815.

6. Finally, the Glorious Revolution marks England's and, thus, Europe's first completely successful break from the Great Chain of Being.

Supplementary Reading:

M. B. Chambers, et al., *Western Experience*, chapter 17, section IV.

M. Kishlansky, *A Monarchy Transformed: Britain, 1603–1714*, chapters 8–13.

Questions to Consider:

1. Was the Restoration Settlement doomed to failure?

2. Was the Revolution of 1688–1689 a liberal revolution or a reassertion of religious bigotry?

Lecture Twelve—Transcript
English Constitutionalism—1649–89

In the last lecture, we saw how the Tudor state inherited by the Stuarts collapsed into civil war and revolution. As in France, the revolutionaries would seek to replace 1,000 years of monarchy with something less traditional; but again as in France, the monarchy would eventually be restored.

The restored Stuarts would prove just as weak as their predecessors. That would lead to another revolution in 1688, which would produce a constitutional monarchy, relative religious toleration, and a serious challenge to France for European domination as well. My task in this lecture is to explain how England became a constitutional monarchy and Europe's greatest hope to stop the juggernaut of Louis XIV.

The government that was established in 1649 was known as the Commonwealth, involving rule by Parliament. Immediately upon the execution of the king, Parliament declared England to be a republic. Like the aristocracy of France, the members of Parliament—the landowners and the merchants who engineered this revolution—now wanted it to stop. They wanted to maintain the Great Chain of Being with themselves at the top, but without having to listen to a king and without having to pay high taxes. They didn't want High Church bishops nosing around in their churches.

But, of course, in killing the king, they had of course violated the Great Chain of Being. Remember that according to the Chain, to break it in any way was to incur the wrath of God. They'd also given the people a model for resistance, and worse, they talked about it. After the king was killed and the Church disestablished, there was no censorship in England. Some 20,000 pamphlets appeared on all sorts of subjects, including wacky ideas such as democracy and freedom of religion. In sanctioning a free press, the revolutionaries gave ordinary people a forum to discuss resistance. In the case of the New Model Army, they even recruited them into that resistance.

Many ordinary people didn't want to go back to hierarchy. As one revolutionary said, "We didn't throw one rider off our backs in order to replace him with another." In particular, a group arose in the army called the Levellers that wanted religious toleration, law reform, and universal manhood suffrage.

Back in 1647, even before the king had been executed, at the Putney debates, the army leadership had debated the form that England's post-war constitution should take. One Colonel Thomas Rainsborough set forth the Leveller position that, "The poorest he that is in England hath a life to live as the greatest he." His corollary was that, "Every man that is to live under a government ought first by his own consent to put himself under that government." Here, half a century before Locke, is the notion of contract and consent bubbling up from the people themselves.

Others took advantage of the new age of freedom to explore religious possibilities. The end of censorship meant freedom in printing the Bible and freedom to interpret it as one saw fit. The result was a whole series of new religious sects. Some of them you've heard of.

They were for example the Baptists, or Dippers. They were descended from the German Anabaptists of the 16th century. They believed that baptism and the choice of faith that it implied should be delayed until adulthood, when one could make a rational choice. This seems reasonable, doesn't it? But contemporaries were outraged at the implications of lots of unbaptized young people. Don't forget that freedom of choice in religion means the end of any notion of a state church that has everybody as its members.

Then there were the Seekers. You didn't stay in this one very long because you were going from congregation to congregation seeking a permanent home.

More alarming to the elite were the Diggers, led by Gerard Winstanley, who believed that the Bible did not sanction private property. They thought that Christ wanted it to be shared in common. Just imagine what the landed gentry of England thought of that one. They established communes, which collapsed because of bad weather and also the hostility of local elites.

Then there were the Ranters. They were more alarming still. They believed that nothing was a sin unless you conceived it to be a sin. According to Laurence Clarkson, "[S]in hath its conception only in the imagination.... There is no such act as drunkenness, adultery and theft in God.... What act soever is done by thee in light and love, is light and lovely, though it be that act called adultery.... No matter what Scripture, saints, or churches say, if that within thee do not condemn thee, thou shalt not be condemned." Woohoo!

Contemporaries thought that this gave the Ranters an excuse to party, party, party. So everyone, including other sects, condemned the Ranters, leading the Parliament to pass acts against blasphemy and adultery.

They were just as concerned about the Quakers, who, led by George Fox, believed that all people contained God's inner light (the Holy Spirit, or the Spirit of Christ) in equal measure. That's the rub. This inner light was to be obeyed over the dictates of the state, the Church, and even scripture. Because everyone possesses the inner light in equal measure, a peasant must be as good as a lord, and a woman as good as a man. Consequently, Quakers refused to acknowledge earthly authorities such as the state, the Church, and the courts. Rather, they publicly stressed God's impending vengeance on what they called "the great ones of the Earth." Thus, they refused to swear oaths, to tip their caps, to give the wall, or to demonstrate deference to their social superiors in any way. Moreover, they often gave in to their inner light, quaking, ranting, and preaching in ways that most English people found disturbing. Some went naked as a sign. Others shouted down rival preachers. And always, women played an important role in Quaker services, even going out into the world to preach and to testify. In other words, the Quakers rejected the Great Chain of Being root and branch.

As this should tell you, people were reading their Bibles and coming up with all sorts of new ideas. One of the reasons they were reading their Bibles is that they were living in precarious times and they were looking for clues. They found those clues in the Book of Revelation. Many people assumed that England was nearing the end times. After all, a 1,000-year monarchy had just ended—the 1,000-year reign of the anti-Christ. The reign of King Jesus could not be far behind.

The Muggletonians believed that Lodowick Muggleton, a tailor from the West Country who had experienced a series of religious visions, was the last prophet named in the Book of Revelation, with the power to save or damn on the spot.

But most disturbing of all to those who believed in order were the Fifth Monarchy Men. They believed that the Bible had foretold five great monarchies on earth. Four of those had already fallen: Babylon, Persia, Greece, and Rome. Since the fifth was going to be the kingdom of King Jesus, that meant that the current government—the government of the Commonwealth—must only be an interim arrangement; that Christ's Second Coming was imminent; and that the best way to prepare for it would be to impose Mosaic Law on the whole country.

Some were prepared to go farther, ushering in the Second Coming by force. Do you remember when religion used to be a bulwark of the state? Now religion seemed to be advising people to disobedience.

Religious toleration and a free press had produced religious and political diversity; or, to contemporary eyes, chaos. The English ruling elite was horrified by the sects, and they began to think better of their little experiment with toleration and free speech. But, in fact, and somewhat ironically, the Commonwealth would be dissolved by radicals. In 1653, the army was upset. It was upset at being sent to Ireland to pacify Catholics, which they did with a bloody vengeance. It was upset at not being paid. It was upset at the slow pace of reform. So they sent Parliament home.

After a number of radical experiments, the army leadership eventually opted for a conservative solution. They named its current commander, Oliver Cromwell, Lord Protector of England. Oliver Cromwell ruled England from 1653–1658. In some ways, he can be seen as an anticipation of Louis's policies.

First, Cromwell was pretty good at the godlike thing. Though he was not a king, he assumed many of the trappings of kingship. He had a natural dignity that suited that. Cromwell was in control, mostly. He was a strong decisive leader and a tireless worker. He divided England into 11 military districts, each supervised by a major general, not unlike the French *intendants*. Their job was to enforce law and order, regulate the Poor Law, and guarantee religious toleration.

But like the Anglican bishops who used to harry Puritan communities, they were also supposed to keep an eye on Anglicans and Royalists. They were supposed to suppress rebellion and riot, blasphemy and swearing, drunkenness and gambling, fornication, adultery, indecent fashions, alehouses, playhouses, Sunday sports, and even Christmas celebrations. This is rule by Puritans, remember. This made them terribly unpopular.

Parliament's complaints and grumbling over money also gave Cromwell fits. Like Charles I, he frequently sent them home.

What about religious conformity? Not exactly—Cromwell was a Puritan, but he was what is called an "independent Puritan." He believed in toleration for all Protestant sects. He also readmitted the Jews into England, which he saw as part of the Second Coming.

But Anglican and Catholic worship not tolerated; in fact, the major generals were supposed to target them. In foreign policy, Cromwell obviously had an army. England finally got its aggressive, Protestant foreign policy. He crushed rebellions in Ireland and Scotland. In Ireland, he used terror to produce submission, massacring Catholics at Drogheda and Wexford, confiscating land, and burning crops. These actions led to the deaths of perhaps 250,000 and, by some estimates, as many as 600,000 people out of a total population of two million.

The Scottish pacification was much milder. They were after all fellow Protestants. Cromwell fought a trade war with the Dutch. He also fought Spain and took Jamaica from them. In other words, England had a successful foreign policy for once; but it cost money.

Oliver Cromwell was the first solvent ruler of England since Henry VII, but at tremendous cost. His government passed excise taxes on necessities such as beer, which hurt the poor. He confiscated Royalist, Anglican, and Catholic lands. This resulted in an annual revenue of £2 million, but much grumbling and resentment. This was a far higher tax burden than that imposed by Charles I, against whom these people had rebelled to keep their taxes low.

Oliver Cromwell succeeded in giving England good, strong government. He anticipated many of Louis XIV's rules of Absolutism, but he died in 1658 worn out with care, unable to work with Parliament, and unpopular with Anglicans and Catholics because of the confiscations and harassment. As in France, after over a year of instability, the English people—or at least their ruling elite—decided to go back home again. England wasn't ready for good government, so it invited back the Stuarts.

In 1660, Charles I's son, Charles II, was restored to the throne of his fathers. Charles II would rule England from 1660–1685. He was then succeeded by his brother James, who ruled from 1685–1688. In many ways, they were much like their father and grandfather. Charles II was witty, affable, and a great conversationalist. When told that the Countess of Castlemaine had converted to Catholicism, he replied, "He never concerned himself with the souls of ladies, but with their bodies, in so far as they were gracious enough to allow him." There are lots and lots of quotations like that from Charles. He would have made a terrific talk show host.

But perhaps not surprisingly, he could also be surprisingly undignified. Samuel Pepys was once shocked at the king's amusement at the sight of ducks, er, trying to make more ducks in St. James's Park.

Above all, Charles was made cynical, perhaps by his father's fate. He decided to give himself over entirely to pleasure: the theater, music, boon drinking companions, and a virtual harem of mistresses—the Countess of Castlemaine, beautiful and ambitious; the Duchess of Portsmouth, French, Catholic and, therefore, hated; and Nell Gwynne, English, common, "pretty, witty Nell."

Nell reminds me of one of my favorite stories of Western civilization. I can't resist telling it. One day a royal carriage was rolling down the High Street in Oxford where the king was staying, and it was stopped by an angry crowd. They thought that the carriage contained the Duchess of Portsmouth, who was widely believed to be whispering in the king's ear all sorts of things favorable to Catholicism. They stop the carriage, they start rocking it, and it's pretty clear that they're going to drag this woman out, probably to her death. Out popped the head of "pretty, witty" Nell Gwynne, who said, "Calm yourselves, good people, for you are mistaken. I am the Protestant whore!"

James II, who succeeded Charles in 1685, was a little more dignified. Good, you get godlike points there. He was a distinguished military man who had shown courage under fire. He was at the same time less witty and more of a plodder. He was famous for the reputed ugliness of his mistresses, which court wits explained as the penance imposed on him by his Catholic confessors. Even the Countess of Dorchester admitted, "We are none of us handsome, and if we had wit, he had not enough himself to discover it."

The words "Catholic confessors" should tell you something. James II was a Roman Catholic and that would spell trouble. In fact, both men admired their cousin, Louis XIV, in more than just his Catholicism. (By the way, we've caught up to Louis XIV chronologically in this lecture. For those of you who don't have a Stuart genealogy at hand, both James and Charles were cousins of Louis on their mother's side—Princess Henrietta Maria.)

Though Charles was lazy, James was a hard worker like Louis XIV. But unlike Louis, neither Charles nor James had an efficient local bureaucracy at their disposal. They had to rely on unpaid English nobles and aristocrats to do their bidding in the countryside.

Above all, though restored to the powers of their father, the brothers still had to deal with a powerful Parliament. I'll give you a few examples. In 1673, Parliament forced the king, Charles II, to abandon an unpopular war with the French against the Dutch—that is to say, he was fighting on the French side—and also a policy of religious toleration that he wanted to try out. They did this by threatening to withhold funds. Remember, you can always do that to a king of England.

In 1679–1681, the world's first organized political party—the Whigs—attempted to force Charles to exclude his brother James, then merely Duke of York, from the succession because he was a Catholic. So clearly, money, religion, and control continue to be issues during these reigns.

As all of this implies, neither Charles nor James was particularly wealthy, at least at first. At the Restoration, Charles II was voted a revenue that was supposed to yield £1,200,000 a year; but the taxes Parliament voted didn't always yield that amount. Worse, like his father and grandfather, he loved to spend money on art, on architecture, on his mistresses, and on his 14 acknowledged royal bastards. (If Charles was not the father of his country, he was at least the father of a fair proportion thereof.) Parliament was unwilling to finance these things, so Charles turned to bribes from Louis. In return for the bribes, he promised a pro-French foreign policy.

In 1685, James was luckier. After Parliament's attempts to displace him from the succession, there was a Royalist (or Tory) reaction in his favor. They were sorry. Some Whigs tried rebellion, which only made Parliament more cooperative. As a result, it voted James a revenue of £2 million.

James's biggest problem would be religion. Remember that England was Anglican. There were a few Catholics and more Puritans, but both were virtually outlawed by past history. That is, Catholics had tried to kill the sovereign in the 16th and 17th centuries (under Elizabeth and James). Puritans had actually managed to do it in 1649. So both of those groups were sort of beyond the pale. Scotland was mainly Presbyterian, with a poor Catholic minority in the Highlands. Ireland was mainly Catholic, but all of the power and 80% of the land was in the hands of Protestant settlers.

Both Charles and James were actually attracted to Catholicism. You see, during the English civil wars, they had had to grow up somewhere. They'd escaped the country. They grew up at the court of Louis XIV. There they saw what Absolutism and Catholicism could do for a king.

But Charles was too smart. He knew his people too well to ever do much about this inclination. As we have seen, the English hated Catholics. Remember the Spanish Armada of 1588? Mary Tudor burning Protestants at the stake between 1555–1558? The Catholic plot to blow up the houses of Parliament in 1605? Catholicism was associated in the English mind with France and Absolutism. It was virtually outlawed. For the king to embrace Catholicism would have been like for an American president of the 1950s and 1960s to embrace Communism.

Charles tried to introduce a bill for toleration in 1672, but he was forced to back down by Parliament. Having learned his lesson, he was content to remain a nominal Anglican until he converted to Rome on his deathbed in February 1685.

James was not the smarter brother. As Duke of York, rather than dissimulate, he openly worshipped as a Catholic; hence, the Whig attempt to bar him from the throne. Once he became king, James tried to pack Parliament to legalize Catholicism, possibly in the hope of making it the state religion again. Most English people seemed to hate this.

So, as my students like to ask, why didn't they just rebel? There were two reasons, one borne of the past and one centered on the future, for the fact that the English did not at first rebel against James.

First the past: no one wanted another civil war. The English ruling elite, most of whom were Anglican Tories, remembered full well the chaos of 1637–1660. In a way, this just proved that the Great Chain of Being was right. So, urged on by High Church Anglican preachers, they had resolved never again to oppose a monarch with violence. Anyway, they might not have to, and that had to do with the future.

The second reason that most English men and women were willing to put up with James II and his policies was that they anticipated a short Catholic reign. James II was 52 at his accession and he had never been in great health. When he died, he would be succeeded by one of his two daughters: Mary or, if she should die, Anne.

Mary and Anne had been raised when Charles II was still king. You remember that Charles is the smarter elder brother. He had insisted that they be raised as Protestants. Moreover, each had been safely married to a Protestant husband. Anne, the younger, was very happily married to the otherwise unremarkable, but safely Lutheran, Prince George of Denmark, a man of whom Charles II said, "I've tried him drunk. I've tried him sober. There's nothing in him."

But Mary's husband was something else entirely. Thanks to a diplomatic coup in the 1670s, Mary was married to William of Orange. Do you remember William of Orange? The stadholder of the Netherlands? The defender of Protestantism? Louis XIV's worst nightmare?

So, in 1686–1687, the unpleasant Catholic experiment looked to be a short one. Why risk another English civil war? Good Protestants could endure the present Catholic reign as they had that of Bloody Mary in 1553–1558, anticipating the safely Protestant Mary and her husband William would succeed to the throne.

In England, in the summer of 1687, the Great Chain of Being still held. It began to crack at the end of the year when James's young second wife, Mary Beatrice of Modena (I'm sorry that everybody in this lecture seems to be named Mary, James, or Charles) announced that she was expecting. Everyone in England knew that a female child would have almost no significance for the succession, because that female child would come after Mary and Anne. But according to the laws of primogeniture, which have only recently been abrogated by the current Queen Elizabeth II, a male child would take precedence over his elder sisters. There was no doubt that without Charles to thwart him, James would raise this child a good Catholic.

The prospect of a Catholic succession, followed by a long reign, was intensely frightening to Anglicans and Puritans alike. Catholics at court were convinced that Mary Beatrice's pregnancy was a miracle and that God would give her a boy. Protestants wondered how the Catholics could be so sure.

The Queen's pregnancy came to term a month prematurely in the early summer of 1688. James summoned all his loyal courtiers to be present at the birth. I should explain that royal births really were always moderately public occasions. That may seem distasteful to us, but you had to know that the king had a legitimate heir. In this case, James wanted plenty of witnesses of God's favor for the "One True Faith."

But with his usual political acumen, James only invited Catholics and time-serving Anglicans, neither of whom the country was likely to trust. In other words, he can invite all the people he wanted, but the country wasn't going to trust what they said. So, while Catholic courtiers flocked to St. James's Palace for the lying in, Protestant peers got out of town.

On June 10, 1688, Mary Beatrice gave birth to a boy, dubbed James Francis Edward. Court Catholics were overjoyed. Court Protestants—and there were a few—at the moment of birth decided to give the queen privacy by turning away. Their thoughtfulness allowed them to claim later that the birth was faked, and that the child had been smuggled up the backstairs in a warming pan.

The king was actually reduced to the indignity of declaring to the Privy Council that, "Yes, this really is my boy." He ordered bonfires and bells, but there was little rejoicing in the country. The diarist John Evelyn wrote, "A young Prince born, etc. (which will cause dispute)." That was an understatement. In fact, just a few nights before the birth, a cabal of seven noblemen wrote to William in the Netherlands, inviting him to invade their country. It was now or never.

After several months of careful preparation, William of Orange landed in southern England at Torbay on November 5, 1688—the anniversary of the failed Catholic gunpowder plot. Now thanks to Parliament's generosity, James did have an army, the last resort of

Absolutism. He had tried to staff that army with Catholic officers, but there weren't enough to go around, and the infantry was mainly composed of Protestants.

Maybe for this reason, James hesitated to march on William. As he hesitated, more and more Protestant officers, noblemen, and justices of the peace went over to William, and they brought the militia with them. Rather than face his own son-in-law with an army he couldn't trust, James II fled to France on December 11, 1688.

He actually thought he could paralyze the British government by throwing the Great Seal of England into the Thames. But he failed to reckon on that British ability to just carry on regardless, which is, of course, profoundly modern and rational. After a certain amount of debate, Parliament on February 13, 1689, asked William and Mary take the Crown as William III and Mary II.

The significance of the Glorious Revolution of 1688–1689, as these events came to be called, is that it began to solve most of the problems plaguing English monarchs since the reign of Henry VIII. It did so in a way that was very different from Louis XIV's solution.

First, the problem of sovereignty: clearly, Parliament was sovereign; the king was not a god. Power came from Parliament and the people they represented, not the Supreme Being. It could be taken away by a revolution. It could be bestowed on another, even a Dutchman.

As for the problem of control, the English king clearly remained powerful with most of his executive powers intact. (You'll see that in subsequent lectures.) But his financial and diplomatic situation dictated that he could no longer rule without Parliament. That meant, in turn, that he had to choose ministers with which Parliament could work. By the way, Parliament has met every year since 1689. So in 1688, England was well on its way to a constitutional monarchy.

Then there's the problem of finance. In fact, the revolution would lead to a series of wars with France, which would force the Crown and Parliament to finally solve the former's money problems by tapping the growing wealth of the English economy. (We'll talk about that in a subsequent lecture.) But English kings themselves would stay poor. In other words, the English were about to fund their government very generously, but not their king, who would be restricted to a fairly narrow civil list. The idea of separating government from the governor—of separating the kingdom from the king—was very modern. Compare it to Louis's boast: "I am the state." William was not the state. There was a state, but it wasn't him.

As far as the problem of religion is concerned, clearly England would not be Catholic—or solely anything else from now on. It's true that it was officially Anglican, but Parliament would have to grant a toleration to Puritans because they had supported the revolution. Interestingly, even Catholics would see some of the heat come off as they ceased to be a threat. In other words, once James stopped pushing their agenda, Catholics were no longer viewed as so much of a threat, and things begin to get better for them. Again, this is a far more modern live-and-let-live solution than Louis'.

Finally, there's the problem of foreign policy. William's accession would bring the British kingdoms into the fight against France. Louis couldn't stand by and see a fellow Catholic monarch deposed and his mortal enemy, William of Orange, gain the wealth and power of England to be used against his grand crusade. Now the road to Spain runs through the Netherlands with a boat trip across the Channel.

In fact, the ensuing Nine Years' War would be the first of seven colossal conflicts pitting Britain against France between 1688–1815. But that is a story for another lecture. In the meantime, in the end, the Glorious Revolution marks a successful break from the Great Chain of Being. Englishmen and women, not God, had chosen a king. They would eventually be sovereign through Parliament. They were masters of their own property. They could choose their religion (as long as it was Protestant for the moment). They could take on the might of France. Having broken their chains, they would now begin to flex their muscles. Whoever won this fight would dictate the next century of European history.

Timeline for Modern Western Civilization, 1450–2000

Notes:

1. Eras, prolonged wars, and lifespans of major figures are listed in bold before the events that take place during that time.

2. Events taking place in the same year are listed on separate lines unless they are related in some way.

ca. 1450	Johannes Gutenberg invents a printing press.
1455–1485	**English Wars of the Roses.**
1469	Marriage of Ferdinand of Aragon and Isabella of Castile.
1478	Spanish Inquisition begins.
1479	Ferdinand and Isabel jointly assume the throne of united Spain.
1485	Henry VII founds the Tudor dynasty in England.
1491	Treaty of Pressburg gives Bohemia and Hungary to the Habsburgs.
1492	Columbus encounters the Americas.
1494	Treaty of Tordesillas between Spain and Portugal to divide the New World.
1498	Vasco de Gama returns from the Far East.
1509–1547	**Reign of Henry VIII (England).**
1517	Luther launches the Reformation.
1519–1556	**Reign of Charles V (Holy Roman Emperor).**
1521	Edict of Worms declares Martin Luther a heretic and outlaw.

1524	The Peasants' War.
1526	The Diet of Speyer relaxes pressure on Lutherans; reversed three years later.
1530–1531	German Protestant princes form Schmalkaldic League.
1532	Machiavelli's *The Prince* published.
1532	Galileo's *Dialogues on the Two Chief Systems of the World* published.
1533–1534	England breaks from Rome with Act in Restraint of Appeals (1533) and Act of Supremacy (1534).
1534	Protestants flee Paris after the "Affair of the Placards."
1543–1563	Council of Trent.
1543	Copernicus's *On the Revolutions of the Heavenly Bodies* published.
1546–1552	**War of the Schmalkaldic League.**
1552	Peace of Passau.
1555	Peace of Augsburg.
1556–1598	**Reign of Phillip II (Spain).**
1558–1603	**Reign of Elizabeth I (England).**
1562–1598	**Wars of Religion in France.**
1564–1623	**Life of Shakespeare.**
1567–1608	**Dutch Revolt against Spain.**
1571	Turkish navy defeated at Battle of Lepanto.
1588	The Spanish Armada sails, fails.
1589	Henry IV founds the Bourbon dynasty in France.

1594–1603 .... O'Neill Rebellion in Ireland.

1598 .... Edict of Nantes grants toleration to Huguenots (French Protestants).

1603 .... James I founds the Stuart dynasty in England and Ireland.

1605 .... Bacon's *The Advancement of Learning* published.

1606–1669 .... **Life of Rembrandt.**

1607 .... Jamestown founded.

1618–1648 .... **Thirty Years' War.**

1618–1621 .... Kepler's *Epitome of Copernican Astronomy* published.

1620 .... Bacon's *Novum Organum* published.

1625 .... Kepler's *Rudolphine Tables* published.

1637–1660 .... **The British Civil Wars.**

1648 .... Peace of Westphalia (Treaties of Münster and Osnabrück).

1643–1715 .... **Reign of Louis XIV.**

1649–1652 .... The *Fronde*.

1649 .... Trial and execution of Charles I (England).

1652 .... Hobbes's *Leviathan* published.

1653–1658 .... **Protectorate under Oliver Cromwell.**

1660 .... Restoration of the Stuart monarchy in England.

1683 .... Austrians defeat Ottomans at Battle of Zenta.

1685 .... Revocation of the Edict of Nantes.

1687	Newton's *Principia Mathematica* published.
1688–1689	Glorious Revolution in England.
1688–1697	**Nine Years' War (War of the Grand Alliance)**, known in North America as King William's War.
1690	William III defeats James II at Battle of the Boyne in Ireland.
1690	Locke's *Two Treatises of Government* and *Essay Concerning Understanding* published.
1697	Treaty of Ryswick ends Nine Years' War.
1700–1721	**Great Northern War challenges Sweden.**
1701–1714	**War of the Spanish Succession**, known in North America as Queen Anne's War.
1704	Battle of Blenheim.
1713–1714	Peace of Utrecht (Treaty of Rastatt, Treaty of Baden) ends the War of the Spanish Succession.
1733	Voltaire's *Letters on England* published.
1733–1735	War of the Polish Succession; concludes with Treaty of Vienna (1738).
1739–1742	War of Jenkins's Ear.
1740–1780	**Reign of Maria Theresa (Austria).**
1740–1786	**Reign of Frederick the Great (Prussia).**
1740–1748	**War of the Austrian Succession.**
1746	Battle of Culloden.

1748	Treaty of Aix-la-Chapelle.
1751–1780	Diderot's *Encyclopedia* published.
1756–1763	**Seven Years' War; concludes with Treaty of Paris.**
1759	Battles of Minden, Fort Duquesne, Quebec.
1759	Voltaire's *Candide* published.
1762	Rousseau's *Social Contract* and *Emile* published.
1770–1827	**Life of Beethoven.**
1773	Boston Tea Party.
1773–1774	Pugachev's failed Peasant Rebellion leads to renewal of serfdom in Russia.
1774	British Parliament passes Quebec Act.
1775–1783	**American Revolutionary War.**
1776	U.S. independence.
1776	Smith's *Wealth of Nations* published.
1777	Battle of Saratoga.
1781	Battle of Yorktown.
1783	Treaty of Paris.
1789	French Revolution begins.
1791	Pillnitz Declaration supports the French king against the French Revolution.
1792	Wollstonecraft's *A Vindication of the Rights of Women* published.
1792	Louis XVI rejects the Constitution of 1791.

1792–1801	**French Revolutionary War.**
1792	Battle of Valmy.
1793–1794	Reign of Terror.
1798	*Essay on the Principle of Population* by Thomas Malthus
1799	Napoleon Bonaparte seizes power in France.
1801	Treaty of Amiens.
1803–1815	**Napoleonic Wars.**
1805	Battles of Trafalgar, Austerlitz.
1807	France signs Treaties of Tilsit with Prussia and Russia.
1812	Napoleon's Russian campaign fails.
1815	Battle of Waterloo; Congress of Vienna.
1815	Holy Alliance.
1819	Peterloo Massacre in Manchester, England.
1819	Carlsbad Decrees stifle freedom at German universities.
1820	Troppau Protocol seeks to suppress revolution in Naples.
1820–1823	Revolutions in Spain, Portugal, Italy.
1821–1829	**Greek War of Independence**, concludes with Treaty of Adrianople.
1825	Decembrist Revolt fails in Russia.
1830	Revolutions in France, Belgium, German states, Spain, Portugal, Italian states; French invade Algeria.

1832 ....Reform Act (Britain).

1832 ....Sadler commission investigates child labor (Britain).

1833 ....Factory Act reduces working hours (Britain).

1839–1842 ....Opium Wars.

1845–1847 ....Great Famine (Ireland).

1848 ....Revolutions in France, German states, Italian states, Austria-Hungary; Marx and Engels's *Communist Manifesto* published.

1851 ....Crystal Palace Exhibition, the first world's fair.

1853–1856 ....Russia defeated in Crimean War.

1857–1858 ....Indian Mutiny.

1859 ....Darwin's *Origin of Species* published.

1861 ....Unification of Italy; emancipation of Russian serfs.

1863–1864 ....Dano-Prussian War.

1866 ....Austro-Prussian War.

1869 ....Opening of the Suez Canal.

1870–1871 ....Franco-Prussian War; unification of Germany

1872–1901 ....**Nietzsche's major publications.**

1872 ....Three Emperors' League (Germany, Austria, Russia).

1876 ....Wagner's *Der Ring des Nibelungen* premiers.

1878 ....Russia imposes Treaty of San Stefano on Ottoman Empire.

1881	Assassination of Alexander II (Russia).
1881–1973	**Life of Picasso.**
1883	Marx's *Das Kapital* published.
1884	Berlin Conference establishes the Belgian Congo Free State.
1892	Triple Alliance (Germany, Austria, Italy).
1894	Franco-Russian Alliance.
1894–1906	Dreyfus Affair (France).
1904	Entente Cordiale (Britain, France).
1904–1905	Russia defeated in Russo-Japanese War.
1905	First Russian Revolution; Einstein's three major papers published.
1906	H.M.S. *Dreadnought* built.
1907	Triple Entente (Britain, France, Russia).
1914–1918	**World War I.**
1914	Rape of Belgium; Battle of the Marne.
1915	Gallipoli campaign; sinking of the *Lusitania.*
1916	Battle of Verdun, Battle of the Somme.
1917	Russian Revolutions; United States enters World War I.
1918	Treaty of Brest-Litovsk removes Russia from World War I.
1919	Paris Peace Conference and Treaty of Versailles; founding of the League of Nations.

1921	Treaty of Riga sets Polish border with Communist Russia.
1922	Treaty of Rapallo between Germany and Communist Russia.
1923	German inflation.
1923	T. S. Eliot's *The Wasteland* published.
1924	Death of Lenin; power struggle in Russia between Stalin and Trotsky.
1925	Germany signs Locarno Pact against changing boundaries by force.
1927	Heisenberg's Uncertainty Principle.
1929–1939	**Great Depression.**
1930	Freud's *Civilization and Its Discontents* published.
1932	Lausanne Conference absolves German debts.
1936–1939	The Spanish Civil War.
1936	Hitler enters the Rhineland.
1938	Sudetenland Crisis.
1939–1945	**World War II.**
1940	Fall of France; Battle of Britain.
1941	German invasion of the Soviet Union; Japan and the United States enter war.
1942	Battles of Midway, El Alamein, Stalingrad.
1943	Invasion of Italy; Battle of Kursk.
1944	D-Day.
1945	Surrender of Germany; U.S. drops atomic bombs; surrender of Japan.

1945	Founding of the United Nations.
1945–1989	**Cold War.**
1947	Marshall Plan enacted.
1948	Berlin airlift.
1949	NATO founded; first Soviet atomic blast.
1955	Warsaw Pact founded.
1956	Hungarian revolt crushed by the Soviets.
1957	Treaty of Rome establishes the European Economic Community.
1957	Sputnik launched.
1961	Berlin wall erected.
1968	Czechoslovakia's "Prague Spring" crushed by the Soviets.
1980	Solidarity trade union established in Poland.
1985	Mikhail Gorbachev becomes premier of the Soviet Union.
1987	INF Treaty reduces nuclear arms.
1989	Break-up of Warsaw Pact.
1990–1991	Break-up of Soviet Union.
1994–1999	New Balkans Crisis.
1994	Founding of the European Union.

Glossary

Adrianople, Treaty of (a.k.a. Treaty of Edirne): Established Greek independence from the Ottoman Empire, 1829.

aide: French sales tax before the revolution.

Aix-la-Chapelle, Treaty of: Treaty ending the War of the Austrian Succession (1748). Essentially, all sides reverted to their prewar borders.

Albigensians: Medieval heresy that taught that all matter was evil, violently persecuted by the Church.

Anglicans: Conservative or "High Church" members of the Church of England favoring Church government by bishops.

Anschluss: German annexation of Austria, 1938.

Amiens, Treaty of: Treaty ending the French Revolutionary Wars in 1801.

asiento: The right to supply African slaves to the Spanish colonies of the New World, secured for Britain in the Treaty of Utrecht of 1713.

Augsburg, Peace of (1555): Settlement within the Holy Roman Empire allowing each prince to determine the religion within his territory (*cuius regio, eius religio*).

Auschwitz-Birkenau: Established in 1941 in Poland, the most murderous of the Nazi death camps; liberated in 1945.

auto-da-fé: literally "act of faith"; public declaration of sentences imposed by courts of the Spanish Inquisition, with the carrying out of the sentence (e.g., burning at the stake) by secular authorities.

Avignon Papacy, 1309–1374: Also known as the Babylonian Captivity of the Church, the period when the papacy was based in Avignon, a papal holding in France.

Baptists: Protestants who believed that baptism should be left to adult choice. This idea was controversial because it would leave children unbaptized and vitiate any notion of a national church.

Bastille: French royal prison, attacked by a Parisian mob on 14 July 1789, the first violent act of the French Revolution.

Beer Hall Putsch: Attempted Nazi coup to take over the government of Bavaria in 1923. It was crushed easily, and the Nazi leaders went to prison for one year.

Black Death: Probably bubonic plague, which ravaged Europe from 1347 to 1350, killing one-third to one-half of the population and returning periodically until the last outbreak at Marseilles in 1722.

Black Hand: Serbian nationalist terrorist organization that planned the assassination of Franz Ferdinand in 1914.

Blank Check: Kaiser Wilhelm II's offer to back the Austrian emperor, Franz-Josef, militarily should he attack Serbia and be attacked by Russia in 1914.

Blitzkrieg: War of shock and movement, perfected by the German general staff between the wars and deployed by the German military in World War II, which used aircraft to destroy enemy supply lines and to support ground operations involving massed tanks and infantry.

Bloody Sunday: On 22 January 1905, a peaceful crowd sought to petition the czar at the Winter Palace in St. Petersburg. The imperial guard panicked and fired on the crowd, resulting in about 100 deaths, which in turn, precipitated the First Russian Revolution.

blue-water strategy: A military strategy that concentrates on naval forces rather than land forces.

Bolsheviks (from the Russian word for "majority"): By 1903, a faction of the Russian Social Democratic Labor Party that favored a tight, disciplined, and militantly revolutionary party membership. Led by Lenin, the Bolsheviks would form the core of the triumphant Communist Party at the revolution.

Bon Marché, Paris: Generally credited as the world's first department store.

Brest-Litovsk, Treaty of: Treaty between communist Russia and Germany, in which the former ceded vast amounts of territory, population, and natural resources to the latter in 1918. Allowed Germany to shift the bulk of its forces west for a final offensive later that year.

cahiers de doléance: Reports from the countryside, written to the Estates General, about conditions in France in 1789.

Carbonari: Italian for "charcoal burners"; 19th-century Italian nationalist partisans.

CHEKA: First incarnation of the Soviet secret police, with antecedents in the czarist secret police of the 19th century (see **Third Section**); subsequent incarnations included the GPU, OGPU, NKVD, NKGB, and (from 1953) the KGB. See also **NKVD**.

COMECON: Council for Mutual Economic Assistance; economic association of Communist countries created in 1949, disbanded in 1991.

Commercial Revolution: General expansion of European trade, much of it with North American colonies, China, and India, in the 17th century. Benefited the Dutch, the French, and most of all, the British.

Common Market: Popular name for the European Economic Union established in 1957 that provided for free trade across members' borders.

conciliarism: Late medieval reform movement which responded to the Great Schism by proposing that church councils, rather than the Pope, should have the power to determine policy for the Catholic Church; rejected by Pope Martin V (1417-31) and later condemned by the Fifth Lateran Council (1512-1517).

Congress of Vienna: Peace conference after the Napoleonic Wars (1815), dominated by Klemens von Metternich; Robert, Viscount Castlereagh; and Charles, Count Talleyrand, which restored monarchies and redistributed territory to create a buffer around France and, thus, maintain the balance of power. Though hostile to liberalism and nationalism, the Congress of Vienna secured a general European peace for 99 years.

Congo Free State: Established by the Congress of Berlin of 1884, the personal proprietary colony of Leopold II of Belgium was ruthlessly exploited for its rubber. The revelations of the regime's brutality led to the assumption of control by the Belgian parliament in 1908.

Continental System: Tariff union and free trade area organized by Napoleon for his empire in 1806 in order to promote French industry and shut out the British. This system became one of the grievances against the Napoleonic Empire.

corvée: The right, prior to the Revolution, of a French landlord to demand periodic labor from his tenants to build roads, erect barns, and so forth..

Commonwealth of Independent States (CIS): Alliance, created in 1991, consisting of most states that emerged from the former Soviet Union.

Council of Trent: Church Council, convened in 1543–1563, to address the Reformation. Reasserted Catholic doctrine but urged a reformation of the Catholic clergy.

Crystal Palace Exhibition: The first world's fair (1851), designed to show off the wonders of the Industrial Revolution.

dauphin: title referring to the eldest son of a king of France, in use from 1349 until 1830. "Dauphine" referred to the wife of a dauphin.

Dawes Plan: First American initiative to restructure Germany's massive war reparations debt after World War I; its acceptance in 1924 helped put an end to the inflationary crisis that had gripped Germany in the preceding year.

Declaration of the Rights of Man and Citizen: The statement of principles of the French Revolution (1789), guaranteeing personal freedom, equality, and the sovereignty of the people; it was a summary of Enlightenment thought on government.

Deism: View, increasingly popular in the wake of the Scientific Revolution, in which God's active involvement is not regarded as necessary to explain the daily running of the universe. rather, the Supreme Being is regarded as more of a celestial watchmaker who designed the universe, wound it up, and set it going according to unchanging natural laws.

Diggers: Religious sect emerging out of the toleration following the British Civil Wars. They were led by Gerald Winstanley from about 1649–1650 and believed that the Bible did not sanction private property. A combination of government repression and local hostility broke the movement.

Directory: The constitutional arrangement, headed by five directors, that governed France from 1795–1799.

Dreadnought: British warship completed in 1906 whose firepower, speed, and protection were so superior to other warships that subsequent similar vessels were referred to by the same name. The race to build dreadnought battleships by Britain and Germany was one of the long-term causes of the Great War.

Dreyfus Affair: *Cause célèbre* in 1890s France in which a Jewish French army officer, Alfred Dreyfus, was accused, convicted, and imprisoned on a charge of disclosing military secrets to the Germans. Following a campaign led by Émile Zola to have the case reopened, during which Dreyfus was attacked by conservative politicians and the Roman Catholic hierarchy, he was pardoned, then exonerated, and restored to his rank in 1906. Partly as a result of these events, the French Republic passed legislation separating church and state in 1905.

droits du seigneur: Rights of the landlord to various items and services of his tenants in *ancien régime* Europe.

economic determinism: Marxist theory that says that the political, religious, social, and cultural superstructure of any community is based on its economic arrangements. Related to the idea that all history is a story of class struggle.

Edict of Nantes: Granted toleration to French Protestants (Huguenots) in 1598; revoked by Louis XIV in 1685.

Ems Dispatch: Telegram regarding the Spanish succession that Otto von Bismarck edited to be insulting to French interests, precipitating the Franco-Prussian War in 1870.

Entente Cordiale: Alliance between Britain and France, ending centuries of hostility, worked out in 1904.

Estates General: Tricameral French legislature prior to the French Revolution but not convened between 1614 and 1789. The three chambers corresponded to the First Estate (the clergy), the Second Estate (the nobility), and the Third Estate (the commonality). Legislation had to be approved by a majority of the three chambers.

European Union: Restructuring and expansion of the European Economic Union in 1994 to give Europe greater political unity.

evolution and natural selection: Theory presented in Charles Darwin's *The Origin of Species* (1859) to explain variations in fossils and within current species. Darwin's theories, especially the idea that evolution was propelled by survival of the fittest, were quickly accepted by scientists but attacked by theologians and clergymen.

fascism: Political philosophy originating with Benito Mussolini; emphasized nationalism, patriotism, militarism, obedience, and traditional values. Nazism is a species of fascism.

Fifth Monarchy Men: Sect arising during the British Civil Wars who believed that Christ's Second Coming was imminent.

financial revolution: Process whereby the Dutch, then the English, pioneered many of the instruments and techniques of modern high finance, in particular, the servicing of a funded national debt. Vital to the creation of a successful fiscal-military state in Britain during the 18th century.

Fourteen Points: Woodrow Wilson's plan of 1918 to bring Germany to the bargaining table in World War I. Only partially used as the blueprint for the Versailles peace settlement in 1919.

Frankfurt, Treaty of: Treaty ending the Franco-Prussian War (1871). Bismarck's harsh terms embittered France for more than a generation.

Fronde (literally "slingshot"): Revolt of the French aristocracy (1649–1652), which briefly triumphed (1651–1652). "Frondeur" later came to refer to anyone advocating limits to monarchic power, and even later to anyone criticizing any existing powers.

gabelle: French salt tax before the Revolution.

Geheime Staatspolizei (Gestapo): Nazi secret police.

Girondins: Relative moderates in the French Revolution who wanted to work with the king to establish a constitutional monarchy.

Glorious Revolution: Political revolution in England (1688–1689), which displaced the Catholic James II in favor of the Protestant William III and Mary II. Established parliamentary sovereignty and, therefore, constitutional monarchy in England.

Grand Alliance, War of the, 1688-1697: Also known as the Nine Years' War, and in North America as King William's War, a conflict between France under Louis XIV and a coalition of other European powers led by William III fought over the succession to the British crowns and the balance of power on the continent; concluded with the Treaty of Ryswick.

Great Chain of Being: A medieval intellectual system in which every creature and article in the universe was arranged in a strict hierarchy beginning with God.

Great Schism, 1374–1417: Period when rival popes ruled from Avignon and Rome. Ended at the Council of Constance with the election of Martin V.

guardacostas: private naval forces employed by the Spanish government against England during the 18th century. Their aggressive tactics precipitated the War of Jenkins' Ear 1739–42.

heresy: The Catholic Church's term for any belief which disagreed with the tenets of the Church.

Holy Alliance: An alliance devised in 1815 by Czar Alexander I of the great European monarchies (Russia, Prussia, Austria, France, Britain) that was to work in concert to rule their peoples with Christian love while crushing liberalism, nationalism, and rebellions. Generally successful in the 1820s; Britain and France left in the 1830s as they grew more liberal.

Hundred Years' War, 1337–1456: Intermittent conflict between France and England, which was often allied with French barons. After years of English occupation of large portions of France, the conflict ended with the English being driven out.

Hussites: Followers of John Hus in 15th-century Bohemia who demanded communion in both kinds (i.e., bread and wine). Persecuted as a heresy by the Roman Catholic Church.

iconoclasm: Attacks, often of Protestants against Catholic churches, that destroyed statues and stained glass as graven images.

indulgences: Catholic practice by which the Church claims to remit time in Purgatory for good works. Their sale at the beginning of the 16th century infuriated Martin Luther, prompting his 95 Theses (1517), which launched the Protestant Reformation.

Iron Law of Wages: First posited by David Ricardo in 1817, the idea that wages rise and fall in inverse proportion to the size of the labor force.

intendants: French officials who oversaw local affairs for the Bourbon kings.

Jacobins: Radicals in the French Revolution who sought to create a perfectly egalitarian society. In power, they defended France ably but discredited themselves by launching the Reign of Terror.

Jacobites: Supporters of the exiled King James II and his son, the titular James III, known to his opponents as the Pretender. Jacobite rebellions in 1715 and 1745 failed to restore the Catholic Stuarts to the British throne.

Jesuits: members of the Society of Jesus, a Catholic religious order founded by Ignatius of Loyola in 1534 and recognized by the pope in 1540.

Kaiserschlacht ("emperor battle" in German): German plan to win the war in the west in 1918, devised by General Erich Ludendorff. The Germans nearly reached Paris but were stopped by fresh American troops.

Kosovo: Province of Serbia inhabited mainly by ethnic Albanians. The Serbian attempt to suppress this minority in 1999 provoked NATO military action, which led to the fall of the government of Slobodan Milosevic.

Kristallnacht: Widespread violence against Jews, Jewish businesses, and synagogues in Germany and Austria on 9 November 1938, in response to the murder of a German diplomat in Paris by a Jew.

kulaks (from Russian for "fist"): pejorative term for relatively wealthy Russian peasants, regarded in the Soviet Union as stingy class enemies of the Communist Revolution.

Kulturkampf (Culture War): Otto von Bismarck's program to reduce the role of the Roman Catholic Church in German life.

laissez-faire: Economic policies that eschew government regulation of trade and industry; generally associated with Great Britain at the end of the 18th and the beginning of the 19th centuries.

levée en masse*:* Conscripted citizen army established by the Jacobins to defend France in 1793.

Levelers: Radical members of the New Model Army during the British Civil Wars who demanded universal manhood suffrage, law reform, and "the sovereignty of the people." They were suppressed by the Commonwealth regime.

Little Entente: Alliance against German expansion created in 1920 by Czechoslovakia, Romania, and Yugoslavia, and later joined by France and aided by Poland.

Lollards: Followers of John Wycliff in 14th- and 15th-century England who wanted a deemphasized Church hierarchy, greater lay participation in the liturgy, and Scripture translated into the vernacular. Believed to have been persecuted out of existence by the time of the Reformation.

Lusitania: British luxury liner torpedoed by a German U-boat in May 1915 with tremendous loss of life, including 125 Americans. American threats to enter World War I as a result led the Germans to halt unrestricted submarine warfare for nearly two years.

MAD (mutually assured destruction): The guarantee that use of nuclear weapons by either superpower would result in an automatic, overwhelming, and fatal response. In theory and, so far, in fact, the guarantee of mutual destruction has prevented the use of these weapons.

Mein Kampf: Hitler's autobiography/political manifesto in which he lays out the Nazi program, published in 1926.

Mensheviks (from the Russian word for "minority"): A loosely organized faction of the Russian Socialists, including intellectual moderates. Individual Mensheviks were eventually absorbed into or purged from the Bolshevik-led Communist Party at the revolution.

mercantilism: Economic system, especially associated with 17th-century Western Europe, in which the government plans the economy, encourages local industry, protects it with high tariffs, and acquires colonies for raw materials and markets. Largely discredited by Adam Smith in *The Wealth of Nations* (1776).

middling orders: Social rank below the aristocracy referring to those who generally did not work with their hands and lived comfortable lives but did not have titles and usually did not have lands. Before the Industrial Revolution, they included merchants, financiers, mayors, aldermen, burghers, and professionals such as lawyers, doctors, military and naval officers, clergy, estate stewards, and majordomos. They amounted to perhaps 10 percent of the European population. The Industrial Revolution of the 19th century split the middling orders into an upper group that directly benefited from the new factory system, and a lower group unable to invest in, or compete with, the new system.

Mississippi Company, also Mississippi Scheme: Plan developed by a Scottish speculator named John Law and backed in 1719 by the Duc d'Orleans, regent to Louis XV, to establish a company for investment in the French territory of Louisiana and a Banque Royale to issue notes and stock. The plan collapsed in a rash of speculation.

Muggletonians: a sect of English Puritans who believed that Lodowick Muggleton (1609-1698), a tailor from the West Country who had experienced a series of religious visions, was the last prophet named in the Book of Revelation, with the power to save or damn on the spot. Muggleton denied the Trinity, denounced the heliocentric view of the solar system, and claimed that Eve had been the incarnation of evil.

National Assembly: The Third Estate, plus aristocratic and clerical supporters, once it had retreated to a Parisian tennis court to give France a new constitution in 1789.

National Convention: The body that governed France from 1792–1795.

National Socialist German Workers Party (Nazis): Germany's fascist party in the 1920s–1940s, led by Adolf Hitler.

New Economic Policy: Lenin's tempering of communization (1921–1924).

NKVD: Stalin's secret police, regular police, purge operations, and prison camps combined in 1934 under a "People's Commissariat for Internal Affairs" headed first by Nikolai Yezhov and then by Lavrenty Beria.

No Man's Land: Area between the two trench systems on the Western Front of World War I. So called because no man could long survive the hail of machine-gun bullets and artillery shells that left a scene of desolation and carnage.

Paris Commune: An elected body, run by the *sans-culottes*, that shared governmental power with the National Assembly during the French Revolution. Separately, also later used to refer to the socialist government that governed Paris for two months in the spring of 1871 following France's defeat in the Franco-Prussian War.

Paris, Treaty of: Ended the Seven Years' War in 1763 by awarding Silesia to Prussia and most of Canada and other heretofore French possessions to Great Britain.

Paris, Treaty of: Ended the American Revolutionary War in 1783 by recognizing American independence.

parlements: French legal institutions that often acted as a brake on royal power before the French Revolution.

Passau, Peace of, 1552: France and Maurice of Saxony negotiated with the Holy Roman Empire for the release of Protestant princes, which prepared the way for the **Peace of Augsburg** in 1555.

Pax Britannica (literally, the "British Peace" in Latin, harking back to the Pax Romana of ancient times): Refers to the period in the late 19th century when the British Empire was at its height and the Royal Navy enforced order around the globe.

Peasants' War: Failed religious, political, and economic revolt by German peasants during 1524-1526, sparked by the attacks on the church by Martin Luther and other reformers. Luther himself denounced the revolt.

perestroika: Attempted restructuring of the communist system by Mikhail Gorbachev, intended to save communism but actually helped to precipitate its demise in Eastern Europe.

philosophes: Eighteenth-century Enlightenment philosophers.

Phony War: Period from 1939–1940 when neither the Allies nor the Germans launched offensives.

Positivism: The belief, associated with Auguste Comte, that a scientific approach to human problems would lead to their solutions and continuous human progress.

Pragmatic Sanction Decree, 1713: Decree by which Maria Theresa was recognized as heir to the Austrian throne.

Prague, Treaty of: Treaty ending the Austro-Prussian War of 1866, which saw the creation of the North German Confederation.

Pogroms (from Russian for "wreaking of havoc"): Spontaneous anti-Semitic massacres in czarist Russia, often tolerated by the government.

polysynody: system of French government, used briefly after the death of Louis XIV in 1715, in which traditional ministers were replaced by eight councils staffed by the ancient aristocracy ("the nobility of the sword").

Pugachev's Rebellion: Peasant rebellion in Russia (1774) led by Yemelyan Ivanovich Pugachev, brutally suppressed by the forces of Catherine the Great.

Purgatory: Roman Catholic belief that, at death, souls who are not damned but not of sufficient perfection to merit heaven go to this place to become so. Catholics believe that the prayers of the faithful and the indulgences granted by the Church for good deeds in life are efficacious in reducing the amount of time a soul spends there.

Puritans: English Protestants who sought the continued reform of the Church of England after its establishment in 1559–1563.

Quakers: Religious sect emerging out of the toleration following the British Civil Wars and led by George Fox. They believed that each human being possessed God's inner light in equal measure, regardless of gender or social rank. This inclined them, notoriously, to flout gender roles, deny deference to social superiors, refuse to swear oaths, and "quake" with their inner light at services.

Ranters: Religious radicals emerging out of the toleration following the British Civil Wars, who believed that those in tune with God can commit no sin. This idea was thought to give Ranters license to perform all manner of debauchery. Though much feared and reviled at the time, historians now debate their existence.

Realism: Nineteenth-century artistic movement emphasizing the accurate depiction of life, especially among working people in both city and country.

Realpolitik: Belief, associated with Otto von Bismarck, that international diplomacy should be based on practical considerations, not religious or moral sentiments.

Reform Act: British statute of 1832 that extended the vote to the middle class.

Revolt of the Netherlands, 1567–1608: Protestant Dutch response to Philip II's decision to impose the Inquisition on the Netherlands; it eventually resulted in independence for the northern provinces.

Risorgimento ("resurgence"): Abortive movement in 1848 to unify Italy.

Ryswick, Treaty of, 1697: Treaty ending the Nine Years' War, by which Louis XIV recognized William III as the rightful king of England, Scotland, and Ireland; gave back European territory taken since 1678; and agreed to work out with William a partition of the Spanish Empire after the death of Carlos II.

salon: Originating in France during the 17th and 18th centuries, any literary, artistic, or intellectual gathering of distinguished guests, often from a variety of fields, in a drawing room or large reception hall and organized by a prominent hostess or host. Crucial to advancing the Enlightenment and often led by women.

salutary neglect: British policy of non-interference in the internal affairs of Britain's North American colonies.

sans-culottes: Urban workers, mainly in Paris, who radicalized the French Revolution. So called because, being people who worked for a living, they wore trousers, not knee-britches.

Schlieffen Plan: Devised by General Alfred von Schlieffen and finalized in 1905, Germany's plan to win a general European war quickly by attacking France first, then Russia. The defeat of France was to be accomplished by a feint through the Ardennes, the main attack coming through neutral Belgium. The plan failed on implementation in 1914, leading to the stalemate on the Western Front.

Schmalkaldic League: League of Protestant nobles who fought Charles V for religious autonomy within the Holy Roman Empire in the mid-16th century.

Schutzstaffel (SS): Elite Nazi military units, often associated with concentration camp duties and battlefield atrocities.

Sejm: Historical term for the entire parliament of Poland, consisting of two chambers as well as the king (who was regarded as considered a third legislative chamber). Veto was possible by any one aristocrat (liberum veto). After 1918, Sejm referred only to the lower chamber.

Spanish Armada: Philip II's failed attempt to invade England in 1588, defeated by the Royal Navy and a Protestant wind (i.e., the weather).

Spanish Crusade: Effort, led by King Philip II beginning in the 1560s to stamp out Protestant heretics.

Spanish Inquisition: Effort launched in 1478 by the united Spanish monarchy under Ferdinand of Aragon and Isabelle of Castile to eradicate Catholic heresies and root out *conversos* (Jews who claimed to have converted to Christianity while continuing to practice their own religion) and *moriscos* (Muslims who had been forced to convert to Christianity). Later, the Spanish government expelled non-Christians. From 1492, 150,000 Jews were expelled from Spain, leading to the loss to Spain of many physicians, artists, and government officials. From 1502, Muslims were expelled as well. In 1602, even converted Muslims had to leave. The Inquisition continued to operate into the early 19th century.

Social Darwinists: Nineteenth-century social theorists who attempted to apply Darwin's theories of evolution and natural selection to human political, social, and economic relations, resulting in justifications for the European class system, imperialism, and aggression.

Spanish Flu: Worst pandemic in history, killed perhaps 20 million in 1918–1919.

Stamp Act: A British parliamentary statute of 1765, requiring that the American colonists purchase stamps to affix to official documents. The first serious attempt to tax the colonies was met with great hostility and was repealed the next year.

Sturmabteilungen (SA): Nazi storm troopers, eliminated in 1934.

Sudetenland Crisis: Ensued when, in 1938, Hitler demanded, first, autonomy, then independence, and finally, the absorption into

Germany of the Sudetenland, a portion of Czechoslovakia mainly inhabited by ethnic Germans. Britain, France, and Italy agreed to these measures over Czech protests. Early in 1939, Hitler absorbed the rest of Czechoslovakia.

szlachta: Relatively broad class of local nobles and gentry in Poland, whose power was weakened by the partitions of Poland (1772, 1793, 1795) in favor of the most elite portions of the aristocracy.

taille: A hearth tax paid by every French commoner before the revolution.

Three Emperor's League: Alliance designed in 1872 by Bismarck, Julius Andrássy, and Prince Gorchakov to ally the rulers of Germany, Austria, and Russia.

Third Section: Russian secret police established by Czar Nicholas I after the failed Decembrist uprising of 1825.

Tilsit, Treaty of, 1807: Recognized Napoleon's Empire in the West and Czar Alexander I's supremacy in the east.

Tories: English political party that arose in the 17th century. The Tories began as a court party, defending the hereditary succession in the person of James, duke of York. They favored the rights of the monarch, the Church of England, and the interests of landowners. During the 1690s, as they became associated with Jacobitism and lost power, the Tories grew to be more of a country (opposition) party.

Totalitarianism: A form of absolute government admitting no dissent or rival loyalties, usually associated with dictatorship and the use of modern technology to monitor and enforce obedience.

Triple Entente: Alliance among Britain, France, and Russia established in 1907.

Triangular Trade: The commercial system from 1619–1807, whereby British slavers purchased slaves from West African kings, transported them to and sold them in the New World, and transported the sugar, tobacco, or cotton they harvested back to Britain for distribution to all of Europe. This trade was key to Britain's economic superiority in the 18th century.

Triple Alliance: Alliance worked out by Kaiser Wilhelm II among Germany, Austria, and Italy in 1892.

***Unterseeboots* or U-boats**: German submarines, used to sink merchant ships supplying the British Isles in both world wars.

Utopian Socialists: Early-19th-century socialists (Henri de St. Simon, Charles Fourier, Robert Owen) who believed that the aristocrats and factory owners could be persuaded to relinquish control of natural resources and the means of production for the good of all.

Utrecht, Treaty of, 1713: Treaty between Great Britain and France ending their hostilities in the War of the Spanish Succession. Britain acquired Gibraltar, Newfoundland, Nova Scotia, territory in the Caribbean, the asiento, Louis XIV's recognition of the Protestant Succession, and the promise that the crowns of France and Spain would never be united.

Versailles Conference: Peace conference, held at Versailles Palace, to formally end World War I in 1919. The conference was successful in establishing numerous democracies in Europe, but it did not seriously confront the issue of imperialism, and its punitive treatment of Germany contributed to the resentment that would lead to the Second World War.

Versailles Palace: Magnificent palace built by Louis XIV during 1661–1685 to display his power.

War Communism, 1917–1921: Lenin's first quick attempt at communization. Forced collectivization, immediate peace with Germany, and the encouragement of international terrorism led to much loss of life, territory, and international legitimacy. Reversed in 1921–1922 by Lenin's New Economic Policy.

Westphalia, Treaty of: Treaty ending the Thirty Years' War in 1648 that affirmed the principle *cuius regio, eius religio*: the religion of the state is to be that of the ruler. This was, in fact, a step toward religious diversity and toleration in Europe.

Whigs: English political party that arose in the 17th century. The Whigs began as a country (opposition) party, demanding the exclusion of James, duke of York, a Catholic, from the throne; emphasizing the rights of Parliament and of dissenters; and championing a Protestant (pro-Dutch) foreign policy. In the 1690s, they became a party of government and grew less radical.

Yalta Conference: Attended in February 1945 by Sir Winston Churchill, Franklin Roosevelt, and Joseph Stalin to determine the postwar fate of Europe. The decision to recognize the Soviet occupation of Eastern Europe laid the foundation for the Iron Curtain.

Biographical Notes

Adolphus, Gustavus (1594–1632): King of Sweden (1611–1632) who made Sweden a major power and, like Prussian rulers, created an efficient, absolutist, Protestant state that was geared for war and blocked Habsburg ambitions in the Thirty Years' War.

Alexander I (1777–1825): Czar of Russia (1801–1825) who led Russia during the Napoleonic Wars and originated the idea for the Holy Alliance (1819).

Alexander II (1818–1881): Liberal, reforming czar of Russia (1855–1881) who freed the serfs (1861) and reorganized the government and military but was nevertheless assassinated by anarchists.

Alexander III (1845–1894): Czar of Russia (1881–1884); cancelled his father's plans for a more representative government, persecuted non-Orthodox minorities, and sought to impose Russian nationalism on non-Russians.

Anjou, Phillipe, Duke of (1683–1746): Grandson of Louis XIV. His decision to accept the Spanish crown in 1700 led to the War of the Spanish Succession (1702–1714). King Philip V (Felipe V) of Spain (1700–1745).

Anne (1665–1714): Last Stuart queen of Great Britain (1702–1714), her selection of the duke of Marlborough to command her forces in the War of the Spanish Succession produced military victories, while her selection of Robert Harley, Earl of Oxford, to negotiate the Treaty of Utrecht established British commercial superiority.

Bacon, Francis, Baron Verulam and Viscount St. Albans (1561–1626): English government official and philosopher; author of *The Advancement of Learning* (1605), *Novum Organum* (1620), and *The New Atlantis* (1627), he articulated the concept later known as the scientific method.

Beethoven, Ludwig van (1770–1826): German composer, often credited with propelling music into the Romantic age, a democrat and critic of Napoleon.

Bentham, Jeremy (1748–1832): Utilitarian philosopher, author of *Principles of Morals and Legislation* (1798).

Bismarck, Otto von (1815–1898): Chancellor of, first, Prussia (1862–1871), then Germany (1871–1890), architect of German unification, master diplomat, often credited with inventing *Realpolitik* but also with maintaining the peace of Europe in the 1870s and 1880s.

Blake, William (1757–1827): Visionary Romantic poet, critiqued industrial life in such poems as *Jerusalem* (1808).

Bonaparte, Louis Napoleon. See **Napoleon III**.

Bonaparte, Napoleon (1769–1821): French general, consul of France (1799–1804), emperor (1804–1815); a brilliant battlefield tactician, he sought, through military conquest, to unify Europe under his rule. Though a product of the revolution, his rule could be harsh and authoritarian. After his final defeat at Waterloo in 1815, he was sent into exile at St. Helena.

Brezhnev, Leonid (1906–1982): Premier of the Soviet Union (1965–1982), he presided over a period of internal stagnation but made some accommodation with the West in the Cold War.

Burke, Edmund (1729–1797): Irish statesman and author of *The Philosophical Inquiry into Our Ideas of the Sublime and the Beautiful* (1756) and *Reflections on the Revolution in France* (1792). He was a harsh critic of the excesses of the French Revolution. Often credited as a founding father of conservatism.

Calvin, John (1509–1564): Protestant reformer who became the virtual ruler of Geneva; articulated the idea of predestination, that is, that one's personal salvation has already been determined affirmatively or negatively by an all-knowing God.

Carlos II (1661–1700): Last Habsburg king of Spain (1665–1700), he suffered from numerous physical infirmities. His decision to offer the entire Spanish Empire to Louis Phillipe, Duke of Anjou, helped precipitate the War of the Spanish Succession.

Castlereagh, Robert Stewart, Viscount (1769–1822): British statesman and diplomat, architect of the final coalition against Napoleon, and one of the principal framers of the Congress of Vienna.

Catherine the Great (1729–1796): Czar of Russia from 1762–1796, she embraced reform early in her reign, but following Pugachev's

Rebellion (1773–1774), she strengthened the power of landowners over their serfs.

Cavour, Count Camillo di (1810–1861): Prime minister of Piedmont-Sardinia and architect of its modernization and, therefore, of the unification of Italy.

Charles I (1600–1649): King of England, Scotland, and Ireland (1625–1649); his personality and policies helped to precipitate the British Civil Wars of 1637–1660. He was tried and executed on the charge of treason against the people of England in January 1649.

Charles II (1630–1685): King of England, Scotland, and Ireland (1660–1685); he pursued some elements of absolutism but never singlemindedly.

Charles V (1500–1558): Holy Roman Emperor (1519–1556); as Charles I, king of Spain (1506–1556), he spent most of his reign combating, unsuccessfully, the Protestant Reformation and its embrace by many of the princes of the empire. He also spent many years fighting France for control of Italy. Abdicated his thrones in 1556.

Charles VI (1685–1740): Holy Roman Emperor (1711–1740) who in the War of the Spanish Succession sought to become king of Spain and thereby recreate the empire of Charles V. Arranged the Pragmatic Sanction allowing succession by his daughter Maria Theresa.

Charles VII (1403–1461): King of France (1422–1461) who restored the authority of the French monarchy following the Hundred Years' War.

Charles IX (1550–1574): King of France (1560–1574) who accepted the advice of his mother to massacre Protestants on St. Bartholomew's Day in 1572.

Charles X (1757–1836): King of France (1824–1830); attempted to restore elements of the *Ancien Régime* and was forced to abdicate by the July Revolution of 1830.

Charles Albert (1748–1849): King of Sardinia (1831–1849), whose resistance against the Austrians helped inspire the Italian movement for national independence.

Churchill, John, Duke of Marlborough. See **Marlborough, Duke of**.

Churchill, Sir Winston Spencer (1874–1965): Journalist, soldier, statesman, and prime minister of Great Britain (1940–1945, 1951–1955). After an adventurous early career, Churchill served as First Lord of the Admiralty (1911–1915). The failure of the Gallipoli campaign led to a period alternating between minor government posts and the political wilderness, until his reappointment to the Admiralty early in 1939. Most famously led Britain in World War II; his record in labor and Irish affairs is more checkered and controversial. Winner of the Nobel Prize for literature in 1953.

Clemenceau, Georges (1841–1929): Prime minister of France (1917–1920) who pressed tirelessly for victory over Germany in WW1 and rejected moderate treatment of Germany after the war ended.

Colbert, Jean-Baptiste (1619–1683): Advisor to Louis XIV from 1665 whose fiscal and military reforms facilitated France's wars.

Colón, Cristóbal (1451–1506): Italian explorer in the service of Spain who made the European discovery of the New World in October 1492. Thinking that he had landed in Asia, he dubbed the natives "Indians." Made three subsequent voyages to the Americas.

Copernicus, Nicholas (1473–1544): Polish astronomer who wrote *On the Revolutions of the Heavenly Bodies* (1543), which posited a Sun-centered system.

Cromwell, Oliver (1599–1658): Puritan gentleman who became the most successful general of the British Civil Wars, then Lord Protector of England (1653–1658). His regime was well governed and successful, but his sanction of the slaughter of surrendered combatants and civilians in the Irish campaign in 1648 contributed to continuing Anglo-Irish bitterness.

Darwin, Charles (1809–1882): British biologist and author of *The Origin of Species* (1859), which posited the theory of evolution accomplished by natural selection, and *The Descent of Man* (1879), which argued that humans had evolved from primitive primates. His ideas were soon embraced by scientists, but they continue to be controversial among lay people.

Descartes, Rene (1596–1650): Philosopher, scientist, and mathematician who made advances in optics, systematized the study of curves, and devised the alphabetical system for unknown variables (a, b, c, x, y, z, etc.) as well as the system of superscripts for powers.

de Gaulle, Charles (1890–1970): A soldier in World War I, leader of the Free French forces in World War II, and president of France 1958–1969. He famously maintained French independence from its British and American allies in the postwar period.

Dickens, Charles (1812–1870): British novelist, author of *Oliver Twist* (1838) and *Hard Times* (1854), among many other works; famous for his colorful descriptions of life at all levels of Victorian society but especially the poor.

Diderot, Denis (1713–1784): French *philosophe*, compiler of the *Encyclopedia* (1751–1766).

Dostoevsky, Feodor (1821–1881): Russian novelist, author of *Crime and Punishment* (1866) and *The Brothers Karamazov* (1879–1880), among many other works; his novels combine a cosmological vision with searing psychological insight.

Edison, Thomas (1847–1931): American inventor, responsible for more than 1,000 patents, including ones for the electric light, the phonograph, the stock ticker, and important work on motion-picture technology.

Eichmann, Adolf (1906–1962): German soldier, SS man, and war criminal, responsible for carrying out Hitler's "Final Solution" from 1941. After the war, he fled to South America, where he was apprehended in 1960 by Israeli agents; subsequently tried and executed for his crimes against humanity.

Einstein, Albert (1879–1955): German physicist responsible for the special and general theories of relativity and, with them, a new paradigm in physics. Fled Germany in 1933. In 1939, wrote to President Roosevelt to urge, successfully, that the United States develop an atomic bomb.

Eisenhower, Dwight David (1890–1969): Soldier, statesman, and president of the United States (1953–1961). Supreme Allied Commander in Europe (1943–1945); successfully coordinated Allied cooperation in the defeat of Germany. As president, he led the United States and the free world in a crucial period of the Cold War.

Eliot, Thomas Stearns (1888–1965): American-born, British-naturalized poet, author of *The Waste Land* (1922) and other poems that eschewed conventional narrative or lyric voice in favor of psychological monologue. One of the founders of modern 20th-century poetry.

Elizabeth I (1533–1603): Queen of England and Ireland (1558–1603); she ruled successfully during a period of religious and political strife, establishing a compromise settlement for the Church of England and presiding over the defeat of the Spanish Armada in 1588 and the Catholic Irish rebels in 1603.

Engels, Friedrich (also Frederick) (1820–1895): Son of a middle-class factory owner, he was shocked at conditions in Manchester and wrote *The Condition of the Working Class in England* (1845). Subsequently Karl Marx's writing partner.

Eugene of Savoy (1663–1736): Prince and allied general during the War of the Spanish Succession (1702–1714) and Marlborough's partner in the victory at Blenheim; he subsequently drove the French out of Italy.

Ferdinand V of Castile (or II of Aragon) (1452–1516): King of Spain 1479–1516 (jointly with Isabella, 1479–1504). He completed the conquest of Granada and the unification of Spain and sponsored Columbus's voyages but also invited the Inquisition to enter Spain (1480) and persecuted and eventually expelled Muslims and Jews.

Fleury, André-Hercule de, Cardinal (1653–1743): Statesman, tutor to Louis XV, and eventual *de facto* prime minister of France (1726–1743), he pursued a policy of peace with Britain.

Francis I (1494–1547): King of France (1515–1547), he pursued a series of wars against England and the Holy Roman Empire. A great patron of the arts and letters who encouraged the Renaissance in France.

Francis II (1544–1560): King of France (1559–1560); married Mary Stuart, queen of Scots in 1558, was dominated by her anti-Protestant advisors, and provoked Huguenots to mobilize.

Franco, Francisco (1892–1975). Soldier, Spanish fascist leader, and dictator (1939–1975). Though he presided over a repressive regime, his decision to designate the Bourbon Juan Carlos as his successor in

1969 facilitated a transition to constitutional monarchy and democracy.

Frank, Anne (1929–1945): German-born author. Her family, which was Jewish, fled to the Netherlands in the 1930s. After the Nazi occupation of the Netherlands in 1941, the Franks hid in a secret room in a warehouse, where they were discovered by the Gestapo in August 1944 and sent to concentration camps. Anne died at Bergen-Belsen in 1945. Her father survived and published her diary, translated into English as *The Diary of a Young Girl*, in 1947.

Franz Ferdinand (1863–1914): Statesman and heir to the Austrian throne, he was assassinated in Sarajevo, Bosnia-Herzegovina, by Gavrilo Princip, a Serb nationalist terrorist. The assassination precipitated World War I.

Franz-Josef (1830–1916): Austrian emperor (1848–1916) and king of Hungary (1867–1916). He put down the Revolution of 1848 in the empire and suppressed the Italian nationalist movement in 1849. Presided over Austria's successful participation in the war against Denmark in 1864 but also Austria's defeat at the hands of Prussia in 1866. Tensions in the Balkans led to frequent clashes with Russia during his reign, culminating in the assassination of his nephew Franz Ferdinand and entry into war in 1914. Domestically, his rule evolved from autocracy to grudging constitutionalism.

Frederick II (the Great) (1712–1786): King of Prussia (1740–1786) and author. After a difficult apprenticeship at the hands of his father, Frederick launched the War of the Austrian Succession in 1740 and subsequently involved Prussia in the Seven Years' War in 1756 and the partition of Poland in 1772, both of which increased Prussian holdings. Domestically, a reformer, encouraging agriculture, industry, and literature.

Freud, Sigmund (1856–1939): Physician, psychiatrist, father of psychotherapy, originator of the concept of the unconscious mind, and author of numerous works, including *Civilization and Its Discontents* (1930).

Galilei, Galileo (1564–1642): Scholar, scientist, and professor at the University of Padua, he was one of the first to turn a telescope to the heavens. His *Dialogues on the Two Chief Systems of the World* (1632) was condemned by the Roman Catholic Church, and he was confined to house arrest.

Garibaldi, Giuseppe (1807–1882): Italian nationalist patriot leader, his defeat of the Kingdom of the Two Sicilies and subsequent acknowledgement of Victor Emanuel II as king of Italy in 1861 led to the unification of Italy.

Goebbels, Josef (1897–1945): Nazi propaganda minister.

Goering, Hermann (1893–1946): Aviator; a flying ace in World War I, Goering organized the Gestapo and then the Luftwaffe for Hitler. Famous for his lavish lifestyle. Convicted of crimes against humanity at Nuremberg in 1946, he committed suicide before he could be hanged.

Goethe, Johan Wolfgang von (1749–1832): Author, one of the seminal figures in the birth of German Romanticism, he wrote *The Sorrows of Young Werther* (1774) and both parts of *Faust* (1808, 1832).

Gorbachev, Mikhail (b. 1931): Statesman, secretary general of the Communist Party (1985–1991), and president of the Soviet Union (1988–1991); launched a reform (*perestroika*) of Russian communism and worked with U.S. President Reagan to ease nuclear tensions. When *perestroika* and *glasnost* ("openness") led to increasing dissent and freedom in Warsaw Pact countries, Gorbachev's decision not to apply military force did much to facilitate the end of Russian and communist domination. Awarded the Nobel Peace Prize in 1990.

Gutenberg, Johannes (?1400–1468): Generally acknowledged as the inventor of the printing press, his production of the first printed Bible is a landmark in the history of communications.

Henry "the Navigator" (1394–1460): Prince of Portugal who established a naval academy at Sagres that trained European explorers of Africa.

Henry IV (1553–1610): King of Navarre (1572–1589) and leader of the French Huguenots during the Wars of Religion, king of France (1589–1610). Henry had to defend his throne against the Catholic League and Philip II until 1596, despite his conversion to Catholicism in 1593. He pursued absolutism, encouraging industry and reorganizing the finances of France. Granted toleration to the Huguenots with the Edict of Nantes of 1598. He was assassinated in 1610.

Henry VIII (1491–1547): King of England (1509–1547) and Ireland (1540–1547); he assumed the leadership of the Church of England and married Anne Boleyn in 1533 after the papacy refused his request of a divorce from Catherine of Aragon. Spent the rest of his reign vacillating in religion, wedding and sometimes beheading four more queens, and wrecking the royal finances in a series of fruitless wars with France and Scotland.

Hume, David (1711–1776): A leading exponent of the Scottish Enlightenment; his works include *A Treatise of Human Nature* (1739–1740), *An Enquiry Concerning Human Understanding* (1748), an eight-volume *History of England* (1754–1762), and *Dialogues Concerning Natural Religion* (written in the 1750s but so controversial that they were suppressed until 1779).

Himmler, Heinrich (1900–1945): Nazi politician, head of Hitler's SS.

Hitler, Adolf (1889–1945): Soldier, leader of the Nazi Party, German dictator (1933–1945), instigator of the Holocaust and World War II in Europe.

Hobbes, Thomas (1588–1679): English philosopher and author of *Leviathan* (1651), which argues that human nature is driven by passions, that human beings in their natural state compete viciously for the necessities of life, and that the only way to eliminate that competition is to form an irreversible contract with an absolute ruler.

Hugo, Victor (1802–1885): French Romantic novelist, author of, among many other works, *Les Misérables* (1862). His writings were banned and he was exiled during the rule of Napoleon III.

Ibsen, Henrik (1828–1906): Norwegian playwright, author of, among many other works, *A Doll's House* (1879); his works explore the psychological tensions and tragedies of everyday life.

Ignatius of Loyola (1491–1556): Soldier, Roman Catholic clergyman, and saint. He was wounded as a young man at the siege of Pamplona in 1521; experienced a religious conversion that led him to found the Society of Jesus, an order of priests with military discipline to preach, teach, and combat Protestantism.

Isabella I (1451–1504): Queen of Castille (1474–1504) and Spain (jointly with Ferdinand, 1479–1504). With Ferdinand, she completed the conquest of Granada and the unification of Spain and sponsored

Columbus's voyages, but the pair also invited the Inquisition to enter Spain (1480) and persecuted and eventually expelled Muslims and Jews.

James I (1566–1625): King of Scotland (1567–1625), first Stuart king of England (1603–1625); he ruled faction-ridden Scotland successfully before assuming the English throne. In England, he pursued a pacifistic foreign policy but had difficulty with Parliament, in part because of his financial extravagance.

James II (1636–1685): King of England, Scotland, and Ireland (1685–1688). He attempted to secure toleration for Catholics and Protestant Dissenters, which precipitated the Glorious Revolution of 1688–1689.

Jefferson, Thomas (1743–1826): Landowner, statesman, author of the Declaration of Independence (1776), governor of Virginia (1779–1781), president of the United States (1801–1809). His authorization of the Louisiana Purchase doubled the size of the United States.

Joseph II (1741–1790): Holy Roman Emperor (1765–1790), regent of Austria (1765–1780), and emperor of Austria (1780–1790). He pursued a series of reforms, including an Edict of Toleration (1781); dissolved the contemplative monasteries to endow hospitals; freed the serfs; and decreed the use of German throughout the empire in official documents.

Joyce, James (1882–1941): Irish novelist and proponent of stream-of-consciousness narrative in *Portrait of the Artist as a Young Man* (1916), *Ulysses* (1922), and *Finnegan's Wake* (1928–1937).

Kant, Immanuel (1724–1804): German moral philosopher, author of *Critique of Pure Reason* (1781), *Metaphysics of Ethics* (1797), *Critique of Practical Reason* (1788), and *Perpetual Peace* (1795).

Kennedy, John Fitzgerald (1917–1963): Seaman, statesman, and president of the United States (1961–1963). Kennedy launched the space program, supported civil rights for American blacks, managed to avoid nuclear war in the Cuban Missile Crisis, and worked out the Test Ban Treaty with the Soviets. He was assassinated in 1963.

Kepler, Johannes (1571–1630): German astronomer who perfected the Copernican system by arguing that the planets revolved around the Sun elliptically.

Keynes, John Maynard (1883–1946): English economist, diplomat, and author, most notably, of *The General Theory of Employment, Interest and Money* (1933–1935).

Khrushchev, Nikita (1894–1971): General secretary of the Communist Party (1953–1964) and premier of the Soviet Union (1958–1964). He famously criticized Stalinist terror in 1956. In foreign policy, he alternated between bellicosity and "peaceful coexistence" with the West. Deposed in a coup in 1964.

Koch, Robert (1843–1910): German physician and bacteriologist, he was the first to isolate the bacilli for anthrax, tuberculosis, and Asiatic cholera; awarded the Nobel Prize for physiology and medicine in 1905.

Kohl, Helmut (b. 1930): German statesman, chancellor of West Germany (1982–1990) and Germany (1990–1998). Reduced government spending, supported NATO and European integration, and managed the unification of Germany skillfully.

Lenin, Vladimir Ilyich (1870–1924): Premier of the Soviet Union (1917–1924). Bolshevik leader who spent much of his youth in prison or exile. Upon his return to Russia in 1917, he organized, first the Bolsheviks, then a revolution that toppled the provisional government of Alexander Kerensky. His War Communism (1917–1921) was an economic and social disaster, but the New Economic Policy (1921–1924), which slowed collectivization and restrained international communism, was relatively successful.

Leopold II (1835–1909): King of Belgium (1865–1909), he sponsored African exploration (1879–1884), was the proprietor of the Congo Free State (1884–1908), and presided over terrible abuse of native populations.

Lloyd-George, David (1863–1945): Prime minister of Great Britain (1916–1922) during and after World War I who privately agreed with Woodrow Wilson's call for moderate treatment of defeated Germany but rejected moderation in the Treaty of Versailles.

Locke, John (1632–1704): British philosopher; his *Essay Concerning Human Understanding* (1690) argued for the importance of environment over inherent characteristics in human development. The *Second Treatise on Government* (1690) argued that humans form both a social and a civil contract to escape the state of nature and that the latter can be broken when a ruler fails to protect life, liberty, and property.

Louis Philippe (1773–1850): Duke of Valois, duke of Chartres, duke of Orléans; king of France (1830–1848). He came to power as a result of the Revolution of 1830 and left it as a result of the Revolution of 1848. In between, he began as a democrat and a liberal but grew unpopular as he began to restore royal power.

Louis XI (1423–1483): King of France (1461–1483). Louis XI enhanced his power by reducing that of his nobles, especially the dukes of Burgundy.

Louis XIV (1638–1715): King of France (1643–1715), known as the "Sun King." The nation was administered for Louis XIV by Jules, Cardinal Mazarin, and the *Frondeurs* until he declared himself of age in 1661. Thereafter, he enhanced royal power, built Versailles, and pursued an aggressive foreign policy aimed at securing control of the Spanish throne and empire. After several successful wars, his ambitions were halted and his regime was nearly bankrupted by the War of the Spanish Succession (1702–1714).

Louis XV (1710–1774): King of France (1715–1774), but prior to 1723, during his minority, the kingdom was administered by the duke of Orleans as regent. During his reign, France fought several expensive wars, culminating in spiraling debt and military disaster at the end of the Seven Years' War in 1763.

Louis XVI (1754–1793): King of France (1774–1793); he inherited massive debts and military defeat from Louis XV, to which his ministers responded with reform. Supported the United States in the American Revolutionary War, but this further saddled the government with crippling debt. Called the Estates General in 1789, thus setting in motion the French Revolution. His hesitation over the revolution, culminating in his attempt to flee after the new constitution of 1791, discredited him. Tried in December 1792, convicted, and executed on a charge of treason in January 1793.

Luther, Martin (1483–1546): Augustinian priest and religious reformer; Luther was a professor at the University of Wittenberg when he wrote his 95 Theses against the sale of indulgences. He was excommunicated (1520) and refused to recant at the Diet of Worms (1521); thereafter, he translated the Bible into German and produced other writings elaborating his theology.

Machiavelli, Niccolò (1469–1527): Italian writer on politics, author of *Il Principe* (*The Prince*, 1532).

Malthus, Thomas (1766–1834): British political economist, his *Essay on Population* (1798) argued that the world's population was bound to outrun its food supply and that charity and medicine only exacerbated the problem.

Maria Theresa (1717–1780): Archduchess of Austria, queen of Hungary and Bohemia, succeeded to imperial dominions (1740–1780). She reformed Austrian finances and military and encouraged trade. Facing the War of the Austrian Succession upon her accession in 1740, her foreign policy was largely unsuccessful, resulting in the loss of Silesia to Frederick the Great.

Marlborough, John Churchill, Duke of (1650–1722): British soldier and statesman, captain-general of Queen Anne's forces in the War of the Spanish Succession. Beginning with Blenheim (1704), he won a series of decisive victories against Louis XIV, thus destroying the myth of French invincibility and ensuring British superiority in Europe and beyond for a generation.

Marshall, George C. (1880–1959): American soldier and statesman, U.S. Army chief of staff in World War II; he organized the massive American mobilization, then the relief plan implemented to restore the European economies that bears his name, beginning in 1947. Awarded the Nobel Peace Prize in 1953.

Marx, Karl (1818–1883): German philosopher, architect of international communism in a series of works beginning with the *Communist Manifesto* (1848) and culminating in *Das Kapital* (1883). Marx argued that the material conditions of life in any society lay the foundation for its political, social, and cultural organization; that history is the story of class struggle; and that the working class could win that struggle only by seizing the means of production through revolution, though vague on how this would produce a classless society. His ideas had a powerful influence for the next century.

Matthias Corvinus, Matthias I, later nicknamed Matthias the Just (1443–1490): Hungarian king who ruled strongly from 1458 to 1490, initially under the guidance of a regent from Italy and for a long time with a fascination for the Italian Renaissance. He died without a legitimate heir, and the strong state he built collapsed back into feudalism.

Mazarin, Jules, Cardinal (1602–1661). Chief minister to Louis XIV from 1643; his efforts to raise funds for the war against Spain provoked the last major revolt against French absolutism before the Revolution (the Fronde of 1649–1652). The defeat of that revolt allowed him to strengthen the king's provincial administrators (*intendants*) and prepare the way for an even more effective generation of ministers, led by Jean-Baptiste Colbert.

Mendel, Gregor (1822–1884): Augustinian monk and botanist who, through experiments on peas, discovered Mendel's law about heredity and its transmission through genes.

Metternich, Klemens von (1773–1859): Austrian diplomat, one of the architects of the Congress of Vienna and the next 30 years of conservative reaction in Europe. He fell from power during the Revolutions of 1848.

Mill, John Stuart (1806–1873): British philosopher and member of Parliament, the author of *Principles of Political Economy* (1848), *On Liberty* (1859), *On Representative Government* (1861), and *On the Subjection of Women* (1869). Began as a Utilitarian liberal, but came to articulate a new, more interventionist style of liberalism.

Milošević, Slobodan (1941–2006): Serbian politician, president of Serbia (1988–1997) and reorganized Yugoslavia (1997–1999); a determined nationalist, his plans for a "Greater Serbia" led to the policies of "ethnic cleansing" in Bosnia-Herzogovina in 1992–1994 and in Kosovo in 1998–1999. Subsequently tried for crimes against humanity.

Montagu, Charles, later Earl and Marquis of Halifax (1661–1715): Whig politician, chancellor of the exchequer under William III, and architect of the financial revolution, by which Britain creatively funded its national debt; he raised vast sums of money that paid for the Nine Years' War and the War of the Spanish Succession.

Montaigne, Michel de (1533–1592): Humanist author whose *Essays* advocated rational reforms.

Montesquieu, Charles-Louis de Secondat, Baron de (1689–1755): French *philosophe* of the Enlightenment, author the *Spirit of the Laws* (1748), in which he argued that the most effective forms of government divided power so that each branch could check and balance the others.

Mozart, Wolfgang Amadeus (1756–1791): Austrian composer of, among many other great works, *The Marriage of Figaro* (1785–1786), *Don Giovanni* (1787), and the *Magic Flute* (1790–1791).

Mussolini, Benito (1883–1945): Italian fascist leader and dictator of Italy (1922–1943), one of Hitler's principal allies in World War II.

Napoleon III, Louis Napoleon Bonaparte (1808–1873): President of France (1848–1852), emperor of France (1852–1870). Though viewed initially as a liberal, even as president, he sought to enhance his authority. As emperor, he combined enlightened social policies and extensive public works with an aggressive and expansionist foreign policy. Deposed after bungling into and losing the Franco-Prussian War (1870–1871).

Nelson, Horatio, Lord (1758–1805): British admiral, victor at the Battles of the Nile (1798), Copenhagen (1801), and Trafalgar (1805), where he was wounded mortally. These victories limited Napoleon's ambitions and established British naval supremacy for a century.

Newton, Sir Isaac (1642–1727): British scientist who posited the theory of gravity, three laws of motion, and in the *Principia Mathematica* (1687), a complete cosmological system.

Nicholas I (1796–1855): Czar of Russia (1825–1855); came to power via suppression of the Decembrist uprising and immediately founded a Third Section within the imperial chancery that functioned as secret police against political enemies. Always an autocrat who relied upon an inner circle of military men, he became even more authoritarian after the European revolutions of 1848, and he died during the unsuccessful Crimean War (1853–1855) against the Ottomans, French, and British.

Nicholas II (1868–1918): Czar of Russia (1894–1917); he continued the repressive measures of Alexander III and involved Russia in the disastrous Russo-Japanese War (1904–1905) and World War I.

Abdicated in 1917 and was executed by order of the Communist government in 1918.

Nietzsche, Friedrich (1844–1900): German philosopher; posited the notion that God is dead as a meaningful philosophical concept and that true action is only possible by a Superman above traditional moral laws. His works included *The Birth of Tragedy* (1872), *Thus Spake Zarathustra* (1883–1885), *Beyond Good and Evil* (1886), *On the Genealogy of Morals* (1887), *Ecce Homo* (1908), and *The Will to Power* (1901).

Nixon, Richard (1913–1994). President of the United States (1969–1974); Nixon maintained and extended American involvement in Southeast Asia, pursued detente with the Soviet Union and communist China, and continued liberal social programs. Forced to resign in 1974 after implication in a series of covert unconstitutional acts, including the cover-up for the Watergate break-in.

Owen, Robert (1771–1858): British Utopian socialist who urged factory owners, in *A New View of Society* (1813), to organize communities in which workers would be provided good working and living conditions, as well as a share in company profits. Many such communities were set up, but all eventually failed.

Oxford, Robert Harley, First Earl of (1661–1724): English statesman, architect of the Treaty of Utrecht. Impeached for Utrecht in the next reign, he was acquitted and retired to amass one of the great book and manuscript collections in England, which later formed the basis for the British Museum.

Pankhurst, Emmeline (1858–1928): British feminist who helped found the Women's Franchise League (1889) and the Women's Social and Political Union (1903). She advocated militancy, even violence, to achieve votes for women and was jailed repeatedly.

Pasteur, Louis (1822–1895): French bacteriologist and professor of chemistry who first posited the idea of bacteria, microorganisms that grow in organic compounds and can cause disease. Pasteur developed inoculations for anthrax and rabies.

Peter the Great (1672–1725): Czar of Russia (1682–1725); a great modernizer and reformer; suppressed the rebellion of the *streltsy* guard (1698); won the Great Northern War against Sweden (1700–

1721), resulting in the acquisition of Livonia, Estonia, and parts of Karelia; and established St. Petersburg (1903).

Philippe, Duke of Anjou. See **Anjou, Philippe, Duke of.**

Philippe II, Duke of Orléans (1674–1723). Regent to Louis XV from 1715 to 1723; introduced polysynody in a failed effort to return power to the nobles.

Phillip II (1527–1598): King of Naples and Sicily (1554–1598) and Spain (1556–1598); ruler of vast European and New World holdings. He drove the Turks out of the Mediterranean at Lepanto (1571); imposed the Inquisition on the Netherlands, precipitating the Dutch revolt (1567); launched the failed Spanish Armada (1588); and supported the Catholic League against Henry IV of France (1580). His attempts to stamp out Protestantism wherever he found it bankrupted Spain and led to that country's slow decline in power.

Picasso, Pablo (1881–1973): Spanish painter, famed for his evolution through a variety of experimental styles, including his Blue Period (1901–1904), Cubism (1909–1925), and Surrealism (1925).

Pitt, William, the Elder; from 1766, Earl of Chatham (1708–1778): British statesman, prime minister (1756–1761, 1766–1768); effective war minister during the Seven Years' War; opponent of the attempt to tax the American colonies.

Reagan, Ronald (1911–2004): President of the United States (1981–1989). Reagan's administration marked a turn toward conservative fiscal and social policy in the United States, while he pursued a massive defense build-up designed to oppose the Soviet Union around the globe. Though an ardent Cold Warrior, he negotiated important agreements with Mikhail Gorbachev's regime to scale back nuclear weapons.

Ricardo, David (1772–1823): British political economist, formulator of the "Iron Law of Wages" in his *Principles of Political Economy and Taxation* (1817).

Richelieu, Armand-Jean du Plessis, Cardinal (1585–1642): French clergyman and statesman, virtual ruler of France under Louis XIII (1610–1643). He laid the foundations for absolutism by reducing the power of the French barons and tightening the organization of government. He also encouraged trade, industry, and overseas expansion and pursued an aggressive foreign policy, culminating in French participation in the Thirty Years' War (1618–1648).

Robespierre, Maximilien (1758–1794): Radical French politician, leader of the Jacobins during the French Revolution, virtual ruler of France (1793–1794). He defended France against foreign enemies and pursued egalitarian social legislation, but he was also the principal architect of the Reign of Terror. Eventually, his own supporters turned on him, leading to his execution in July 1794.

Rousseau, Jean-Jacques (1712–1778): Swiss *philosophe*, author of the *Discourses* (1750, 1755), *Emile* (1762), *Social Contract* (1762), and *Confessions* (1782-1789), in which he argued for the primacy of emotion over reason and for small states governed by the general will.

Sartre, Jean-Paul (1905–1980): French existentialist philosopher and novelist; author, among many other works, of *Being and Nothingness* (1943) and *Nausea* (1949). Refused the Nobel Prize for literature in 1964.

Schuman, Robert (1886–1963). Foreign minister of France whose plan for European economic and military unity resulted in the European Coal and Steel Community (1952), which later become the European Economic Community (1958).

Shakespeare, William (1564–1623): English playwright, author of, among many great works, *Richard III* (1593), *Hamlet* (1601), *Macbeth* (1606), and *King Lear* (1606) .

Smith, Adam (1723–1790): British political economist, author of *The Wealth of Nations* (1776), which argued against government interference in natural economic processes.

Sobieski, Jan III (1629–1696): Elective king of Poland (1674–1696) whose armies broke the Ottoman siege of Vienna in 1683 and whose reign marked a brief revival of Polish power.

Stalin, Josef (1879–1953): Secretary general of the Communist Party (1922–1953) and virtual dictator of the Soviet Union (1924–1953). As victor of a power struggle with Leon Trotsky, Stalin maintained his power through terror, pursuing his enemies in a series of purges into gulags or death. In foreign policy, he urged the West to stand up to Hitler but, when rebuffed, signed a non-aggression pact with Nazi Germany. Taken by surprise by Hitler's invasion in 1941, Stalin led the Soviet Union in World War II, then imposed communist regimes on occupied Eastern Europe.

Stravinsky, Igor (1882–1970): Russian composer of, among other works, the revolutionary ballets *The Firebird* (1909–1910), *Petrushka* (1910–1911), and *The Rite of Spring* (1913).

Sully, Maximilien de Béthune, Duke of (1560–1641). Huguenot financial and political advisor to Henry of Bourbon before and throughout his reign as King Henry IV (1589–1610); credited with policies generating a surplus in the French treasury and a return to economic prosperity.

Talleyrand, Count Charles Maurice de, Prince de Bénévent (1754–1838): French statesman and diplomat, bishop of Autun (1789–1791); active in the French Revolution, served in the governments of Napoleon I and Louis XVIII.

Thatcher, Margaret, Baroness (b. 1925): British politician, prime minister (1979–1990); she cut government spending and social programs, privatized industry, and pursued a strongly pro-American, anti-communist foreign policy. She became known as the "Iron Lady" for her unswerving determination in struggles against labor unions and in prosecuting the Falklands War of 1982.

Tito, Josip (1892–1980): Yugoslavian soldier and statesman, president of Yugoslavia (1953–1980); he organized partisan resistance to the Nazis during World War II. After the war, he led a decentralized communist regime independent of Moscow.

Toland, John (1670–1722). Catholic-born convert to Anglicanism whose *Christianity Not Mysterious* (1696) became a classic of Deism.

Tolstoy, Leo (1828–1910): Russian novelist, author of *War and Peace* (1865–1869), *Anna Karenina* (1875–1877), and *The Death of Ivan Ilyich* (1888).

Trotsky, Leon (1879–1940): Russian Communist leader, negotiated the Treaty of Brest-Litovsk (1918) and organized the Red Army. After Lenin's death, Trotsky lost to Josef Stalin in a struggle for control of the party (1924–1926); he was exiled abroad and murdered in 1940, almost certainly on Stalin's orders.

Van Gogh, Vincent (1853–1890): Dutch painter whose innovative work reveals deep personal psychological struggle, even torment.

Verdi, Giuseppe (1813–1901): Italian opera composer of, among many other works, *Rigoletto* (1851), *La Traviata* (1853), and *Otello* (1887).

Victor Emanuel II (1820–1878): King of Piedmont-Sardinia (1849–1861), king of Italy (1861–1878). He followed the advice of Count Camillo di Cavour in challenging Austria (1859–1861). His forces later took Rome (1870), which became the Italian capital.

Victor Emanuel III (1869–1947): king of Italy (1900–1946). Accepted both Liberal cabinets and the Fascist seizure of power; ordered Mussolini's arrest in 1943, and himself abdicated three years later in an effort to influence a 1946 plebiscite that instead abolished the Italian monarchy.

Voltaire (François-Marie Arouet) (1694–1778): French *philosophe*, author of, among many other works, *Letters on England* (1734) and *Candide* (1759). His relentlessly critical and satirical tone, especially against government and Church corruption, superstition, and religious bigotry, led to his banishment from France.

Wagner, Richard (1813–1883): German composer of vast, psychologically complex operas, such as *Tristan and Isolde* (1865); *Die Meistersinger von Nuernberg* (1868); and *Der Ring des Nibelungen* (1876).

Wallenberg, Raoul (1912–c. 1947): Swedish diplomat who saved 95,000 Jews by providing them with Swedish passports; disappeared in 1945 when the Red Army took Budapest. The Soviets claimed that he died in their custody in 1947, but doubts remain as to his final fate.

Walpole, Sir Robert (1676–1745): British statesman, prime minister (1720–1742). He maintained his power by pursuing peace abroad, keeping taxes low at home, and running a political spoils system in which members of Parliament were rewarded for loyalty with titles, government jobs, pensions, and so on.

Watt, James (1736–1819): Scottish engineer and inventor; he perfected the Newcomen steam engine by attaching a condenser and a fly-wheel, which made possible rapid circular motion necessary to run large factory equipment.

Wellesley, Arthur, Duke of Wellington (1769–1852). British army commander in the Napoleonic wars who held on at Waterloo (1815) until Prussian reinforcements under Blücher joined Wellington's troops to defeat Napoleon.

Wilhelm I (1797–1888): King of Prussia (1861–1871), Kaiser of Germany (1871–1888); his support of Bismarck led to the unification of Germany, but his reign saw a continuous struggle with the forces of liberalism.

Wilhelm II (1859–1941): Kaiser of Germany (1888–1918), his diplomatic missteps and decision to build a navy alienated the Russians and the British and facilitated the outbreak of World War I. Abdicated in November 1918 as Germany lost the war.

William of Orange, William the Silent (1533–1584). Leader of the Netherlands' revolt against Spain, first stadholder, and grandfather of King William III of England.

William of Orange, William III (1650–1702): Stadholder of the Netherlands (1672–1702), king of England, Scotland, and Ireland (1689–1702; in co-rule with Mary II during 1689-1694). William spent nearly his entire life opposing the ambitions of Louis XIV; he engineered the Grand Alliance and defeated Louis in the Nine Years' War.

Wilson, Woodrow (1856–1924): President of the United States (1913–1921); reelected in 1916 on the grounds that he kept the United States out of World War I. His Fourteen Points were only partly fulfilled by the peace settlement of Versailles. While campaigning for ratification of the treaty in October 1919, he suffered a stroke that incapacitated him for the remainder of his term.

Wollstonecraft, Mary (1759–1797): British feminist, often considered the mother of modern feminism, author of *A Vindication of the Rights of Women* (1792).

Wordsworth, William (1770–1850): British Romantic poet, co-author of the *Lyrical Ballads* (1798).

Yeltsin, Boris (b. 1931): Russian statesman, first president of the Russian Federation (1991–2000). His courageous stand against a communist coup in 1991 ensured the continued democratization of Eastern Europe, but as president, he faced great difficulty in attempting to implement free-market reforms. His harsh handling of the Chechnya revolt failed to crush it, leaving a legacy of lasting bitterness.

Zola, Émile (1840–1902): Liberal French author who embraced Realism in writing about peasant and working-class life in such novels as *Nana* (1880), *Women's Paradise* (1883), and *Germinal* (1885); he was active in politics, especially in the campaign to free Alfred Dreyfus.

Bibliography

The primary recommended reading for this course can be accomplished with the second volume of any one of a number of commercially available histories of Western civilization, mostly available as textbooks for university courses. One reliable and readable text is M. B. Chambers, B. Hanawalt, T. Rabb, I. Woloch, and R. Grew, *The Western Experience*, vol. 2, 8th ed. (New York: McGraw-Hill, 2002). For an alternative perspective (both to most Western civilization texts and to that of this course), written from the point of view of Eastern Europe, try chapters 7–12 of N. Davies, *Europe: A History* (New York: Harper Perennial, 1998).

Essential Readings

Brewer, J. S. *The Sinews of Power: War, Money and the English State, 1688–1783*. Cambridge, MA: Harvard University Press (reprint edition), 1990. Explains how Britain financed and won the "Second Hundred Years War" against France by balancing taxation against borrowing, state power against freedom.

Elliott, J. H. *The Old World and the New, 1492–1650*. Cambridge and New York: Cambridge University Press (reprint edition), 1992. Concentrates on how the latter affected the former, challenging European assumptions about geography, theology, and human nature.

Fischer, K. P. *Nazi Germany: A New History*. New York: Continuum International Publishing Group. 1996. An up-to-date survey emphasizing that the Nazis enjoyed broad-based support in their rise to power.

Fussell, P. *The Great War and Modern Memory*. New York: Oxford University Press (25th anniversary edition), 2000. A classic; examines the continuing cultural legacy of World War I, mostly in British literature to argue that the war really marks the beginning of the modern world.

Heilbronner, R. *The Worldly Philosophers: The Lives, Times and Ideas of the Great Economic Thinkers*. New York: Touchstone (7th rev. ed.), 1999. The classic, eminently readable account of the development of modern economics through biographical sketches of its great practitioners.

Service, R. *A History of Twentieth-Century Russia.* Cambridge, MA: Harvard University Press, 1999. Panoramic survey by one of the leading historians of the Soviet Union demonstrates that seven decades of Soviet rule continue to influence Russia today.

Supplementary Readings

Abrams, M. H. *The Mirror and the Lamp: Romantic Theory and the Critical Tradition.* New York: Oxford University Press, 1971. A classic exposition of the Romantic sensibility which sets out to explain our modern conception of the artist as a lonely trailblazer–the lamp of the title.

Allen, W. S. *The Nazi Seizure of Power: The Experience of a Single German Town, 1930–1935.* New York: Quadrangle Books, 1965. Revealing study, based on documentary evidence and interviews, of the Nazi takeover of one German town, Northeim, Hanover.

Alter, P. *Nationalism.* London: E. Arnold, 1989. Concise account covering the last 200 years, organized by type of nationalism (*risorgimento* nationalism, reform nationalism and integral nationalism) rather than by country). Explains well how nationalism can be adapted to a variety of situations and other ideologies of the left or right.

Anderson, F. *Crucible of War: The Seven Years' War and the Fate of Empire in British North America, 1754–1766.* New York: Alfred A. Knopf, 2000. A now standard account with special emphasis on how the British victory created the situation that led to the crises that concluded in American independence. The war also proved a disaster for Native Americans, as they could no longer play Britain and France against each other.

Ashton, T. S. *The Industrial Revolution, 1760–1830.* New York: Oxford University Press (reprint edition), 1998. A classic account which emphasizes the positive results of the revolution for technology and living standards.

Avineri, S. *The Social and Political Thought of Karl Marx.* Cambridge and New York: Cambridge University Press (new edition), 1970. A comprehensive and clear introduction which strikes a balance between Marx's disciples and detractors.

Bailyn, B. *The Ideological Origins of the American Revolution.* Cambridge, MA: Belknap Press (enlarged edition), 1992. Eminently readable, classic account which traces how Locke and many others helped shape the world-view of the Founding Fathers.

Beales, D. *The Risorgimento and the Unification of Italy*. Harlow, Essex, UK: Longman Group United Kingdom, 1982. A brief, critical introductory survey which traces the role of Italian nationalist movements (political, cultural and religious) in the creation of the Italian state.

Bergeron, L. *France under Napoleon*. Trans. by R. R. Palmer. Princeton, NJ: Princeton University Press, 1981. A social history of Napoleon's France which examines Napoleon's domestic policy and its effect on ordinary people, attempting to sort out what echoed past policies, what was new, and what lasted after the Empire fell.

Biagioli, M. *Galileo, Courtier: The Practice of Science in the Culture of Absolutism*. Chicago: University of Chicago Press (reprint edition), 1994. A brilliant exposition of the political context of Galileo's work which argues that he was driven as much by courtly ambition and patronage opportunities as by the desire to know.

Blanning, T. C. W. *The French Revolutionary Wars, 1787–1802*. London: Hodder Arnold, 1996. Concise but comprehensive account argues that it was these wars, not the revolution itself, which destroyed the Ancien Régime, spawned the Terror and Napoleon and engendered the modern world.

Bonney, R. *The European Dynastic States, 1494–1660*. New York: Oxford University Press, 1992. A standard and comprehensive overview of the rise of the modern state, relating this theme to the Reformation, the Wars of Religion, expanding capitalist economies and overseas empires.

Briggs, A. *The Age of Improvement, 1783–1867*, 2nd ed. New York: Longman, 1999. An exuberant history of Britain during the Industrial Revolution which argues that a strong economy enabled the British middle class to demand reform and power.

Browning, C. *The Origins of the Final Solution: The Evolution of Nazi Jewish Policy, September 1939–March 1942*. Lincoln, NE: University of Nebraska Press, 2004. Detailed exposition of the gradual evolution of Nazi policy from discrimination to expulsion to extermination, in large part in response to the exigencies of war and, throughout, with the personal involvement of the *Führer*.

Bucholz, R. and Key, N. *Early Modern England 1485-1714: A Narrative History*. Malden, MA: 2003. Written primarily for an

American audience, this narrative of the history of Tudor and Stuart England relates political developments to social and cultural history.

Burke, P. *The Italian Renaissance*. Princeton, NJ: Princeton University Press (revised edition), 1986. The standard modern survey attempts to explain why the Renaissance began in Italian cities; and how it changed the status of artists.

Campbell, J., ed. *The Experience of World War II*. New York: Oxford University Press, 1989. Well-illustrated compilation by sixteen scholars relies on eyewitness accounts to explain the daily life of the soldier, conditions in prisoner-of-war camps, and the experience of the home front.

Chamberlain, M. E. *Decolonialization: The Fall of the European Empires*. 2nd ed. Cambridge, MA: Blackwell Publishers, 1999. A standard account now updated to take into account the end of the Cold War and subsequent developments.

Cipolla, C. M., ed. *The Industrial Revolution, 1700–1914*. London: Collins/Fontana Books, 1973. A collection of essays addressing a variety of interpretations and aspects of industrialization.

Doyle, W. *The Old European Order, 1660–1800*. 2nd ed. New York: Oxford University Press, 1993. Standard and comprehensive, this book emphasizes economic and social structures and changes, as opposed to the narrative of events.

Egret, J. *The French Pre-Revolution, 1787–1788*. Chicago: University of Chicago Press, 1978. How the *Ancien Régime* fell apart.

Ellis, J. *Eye-Deep in Hell: Trench Warfare in World War I*. Baltimore, MD: Johns Hopkins University Press (reprint edition), 1989. Graphic account of the soldiers' experience, not just in battle, but in the daily grind of waiting for it; well illustrated.

Evans, R. J. *The Feminists: Women's Emancipation in Europe, America and Australia*. London: Croom Helm, 1979. One of the few studies comparing the experience of more than one country.

Ferguson, N. *Empire: The Rise and Demise of the British World Order and the Lessons for Global Power*. New York: Basic Books, 2003. Controversial, tends to take a positive view of empire, emphasizing benefits such as the free movement of goods and rule of law over abuses such as the exploitation of native peoples and devastation of their cultures. Attempts to draw lessons for today's great imperial power, the United States.

Fieldhouse, D. K. *The Colonial Empires: A Comparative Survey from the Eighteenth Century.* 2nd ed. New York: Macmillan, 1982. A comprehensive study going beyond the history of a single empire.

Fitzpatrick, S. *Everyday Stalinism. Ordinary Life in Extraordinary Times: Soviet Russia in the 1930s.* New York: Oxford University Press, 1999. A sequel to her *Stalin's Peasants* (1994), this book uses eyewitness accounts of ordinary people to relate the experience of urban life in the Soviet Union during the 1930s.

———. *The Russian Revolution.* New York: Oxford University Press (2nd reissued edition), 2001. Accessible introduction that emphasizes 1) social conditions on the eve of the Revolution; and 2) that that event was not really complete until Stalin consolidated his power and created the world's first true totalitarian state.

Gaddis, J. L. *We Now Know: Rethinking Cold War History.* New York: Oxford University Press (reprint edition), 1998. Informed by revelations from Soviet and Eastern bloc archives, it argues that the Cold War was unavoidable given the policies and predilections of Josef Stalin.

Gay, P. *The Enlightenment, an Interpretation: The Rise of Modern Paganism.* Magnolia, MA: Peter Smith Publisher, 1996. A standard, magisterial work. which traces the development of Enlightenment thought on reform to the educations of the *philosophes*.

Ginzburg, C. *The Cheese and the Worms: The Cosmos of a Sixteenth-Century Miller.* Baltimore, MD: Johns Hopkins University Press (reprint edition), 1992. Uses the transcript of a single trial of the Inquisition to reconstruct the worldview of a 16th-century villager.

Gutmann, M. *Toward the Modern Economy: Early Industry in Europe, 1500–1800.* New York: Alfred A. Knopf, 1988. Covers the whole continent, not just Britain.

Guttman, R. J., ed. *Europe in the New Century: Visions of an Emerging Superpower.* Boulder, CO: Lynne Rienner Publishers, 2001. A series of essays by leading European politicians and journalists, examining the continent's challenges at the beginning of the new century.

Hale, J. *The Civilization of Europe in the Renaissance*. New York: Scribner (reprint edition), 1995. The standard overview, arranged thematically, rather than chronologically, it emphasizes the decline of Christendom and its replacement with Europe in the sixteenth and seventeenth centuries.

Hampson, N. *Social History of the French Revolution*. London: Routledge, 1987. Lucid and concise.

———. *A Cultural History of the Enlightenment*. New York: Penguin, 1977. A general history.

Hatton, R. N. *Europe in the Age of Louis XIV*. New York: Harcourt Brace College and School Division, 1969. A collection of essays taking a panoramic view of the reign.

Henderson, W. O. *The Industrialization of Europe, 1780–1914*. London: Thames and Hudson, 1969. Standard account of the second Industrial Revolution.

Herlihy, D. *Women, Family and Society in Medieval Europe: Historical Essays, 1978–1991*. New York: Berghahn Books, 1995. A sweeping overview, arranged thematically, of social life at the start of our course.

Hilberg, R. *Perpetrators, Victims, Bystanders: The Jewish Catastrophe, 1933–1945*. New York: Harper Paperbacks, 1993. Written for the general reader, this series of essays is by the dean of Holocaust historians.

Himmelfarb, G. *Darwin and the Darwinian Revolution*. Chicago: Ivan R. Dee, Publisher (reprint edition), 1996. This critical analysis explains the precursors of Darwin's thought and explains its implications for the wider culture.

Hobsbawm, E. J. *The Age of Revolution: Europe, 1789 to 1848*. New York: New American Library, 1964. The classic Marxist account of the period from the French Revolution, through the Industrial Revolution, to those of 1848.

Howard, M. *The Franco-Prussian War*. London: Routledge (2nd rev. ed.), 2001. A lucid masterpiece, providing vivid combat narrative while placing the war in its larger diplomatic, political and societal context.

Hughes, H. Stuart. *Consciousness and Society: The Reorientation of European Social Thought, 1890–1930*. New York: Octagon Books,

1976. A masterful intellectual history which deals with all aspects of turn-of-the century European thought.

Joll, J. *The Origins of the First World War.* 2nd ed. London: Longman, 2000. Comprehensive, clear, and balanced, addressing both strategic visions and popular opinion.

Jones, J. R. *Marlborough.* Cambridge: Cambridge University Press, 1993. A concise and up-to-date treatment taking into account historiographical developments since the publication of Churchill's magisterial biography of his ancestor.

Judah, T. *Kosovo: War and Revenge.* 2nd ed. New Haven, CT: Yale University Press, 2002. An up-to-date, standard account, written by a journalist based in Belgrade during 1990-95, which traces the conflict back to its Medieval roots and explodes propaganda on both sides.

Keegan, J. *The First World War.* London: Vintage, 2000. Lucid and readable, explaining both origins and the experience of war itself with psychological insight into both leaders and led.

———. *The Second World War.* New York and London: Penguin, 2005. Well-written yet detailed one-volume survey with many illustrations; tends to concentrate on the war in Europe.

Kiernan, V. G. *European Empires from Conquest to Collapse, 1815–1960.* United Kingdom: Alan Sutton Publishing, Ltd., 1998. A standard account.

Kindleberger, C. P. *The World in Depression, 1929–1939.* Berkeley, CA: University of California Press (revised and enlarged edition), 1986. Global in scope, this book argues that the causes of the Depression were largely structural, in particular a disastrous reliance on the gold standard, and that, despite the various efforts of governments, full recovery did not occur until the massive spending on armaments prompted by World War II.

Kishlansky, M. *A Monarchy Transformed: Britain, 1603–1714.* New York and London: Penguin, 1997. Bold and lively, the most up-to-date synthesis of the Stuart period, notably gives the later half of the period its due.

Kissinger, H. *A World Restored: Metternich, Castlereagh and the Problems of Peace, 1812–22.* Boston: Houghton Mifflin Company, 1973. Written by Nixon's future secretary of state, sympathetic to the conservative framers of the 1815 settlement.

Kittelson, J. M. *Luther the Reformer: The Story of the Man and His Career*. Minneapolis, MN: Augsburg Fortress Publishers, 2003. The standard introduction to Luther's life and theology.

Kolata, G. *Flu: The Story of the Great Influenza Pandemic of 1918 and the Search for the Virus That Caused It*. New York: Farrar, Straus and Giroux, 1999. A panoramic view that deals clearly with the science, politics, and cultural implications of the great pandemic.

Laqueur, W. *Europe in Our Time: A History, 1945–1992*. New York: Penguin Books (reprint edition), 1993. Comprehensive, authoritative, and balanced, it places particular emphasis on economic, social and cultural developments on both sides of the Iron Curtain.

Lindemann, A. S. *A History of European Socialism*. New Haven, CT: Yale University Press, 1983. Traces the movement from the Utopians to the Marxists.

Lovejoy, A. O. *The Great Chain of Being: A Study of the History of an Idea*. Cambridge, MA: Harvard University Press, 2005. A classic, tracing the idea back to ancient times.

MacCulloch, D. *The Reformation: A History*. New York: Viking Adult, 2004. An award-winning reassessment which covers popular attitudes as well as the actions and thought of leading players, it argues that the Medieval Catholic Church was not as ineffective and corrupt as later reformers portrayed it to be.

Markham, F. *Napoleon*. New York: Signet Books (reissue edition), 1988. Still the standard biography, really a life-and times which places Napoleon and his achievements in a European context, rather than an in-depth psychological study.

Massie, R. K. *Castles of Steel: Britain, Germany, and the Winning of the Great War at Sea*. New York: Random House, 2003. The sequel to *Dreadnought*; carries the story through World War I in the same accessible style.

———. *Dreadnought: Britain, Germany, and the Coming of the Great War*. New York: Ballantine Books (reprint edition), 1992. Reads like a novel but tends to view the naval race as a clash of personalities among great men; other historians would argue that it was more complicated than that.

———. *Nicholas and Alexandra*. New York: Ballantine Books, 2000. Novelistic account of the Russian Revolution; provides a sympathetic portrayal of the doomed royal family, but in concentrating on the personalities at the top, it skims over the real grievances of the Russian people.

Mattingly, G. *The Armada*. Boston: Mariner Books, 1974. Panoramic treatment of the diplomatic, military, and naval situation; reads like a novel; superceded in detail by more recent work, but no one has equaled its sweep.

Middlebrook, M. B. *The First Day on the Somme*. United Kingdom: Pen and Sword Books, 2003. This gripping account of military disaster is based on first person narratives, which are liberally quoted.

Middlekauff, R. *The Glorious Cause: The American Revolution, 1763–1789*. 2nd ed. New York: Oxford University Press, 2005. A balanced treatment of the period from the Seven Years' War to the framing of the Constitution, but the centerpiece is a detailed and vivid narrative of the War of Independence.

Milward, A. S., and S. B. Saul. *The Development of the Economies of Continental Europe, 1850–1914*. London: Allen & Unwin, 1977. Economic history on a grand scale, the standard work on the Second Industrial Revolution.

Moorehead, A. *Gallipoli*. New York: Harper Perennial Modern Classics, 2002. Gripping account written from the Allied point of view argues that Churchill's initial plan was sound; the disaster lay in its execution.

Morgan, P. *Italian Fascism, 1915–1945*. 2nd ed. New York and United Kingdom: Palgrave Macmillan, 2004. A standard introduction that focuses on the actual working of the Mussolini state and its day-to-day impact on its citizens.

Mosse, G. L. *The Fascist Revolution*. New York: H. Fergig, 1999. A set of essays concentrating on the origins of fascism in nationalism, anti-Semitism, and so forth.

Palmer, R. *Twelve Who Ruled: The Year of the Terror in the French Revolution*. Princeton, NJ: Princeton University Press (reprint edition), 1970. A classic, written for non-specialists, which explains Jacobin motivations and thought as well as how the Committee on Public Safety actually worked.

Parker, G. *The Thirty Years' War*. 2nd ed. London: Routledge, 1997. The standard work.

Parry, J. H. *Trade and Dominion: The European Oversea Empires in the Eighteenth Century.* Charleston, SC: Phoenix Press, 2001. A classic by the greatest historian of early modern Europe's overseas empires.

Pflanze, O. *Bismarck and the Development of Germany: The Period of Unification, 1815–1871.* Princeton, NJ: Princeton University Press, 1971. Wide-ranging, definitive treatment which serves as a history of nineteenth century Germany as well as of Bismarck himself. This book roots the tragedies of Germany's 20th century in its 19th century past.

Rearick, C. *Pleasures of the Belle Epoque: Entertainment and Festivity in Turn-of-the-Century France.* New Haven, CT: Yale University Press (reprint edition), 1988. Concentrates on the positive aspects of turn-of-the-century culture, focusing on popular culture, leisure, and a growing antagonism towards a traditional ethic of work.

Riasnovsky, N. V. *The Emergence of Romanticism.* New York: Oxford University Press, 1992. A comprehensive European-wide survey that argues that Romanticism is a unique product of the West, rooted in Christian theology. The book also traces the close relationship between Romanticism and Nationalism.

Rice, E. F., Jr. *The Foundations of Early Modern Europe, 1460–1559.* 2nd ed. New York: W.W. Norton & Co., 1994. A very readable short survey which weaves together the rise of the state, the Reformation, the development of print culture and economic, social and cultural life for people of all ranks.

Scammell, G. V. *The First Imperial Age: European Overseas Expansion, c. 1400–1715.* London: Routledge, 1989. A standard account of the Age of Discovery which strikes a good balance between celebration and indictment of European expansion.

Schama, S. *An Embarrassment of Riches: An Interpretation of Dutch Culture in the Golden Age.* London: Vintage, 1997. A sweeping interpretation of Dutch culture in the 17th century which highlights the tension between Calvinism and the material wealth that this culture came to enjoy so suddenly.

Shapin, S. *The Scientific Revolution.* Chicago: University of Chicago Press, 1998. A brief but challenging overview which emphasizes the shifting world-views which made the Scientific Revolution possible and productive, rather than a blow-by-blow chronology of discoveries.

Sharp, A. *The Versailles Settlement: Peacemaking in Paris, 1919*. New York: St. Martins Press, 1991. The best modern overview concentrates on the problem of Germany and the European settlement, but also covers colonial issues, the Middle-Eastern settlement and Wilson's proposal for a League of Nations.

Sherwin, M. J. A. *A World Destroyed: The Atomic Bomb and the Grand Alliance*. New York: Random House, 1975. Balanced account, aware of all sides of the question, but concentrating on the political/diplomatic rather than the scientific or ethical issues.

Stokes, G. *The Walls Came Tumbling Down: The Collapse of Communism in Eastern Europe*. New York: Oxford University Press, 1993. Based in part on interviews with participants, this dramatic and wide-ranging book traces the decay and collapse of Communism from the days of the Prague Spring of 1968.

Stone, N. *Europe Transformed, 1878–1919*. 2nd ed. Cambridge, MA: Blackwell Publishers, 1999. A critical and comprehensive survey of a complex period that concentrates on politics but takes economic, social and cultural developments into account.

Trachtenberg, M. *A Constructed Peace: The Making of the European Settlement, 1945–1963*. Princeton, NJ: Princeton University Press, 1999. An up-to-date and original overview which argues that a divided, non-nuclear and de-militarized Germany was the key to the stable East/West relations that had been achieved by the early 1960s.

Watt, D. C. *How the War Came: The Immediate Origins of the Second World War, 1938–1939*. New York: Pantheon, 1989. A detailed narrative concentrating on Hitler's plans for German aggression and the successive attempts of the other great powers to fathom and restrain them.

Weigley, R. F. *The Age of Battles: The Quest for Decisive Warfare from Breitenfeld to Waterloo*. Bloomington, IN: Indiana University Press, 1991. Traditional military history in the best sense, this book places decisive battles in their political and economic contexts, but argues that they were often less decisive than their planners envisioned.

Weinberg, G. L. *A World at Arms: Global History of World War II*. 2nd ed. Cambridge and New York: Cambridge University Press,

2005. Balanced and comprehensive, integrates political and economic issues with military factors from a global perspective.

Wiener, M. *English Culture and the Decline of the Industrial Spirit, 1850–1980.* 2nd ed. Cambridge and New York: Cambridge University Press, 2004. Brilliant analysis integrating economic, social and cultural factors explaining why England lost its competitive edge.

Winter, J. *Sites of Memory, Sites of Mourning: The Great War in European Cultural History.* Cambridge and New York: Cambridge University Press (reprint edition), 1998. A comprehensive account of the cultural legacy of the Great War and, in particular, how whole nations coped with the immense grief and dislocation brought be the war.

Wohl, R. *The Generation of 1914.* Cambridge, MA: Harvard University Press, 1981. Posits a generation gap that exacerbated tensions leading to the conflict. The book goes on to argue that the experience and legacy of war was very different depending on when during the conflict one turned old enough to fight (ages 17 to 18).

Internet Resources:

General: http://www.bbc.co.uk/history/ The BBC History web-page is an excellent portal into the history of the West and especially strong on industrialization.

General: http://www.fordham.edu/halsall/mod/modsbook.html Provides numerous primary texts.

Louis XIV: http://www.louis-xiv.de/louisold/louisxiv.html

The French Revolution: http://chnm.gmu.edu/revolution/ Includes 250 text documents)

The Industrial Revolution:
http://members.aol.com/TeacherNet/Industrial.html

World War I: http://www.spartacus.schoolnet.co.uk/FWW.htm Excellent potted biographies of leaders, narratives of events, etc.

World War II: http://www.spartacus.schoolnet.co.uk/2WW.htm The same as for WWI.